The Immigrant and the Community

You are holding a reproduction of an original work that is in the public domain in the United States of America, and possibly other countries. You may freely copy and distribute this work as no entity (individual or corporate) has a copyright on the body of the work. This book may contain prior copyright references, and library stamps (as most of these works were scanned from library copies). These have been scanned and retained as part of the historical artifact.

This book may have occasional imperfections such as missing or blurred pages, poor pictures, errant marks, etc. that were either part of the original artifact, or were introduced by the scanning process. We believe this work is culturally important, and despite the imperfections, have elected to bring it back into print as part of our continuing commitment to the preservation of printed works worldwide. We appreciate your understanding of the imperfections in the preservation process, and hope you enjoy this valuable book.

THE IMMIGRANT
AND THE COMMUNITY

THE IMMIGRANT
AND THE COMMUNITY

BY
GRACE ABBOTT
Director of the Immigrants' Protective League
Chicago, Illinois

WITH INTRODUCTION BY
JUDGE JULIAN W. MACK

NEW YORK
THE CENTURY CO.
1917

Copyright, 1917, by
THE CENTURY CO.

Published, April, 1917

INTRODUCTION

AMERICANIZATION of the immigrant has been a popular slogan for the past few years. Gratitude for the wonderful opportunities offered to him has been counted upon as a sufficient incentive to complete assimilation.

The patriotic zeal of the foreign-born citizens has been manifested in every crisis; the recently arrived immigrants have not lagged behind. And this has lulled us into the comfortable belief that we have earned their hearty coöperation.

A study of the laws, federal and state, and of their actual administration; daily contact for many years with hundreds of newcomers, listening to their tale of exploitation, fraud and abuses, have enabled Miss Abbott to picture most vividly the perils which await these men and women who are ignorant of our language, from the moment they leave Ellis Island, and which we ignorantly or complacently have so long tolerated. This experience has also enabled her to point out the methods of remedying these conditions.

Better legislation, wiser administration, and a keener sense of obligation in every citizen are the essentials. How adequately America's duty to the immigrant has been performed is clearly shown in every chapter of the book.

Hitherto, immigration legislation, except as to the

Introduction

Chinese, has been non-restrictive; over the President's veto, this has now been changed and the illiterate, irrespective of character, mental or physical condition, are to be excluded. This fundamental controversy is for the present, at least, settled; both sides should now enlist in the campaign to secure for those immigrants who pass the tests for admission, that protection from abuse and wrong which their helplessness demands and which an enlightened self-interest would seem to require. And when this shall have been secured, perhaps we shall have learned that it is neither desirable nor possible to fit human beings into a single mold: that true Americanization can best be attained by the development of each immigrant's inherited latent powers; that each of the older nations, through its emigrants, can contribute in the future as each has contributed in the past elements of value: spiritual, moral, mental, physical or æsthetic, essential for the realization of an ideal America.

A frank recognition that diversity does not imply inferiority has enabled Miss Abbott during the past eight years, as Director of the Immigrant's Protective League of Chicago, to gain a sympathetic contact with every immigrant group in Chicago and thus to study the problems of the immigrant, both from America's and from the immigrant's point of view. A complete absence of the prejudice, so common in all ages and all countries, against the stranger, the foreigner, pervades her entire work Only in that spirit can the Americanization of the immigrant be successfully accomplished.

JULIAN W. MACK.

PREFACE

At the present time when our attention is not diverted by the dramatic incidents connected with the arrival of hundreds of thousands of immigrants, we should be able to give serious consideration to the problems created by the immigrants who are in our midst. In other words, we should be asking ourselves what are the complications resulting from a complex population which should be taken into account in our community plans and what are the opportunities which are ours because we are akin to all the world.

During the past eighteen months the hyphenated American has been pointed to as an object of scorn and suspicion and Americanism has been called an "issue" in practical politics. Now is therefore the time to consider in justice to ourselves and to the foreign born what should be done with the immigrant or for the immigrant who is admitted.

In the past we have followed a *laissez-faire* policy. In this discussion of *The Immigrant and the Community*, an effort has been made to show concretely how the immigrant and indirectly the community have suffered both materially and spiritually from our failure to plan for his protection and for his adjustment to American life.

The numbers that will crowd the steerage with the

Preface

re-establishment of peace and the parts of Europe from which they will come cannot now be determined with exactness. But we can be sure that the "new immigration" will bring new aspects of the old problems. It is, for example, reasonable to expect that the proportion of women among those who will seek to enter the United States will be larger after than it was before the war. This will mean that the "Special Problems of the Immigrant Girl" discussed in Chapter III will become more serious.

In general, however, the difficulties encountered by the immigrant will be the same and we can, therefore, on the basis of our past experience make intelligent plans for the future.

The conclusions which are reached in this discussion are based on more than eight years of work with the Immigrants' Protective League and seven years of residence at Hull House, Chicago, seven months' investigation for the Massachusetts Commission on Immigration and a brief study of some of the most important European districts from which the immigrants came to us before the war. A part of the material used in Chapters II, III, IV and IX has already appeared in the *American Journal of Sociology*, the *Journal of Criminal Law and Criminology*, and the *Survey*. Most of it was first organized for a course of lectures at the Chicago School of Civics and Philanthropy.

The help and encouragement of the officers of the Immigrants' Protective League, especially of Judge Mack, Miss Addams and Miss Breckinridge, whose sympathy and understanding of the foreign born grows

Preface

out of wide acquaintance with them, is gratefully acknowledged. I am very glad also of an opportunity to say how much of whatever is valuable in the book has been contributed by my associates on the staff of the League who have assisted in working out from day to day the problems which have presented themselves.

GRACE ABBOTT.

Chicago, 1917.

CONTENTS

CHAPTER		PAGE
I	THE JOURNEY OF THE IMMIGRANT	3
II	THE PROBLEM OF FINDING A FIRST "JOB"	26
III	THE SPECIAL PROBLEMS OF THE IMMIGRANT GIRL	55
IV	PROTECTION AGAINST EXPLOITATION	81
V	THE IMMIGRANT IN THE COURTS	105
VI	THE IMMIGRANT AND THE PUBLIC HEALTH	138
VII	THE IMMIGRANT AND THE POVERTY PROBLEM	166
VIII	THE IMMIGRANT AND INDUSTRIAL DEMOCRACY	196
IX	THE EDUCATION OF THE IMMIGRANT	221
X	THE IMMIGRANT IN POLITICS	247
XI	THE IMMIGRANT AND AMERICAN INTERNATIONALISM	267
XII	THE IMMIGRANT'S PLACE IN A SOCIAL PROGRAM	282
	INDEX	299

THE IMMIGRANT
AND THE COMMUNITY

THE IMMIGRANT
AND THE COMMUNITY

CHAPTER I

THE JOURNEY OF THE IMMIGRANT

THE stories of hardship, danger, and exploitation that the immigrants suffered on their journey to the United States during the early part of the nineteenth century do not make pleasant reading. When the sailing vessel was still the usual means of crossing the Atlantic, travelers were required to furnish their own food and bedding for a journey that usually lasted a month or six weeks, and sometimes days or even weeks longer. Complaints of fearful overcrowding without regard for sex or age, of gross immorality, and of cruelty on the part of officers and crew were made in newspapers as well as before congressional investigating committees.

The death-rate during the crossing was appalling. According to Friedrich Kapp, chairman of the New York Board of Emigration Commissioners, a death-rate of 10 per cent. was not uncommon, while sometimes as many as one third of the entire number died. Often, for example, the Irish famine victims, whose power of resistance had already been shattered, escaped from their stricken country only to die at sea.

Conditions of passenger traffic across the ocean were,

The Immigrant and the Community

however, greatly improved as a result of the statutes regulating steerage conditions passed by the United States in 1819, 1846, 1847, 1855, and 1860, and similar legislation adopted at about the same time by England, Holland, and the German cities. The shortening of the journey by the use of steam and the competition of rival companies also resulted in more comforts for the immigrant.

But the journey is still very far from being what decency demands. In ships which still have what is known as the "old-type steerage" as many as three hundred persons often sleep and live during the crossing in the large dormitories which have rows and rows of double-deck berths. These berths are six feet long, two feet wide, and are two and one-half feet apart. Into thirty cubic feet of space, therefore, the immigrant must pack himself, his hand luggage, his towels and other toilet necessities, and the eating utensils which the ship furnishes him.

The misery of these conditions is greatly aggravated on bad days when the immigrants cannot use the small open deck allotted to them, when the hatches are closed, and the three hundred steerage passengers spend day and night in their berths, sometimes compelled to sleep in their clothes because the bedding furnished them is insufficient

A number of excellent reports on steerage conditions have been made in recent years which are based on experiences of men and women who traveled as immigrants both to and from Europe. As is to be expected, all the investigators who have made the trip and know these conditions at first hand have agreed that this old-style

The Journey of the Immigrant

steerage should be abolished. The law should require more deck space, more and better food, and better sleeping quarters. Now, when immigration is in a sense at a standstill, would seem to be a time to set a new standard, so that with the new immigration, which will probably come after the war, safe, sanitary, and reasonably comfortable quarters can be assured for all those who come. The steerage with its huge and promiscuous dormitories should become a thing of the past, and the four- or six-passenger cabins that are now found in the third-class accommodations of some of the boats should be substituted. There is also general agreement that the treatment of the immigrants by the crew, complaint of which is frequently made by the immigrant women, would be much improved if a government inspector traveled with every boat, or if it were known that he might be on any boat disguised as an immigrant.

In the early nineteenth century, the trials of the immigrant did not end with the fearful journey across the Atlantic, for wherever they landed they were met by a small army of exploiters. Runners who spoke their language piloted them to boarding houses where they were held until their little money was exhausted, or employment agents and bogus railroad representatives robbed and misdirected them. Before the regulation of immigration was taken over by the United States, a number of the States had taken steps to prevent these abuses. New York especially had developed machinery that had for its object the guarding of the newly arrived immigrant from fraud and exploitation, not only at the port of New York but in cities in the interior of the State.

The Immigrant and the Community

The statute enacted by New York in 1848 [1] and improved in 1849 [2] established a strict control of immigrant boarding houses, runners, and passenger and baggage agents, and provided for the appointment of officials who were to give advice to the immigrants and put them on their guard against fraud and imposition. A further act of 1855 [3] required transportation companies to furnish the mayors of different cities with a statement of the rates and charges for conveying immigrants; and one of 1868 [4] gave the Commissioner of Immigration supervision over the sale of passenger tickets to immigrants. In their efforts to protect the immigrants the state authorities in New York coöperated with private agencies, especially the German and Irish societies formed to assist the immigrants of those nationalities who were coming in such large numbers at that time.

The decisions of the United States Supreme Court holding the state head tax on immigrants unconstitutional [5] ended state regulation and compelled the United States Government to take over this work. Since then public attention has in the main been so fastened on the 2 or 3 per cent. of the immigrants who are excluded as undesirable that little thought has been given to the 97 or 98 per cent. of them who are admitted, although self-interest alone should long ago have suggested that special precautions be taken by the United States for the protection of the morals and the health of the immigrant who is permitted to remain.

[1] Laws of New York, 1848, Chap 219.
[2] *Ibid*, 1849, Chaps 321 and 350
[3] *Ibid*, 1855. Chap 474.
[4] *Ibid*, 1868, Chap. 793
[5] 11 Peters, 102; 7 Howard, 283; 92 U. S 259.

The Journey of the Immigrant

Much improvement in the methods of inspection, detention, and release of immigrants at the various ports of arrival has been made in recent years. Because of the more efficient organization of the service, immigrants are now treated with humane consideration by government officials; runners from cheap hotels, expressmen, employment agents, and all those who might profit by their ignorance and dependence are generally denied access to them. The moral exploitation of the girl is guarded against by an examination of the persons to whom she is released.

But in contrast to these improvements made at the ports, there is, for the girl destined to Chicago and other interior points, no corresponding protective machinery. She is carefully guarded by the federal authorities until she is placed on the train, but the Government then considers that its responsibility is at an end. It is not considered a matter of national concern whether she is sent to her destination by the most direct or by a long, circuitous route. She may be approached by any one while traveling and persuaded to leave the train. Through her own mistake or intention or the carelessness of railroad officials, she may be put off before she reaches her destination.

Immigrants are no longer sold bogus railroad tickets at the ports as they were before the railroads had official representatives at Castle Garden, but they still do not always get a square deal from the railroads. The steamship companies hold the key to the present situation because relatives and friends who send prepaid tickets from the United States as well as those who purchase their

The Immigrant and the Community

transportation abroad are usually persuaded to buy through tickets to the final destination. This means that most of the immigrants land with an order which shows that they have paid a steamship company for a railroad ticket to their destination. The steamship companies have, therefore, the power of saying whether all those who come on their boats with these orders shall travel over one railroad or whether this patronage shall be more generally distributed By a "friendly" agreement between the steamship companies and practically all the railroads of the country, a railroad office, maintained under the joint control of the railroads at Ellis Island, is recognized by the steamship companies and each railroad is given its share of the patronage. This agreement is based, however, upon the business ideal of fairness to the competing railroads and not upon consideration of the comfort of the immigrants. In order that all the roads may enjoy their share of the traffic, immigrants are sometimes sent by the most indirect routes to their destinations. For example, those who are coming to Chicago are often sent from New York by boat on the Old Dominion Line to Norfolk, Virginia, and from there on by the Chesapeake and Ohio and connecting lines to Chicago.

In the year ending June 30, 1916, immigrants were sent by nine different routes from New York to Chicago, but nearly three times as many were sent around by Norfolk, Virginia, as by any other single route Instances less flagrant but which result in much discomfort and sometimes real suffering also occur.

Immigrants constantly arrive in Chicago on their way

The Journey of the Immigrant

to the Pacific coast who could make the journey without a single change but are given tickets at Ellis Island which call for several changes *en route*.

A Norwegian girl arrived in May of 1916 on the *Kristianiafjord* and was going to a town in Iowa. No change should have been necessary after she left Chicago, but she was put on a train that left the city in the afternoon and then put off at a railroad junction in Illinois at nine o'clock at night to wait for another train. She sat up all night in the railroad station and then spent the next day waiting for her train, alone and frightened because she was unable to speak a word of English and did not know how to make herself safe and comfortable. The railroad agent made no effort to protect her from three men who he saw were annoying her. To add to the anxiety that any girl would feel under these circumstances, she was robbed of the little money she had carefully saved because she did not want to reach her relatives quite empty-handed.

Passengers on the immigrant trains frequently expect to arrive in a much shorter time than the indirect route requires, and they do not provide themselves with the additional food which the roundabout journey makes necessary. No arrangement is made for them to purchase food *en route,* so they sometimes arrive hungry and exhausted. One tired Bohemian mother who came to the office of the Immigrants' Protective League with her four little children had had the difficult task of keeping them quiet when they had had no food for the last thirty-six hours of their trip.

Some improvement has been made recently in the rout-

The Immigrant and the Community

ing of the immigrants, but Mr. Frederic C Howe, the present Commissioner of Immigration at Ellis Island, who is very much interested in eradicating this and all other abuses, thinks that the evils of the present system cannot be cured until the Immigration Bureau is authorized by Congress to take entire charge of this matter.

This neglect on the part of the United States to take any measure to protect the immigrant after he has been admitted to the United States was especially inexcusable. The Government's experience with the ocean-going steamers gave every reason for anticipating that, in the absence of regulation and inspection, overcrowding, insanitary conditions, and inadequate provisions for the women and girls were sure to be found on the boats which carried immigrants from New York to Fall River, or on the immigrant trains which took so many scores of thousands west each year during the periods of heavy immigration which preceded the war

The Massachusetts Commission on Immigration, an investigating commission appointed in 1913, received complaints about conditions on the Fall River boats on which, in accordance with an agreement with the transatlantic steamship companies, all the immigrants were then sent from New York to Boston or from Boston to New York.

Investigators for the Commission who were sent to make the trip as immigrants reported shocking conditions: "beds filthy, ventilation incredibly inadequate, and the overcrowding serious." Worse than this, the immigrant men were the butt of coarse and cruel jokes and pranks, and the Polish girls were compelled to defend themselves

The Journey of the Immigrant

against the advances of the crew who freely entered the women's dormitory and tried to drag the girls into the crew's quarters.

The steamship company was directly responsible for these conditions, but the United States Government was equally to blame for taking no precautions to insure decency on these boats inasmuch as its experience in regulating ocean travel since 1819 had shown the necessity of official regulation and supervision.

In the hope of securing immediate improvement, the Massachusetts Commission submitted the result of its investigation to the officers of the steamship company, and steps were at once taken by the company to improve conditions. By the time its report was submitted to the legislature, the Commission was therefore able to report that the boats were being rebuilt so as to provide outside ventilation for both men's and women's quarters, more sanitary washrooms, and complete separation of the crew's quarters from the quarters of the immigrant women. Furthermore, an immigrant steward and a stewardess were placed in charge of the immigrant service. All this promised much greater safety and comfort for the immigrant. But the Commission called attention to the fact that if conditions were to be kept decent, legislation regulating these boats and continuous inspection were necessary. The temptation to overcrowd dangerously and in consequence to lower the moral safeguards is great. A permanent commission on immigration was not created in Massachusetts, however, and the United States Government, although it holds that the way in which immigrants travel before they are admitted is a

The Immigrant and the Community

matter of national concern, still takes the position that after they are admitted it is quite indifferent as to what they suffer from carelessness, neglect, or exploitation.

The railroad journey also needs supervision. At present, it is practically impossible to trace the girls who leave New York but who never reach their friends in Chicago. Sometimes it is possible to reach some conclusion as to what became of them, but these conclusions only point to the necessity for safeguarding the journey. For example, two Polish girls, seventeen and twenty-two years of age, whose experience before they started for America had been bounded by the limits of a small farm in Galicia, were coming to their cousins who lived back of the Stockyards in Chicago. Their names and addresses had been sent to the Immigrants' Protective League on one of the lists of unaccompanied girls received regularly from the ports of entry. When one of the visitors of the League called at the house, she found the cousin and the entire household much alarmed because the girls had not arrived. Through inquiries of others who came on the same boat, it was learned that the girls had become acquainted on the way over with a man from Rochester and that he was "looking out for them." The only official information which could be secured was a description of the railroad tickets that the girls held when they left Ellis Island. Investigation by the railroad showed that on that date one ticket had been sold to Rochester and two Chicago tickets had been used only as far as Rochester. The girls had completely disappeared, and there was no official responsibility for their failure to arrive in Chicago.

The Journey of the Immigrant

Sometimes the girls, to whom nothing really serious happens, are for a time in an extremely dangerous position. For example, one seventeen-year-old girl was put off the train at South Chicago by mistake and wandered about for several hours at night. Finally a man offered to take her to her friends. He proved worthy of the confidence she had in his kindly intent, and she was conducted safely to the Northwest Side, many miles from where she had been left. Another girl, nineteen years old, who came in by way of Quebec, became separated from her sister and friends at Detroit. She was taken to a police station for the night and in the morning continued her journey. She arrived in South Chicago without money or the address of her relatives. She was therefore taken to the South Chicago Police Station and after spending a night there was taken to the Women's Annex of the Harrison Street Police Station. The police regarded it as impossible to find the girl's friends, so the matron of the Annex found her work in a downtown hotel. A visitor of the League returning from South Chicago reported great excitement in one neighborhood over the fact that an immigrant girl had been lost at Detroit. This report was connected with the story of the police matron, and a visit to the hotel proved the identity of the girl. Except for this she would have been alone in Chicago, ignorant of our language and the dangers of the city, with no one to turn to in case of sickness or unemployment.

Several girls have told of being approached on the trains and invited by strange men to get off at "some big city and see the town," but they wisely concluded to con-

The Immigrant and the Community

tinue their journey without these gay excursions into the unknown.

More immigrants have been arriving at great distributing centers like Chicago, Pittsburgh, or Cleveland than came to the port of New York during the days when the State of New York was adopting its comprehensive program for the protection of the immigrants. During the early part of the nineteenth century it is said, that "the hapless strangers, ignorant of the customs and laws of the country, often unable to speak the language that would procure police assistance, more liable by reason of their 'outlandish' dress and manners to meet ridicule than sympathy from the masses of native citizens, were browbeaten and fleeced without mercy."[6] This reads like a description of the situation in which those who have been coming in the twentieth century have found themselves on getting off an immigrant train in Chicago.

Any woman can understand the nervous apprehension which the immigrant girl must feel as she comes into one of Chicago's bewildering railroad stations, but very few realize how well grounded her fears are. Eager friends and relatives find it almost impossible to meet the immigrants because immigrant trains are sidetracked for all other kinds of traffic, so that it is extremely difficult to determine just when they will reach Chicago. Merely talking with the girls about their experiences is not so convincing as seeing the actual situation which they meet on leaving a train in Chicago.

On one occasion, for example, the train was due at

[6] T. W. Page. "The Transportation of Immigrants and Reception Arrangements in the Nineteenth Century," *Journal of Political Economy*, Vol. 19, p 744.

The Journey of the Immigrant

seven thirty in the morning, but finally arrived shortly after four o'clock in the afternoon. It had been reported as coming at various hours so that three trips were made to the station, although each time inquiry had been made by telephone and assurance given that the train was reported due at once. Several hundred immigrants got off the train when it finally came. Many of them were very young, and one felt their disappointment as they peered eagerly and anxiously for the father or sister or friend they expected to see. Those who were going north or west of Chicago came out the main gate already ticketed by a representative of the transfer company and were taken as American travelers are to another depot without any confusion. But those who were to remain in Chicago were directed into a small immigrant waiting-room which opened on a narrow side street. Here they were hastily sorted into groups and then pushed out the door into the midst of ten or twelve expressmen, who were crowding and pushing and quarreling over the division of spoils. In a short time the struggle was over and they had all been loaded into the waiting wagons. By this time it was almost dark and they drove away.

This unsupervised, irresponsible method of disposing of these people explains the plight of the Irish girl who had started on a wagon with a group of other immigrants for the South Side. After going some distance, the expressman discovered she had a North Side address; so, charging her four dollars, he put her off the wagon and left her without any suggestion as to what she should do. It explains, too, the disposition that was made of a Polish girl of seventeen who was taken at three o'clock

The Immigrant and the Community

in the morning to the place where her sister was supposed to live. The address proved to be incorrect, however, and the woman who lived there angrily refused to let her stay until morning. The girl had no money and wept disconsolately when the expressman told her in a language she did not understand that " nobody could find her sister if nobody knew her address and that he was n't going to take her back to the depot for nothing." The saloon-keeper next door finally offered her a refuge, and she lived with his family behind the saloon three days before her sister, who was making daily trips to the depot, was found.

Not long before this, a girl had been brought to the office of the Immigrants' Protective League who had arrived in Chicago on Sunday afternoon and because her friends could not be found had been taken to the Annex of the Harrison Street Police Station, where, like many immigrant girls, she had received her first initiation into Chicago life. She had the name and address of the girl friend who lived in Chicago and had promised to get her work, written in the front of her prayer-book, and she could not understand that it was incorrect. She tearfully insisted on accompanying the Polish visitor of the Immigrants' Protective League on the search for her friend and grew more and more discouraged as one clue after another was tried and failed. Finally the girl said that her friend worked in a bed-spring factory. Starting out anew on this clue, she was found in the third bed-spring factory they visited. Then the friend explained that one number had been left off the address which the girl had so carefully written in her prayer-book.

The Journey of the Immigrant

Since the summer of 1908, the Immigrants' Protective League has received from the various ports of entry the names and addresses of the unaccompanied women and girls who are coming to Chicago. The plan has been to have these women and girls visited by a representative of the League who was able to speak their language and was prepared to help them in making a beginning of their life in Chicago. Since 1908, 20,304 girls have been thus visited by the League — not all those whose names were received, because the resources of the League were not such as to enable us to do this during the seasons when immigration was heaviest. It was through these visits that we learned that some girls did not reach their relatives and friends, and that an extension of the care and supervision which is given girls at the ports of entry should be extended to the interior. For example, in one year of normal immigration when 3338 girls were visited, 434 of the addresses sent us were obviously incorrect and no visit was attempted. We found some trace of 364 others, but after several visits the attempt to locate them was abandoned, although we had not followed up every possible clue. But 554 could not be located, although every possible effort was made to find them. In thirty-four instances, we found the persons whose names and addresses the girls had given at the port, but they were not expecting the girls and knew nothing of what had become of them. Typical cases of failure to find the girls whose names were received from the ports will illustrate the reasons for anxiety. A Lithuanian girl of eighteen, for example, gave the address of a local steamship agency, and subsequently we learned that she had

The Immigrant and the Community

been called for by a notoriously disreputable man and taken to a rooming house. We traced her to two other addresses but were not able to find her. In another case, investigation of an address which a twenty-year-old Polish girl gave revealed the fact that three years previously a telegram had been received from the port announcing the arrival of a girl who was unknown to any one at the address given. No girl had come. The next year this had happened again. This particular year neither the telegram nor the girl had arrived, and although the name and address was correct no explanation of the use of the name could be given. The evidence which we have had year after year has convinced us that many of these girls whom we were unable to locate undoubtedly reached their relatives and friends; many others, although they did not succeed in doing this, have, by the merest chance, found people who were kind to them and helped them in securing work and in making their connections in Chicago; but from much evidence we are sure that a considerable number cannot be accounted for in these ways.

Whether in cases like those last cited the giving of the incorrect name and address was intentional on the part of the girl, the result of some mistake, or serious deception, federal protection and supervision is the only way of reducing the resulting danger to the community and to the girls. In the administration of the immigration law the girls are required to give the name and address of some one to whom they are coming as a condition of admission. But experience has shown how little protection there is either for the community or for the girl in this requirement.

The Journey of the Immigrant

In 1910 the Immigrants' Protective League was given by the Chicago and Western Indiana Railroad the use of a building across from its depot, and all the immigrants who arrived at that station were sent across to the League's waiting-room. As this was the terminal used by the Erie, the Wabash, and the Grand Trunk railroads, more than three times as many immigrants arrived at this as at any other station in the city. The plan worked out by the League was that its officers, speaking the languages of the immigrants, should arrange to send them to their friends. If possible, relatives were to be reached by telephone; if this could not be done, they were to be sent sometimes with a cab or expressman, sometimes in charge of a messenger boy, or, when they were able to speak English or had some knowledge of how to get about in a city, they were to be directed or taken to a street car; and finally all those who were peculiarly helpless or who had doubtful or suspicious addresses were to be sent out accompanied by one of the officers of the League. This plan was followed for four years. Cards printed in their native languages were given the immigrants as they left the League's waiting-room, telling them what they were to do in case of an overcharge or neglect on the part of the driver or messenger. The name and address of each immigrant, the number of the expressman or cab driver, the name of the relative or officer or messenger boy to whom each was intrusted, as well as any charges made, were carefully recorded

As was anticipated, the expressmen and cabmen opposed this supervision as an invasion of the right to exploit the immigrant which they thought the city had guar-

The Immigrant and the Community

anteed them when they paid their license of one dollar and a half. With their official-looking badges and caps and their stock of foreign phrases, the drivers and runners would secure the attention of the immigrants and then by a combination of force and persuasion would load them on their wagons and drive off with them. During the first six months of the League's work at this station, although a vigorous fight was kept up with the drivers by night as well as by day, we were able to get hold of only 1903 immigrants, the next year 5204 reached our waiting-room and their delivery was arranged for in the orderly manner planned. In 1912 the number increased to 15,-537. By 1913 we had convinced the exploiters that we were really in earnest and that prosecutions would be pushed and licenses suspended, and during that year 41,-322 immigrants were cared for in the League's waiting-room and their delivery arranged for by officers of the League.

Although complaints of abuses were very much less frequent in 1913 than in former years, it was still necessary for us to report thirty-three drivers of express wagons and cabs to the Inspector of Vehicles, who promptly imposed the penalties prescribed by the city ordinance for overcharges and similar offenses.

A very large number of the immigrant trains were found to arrive between midnight and six o'clock in the morning. Some of the immigrants had addresses to which they could not be taken at night, and others having dangerous or doubtful addresses could not be sent out until an investigation had been made in the morning. So the Immigrants' Protective League found it necessary to

The Journey of the Immigrant

keep many of the immigrants over night, and some bedrooms were therefore provided on the second floor of its building. In one year ninety five arrived who had lost their addresses, and it was necessary for us to spend much time in the search for their relatives or friends.

In undertaking this work, the Immigrants' Protective League had two objects: first, to give to the very large numbers arriving at this depot the assistance they so badly needed; and second, and more important, to demonstrate that official supervision was both necessary and practical. The limitations upon the work of a private organization were evident from the beginning. We lacked the authority necessary to make the protection as effective as it should be made; the space we had was quite inadequate to prevent serious overcrowding of the waiting-room; and it was impossible to secure, through private subscription, funds adequate for doing work which so clearly belonged to the Federal Government. Moreover, the organization did not feel justified in appealing to interested citizens to donate the money for this work when the head tax which the Government levied upon the immigrant was much more than enough to pay for really adequate protection and assistance during the first period of adjustment. The need of the Federal Government's undertaking this work was therefore constantly urged; and in 1913 a law was passed by Congress that authorized the Secretary of Labor to establish immigrant stations at points in the interior, and an appropriation was made for the maintenance of such a station in Chicago. This law also authorized the Secretary to detail immigrant inspectors to travel on immigrant trains.

The Immigrant and the Community

With some difficulty, a location was found for the station in 1913, and the receiving-room, dormitories, bathrooms, and laundry were furnished and ready for use in January, 1914. The following summer, certain additional officers were assigned to the Chicago Station to undertake this work, but these were later withdrawn.

The delay in the operation of the Station was declared in the Annual Report of the Secretary of Labor for 1914 to be due to the fact that the immigrants were required to pay a local transfer agency for transportation from the railway stations to the Immigrant Station. This difficulty was removed during the summer of 1914 through the agreement by all the railroads carrying Chicago-bound immigrants to transfer them from the terminal stations to the Immigrant Station without extra charge. But this agreement has not been utilized by the Federal Government except when the immigrant on his arrival at Ellis Island asks to be transferred to the Federal Station in Chicago.

The large receiving-room, after being locked for a year, is now being used for the much-needed labor exchange work that the Department of Labor has recently undertaken. But the dormitories, bathrooms, laundry rooms, etc., have never been used. The Government has been paying rent for this unused space for more than two years. This illustration of the way in which an administrative department of the Government can refuse to carry out the laws passed by Congress should be interesting to students of political science

That the duty of protecting and caring for the immigrant on his journey belongs to the federal rather than

The Journey of the Immigrant

the local government is obvious. The former controls the admission of immigrants and is informed as to the number arriving. Protection and supervision of release is given the immigrants who arrive at the ports of entry, and it is logical, therefore, to ask an extension of this care to the interior. The protection needed by immigrants arriving in Chicago is also needed in Pittsburgh, Cleveland, St. Louis, and other important centers of arrival and distribution. Official inspectors, both men and women, should travel on immigrant trains to insure considerate treatment on the part of the railroads and to protect the immigrant from the organized exploitation which develops when there is no official supervision.

The first federal statute that provided for regulation of immigration (1882), as well as the statutes of 1903 and 1907, authorized the Commissioner-General of Immigration " to establish such regulations, not inconsistent with law, as he shall deem best calculated for protecting the United States and the immigrant *from fraud and loss,*" and gave him authority to enter into contracts for the support and relief of such immigrants as may fall into distress or need public aid. These provisions were not made without a quite definite understanding of the need for the protection which was here authorized. It may be assumed that the provision in the federal statutes recognizing the duty of the Government to guard the immigrant from fraud and loss was suggested by the similar functions of the New York officials. In view of this, it would seem that a moral duty rests on the Federal Government to give proper consideration to the protective aspect of immigrant control.

The Immigrant and the Community

National and even international attention has been drawn to the prosecution of so-called "white slavers." Important as this work is, it should not be the only form of control attempted. For in prosecutions we must, of necessity, wait until the girl has been ruined, and no fine or penitentiary sentence inflicted upon the man or woman responsible for her downfall can undo for her or for society the damage that has been wrought. Some constructive, preventive measures should be undertaken as well. First among these, perhaps, should be the guarantee to every immigrant girl of a safe arrival at her destination.

In his annual report for 1915, the Commissioner-General of Immigration calls attention to the fact that "since the law providing for the collection of a head tax from all arriving immigrants has been in force, up to the end of this fiscal year (1915) there has been collected over $9,000,000 in excess of the expenditures for the immigration service." The Immigration Bill which has just been passed over the President's veto increases this head tax for adults from four to eight dollars. And so it is probable that in the future larger sums will be collected. The obligation of regarding the money collected in this way as a trust fund to be used in behalf of the immigrant cannot be too strongly insisted upon.

The first evidence of the " new nationalism " should be in the nation's affording the kind of protection which shall give to the immigrant such ideas of America as we should like him to have when he begins his life among us. Only too frequently, under present conditions, the idealistic pic-

The Journey of the Immigrant

ture of America which he brings with him is destroyed immediately on his arrival, and instead he begins with a knowledge of some of the ugliest and meanest aspects of our life.

CHAPTER II

THE PROBLEM OF FINDING A FIRST "JOB"

THE importance of the employment agency in the industrial or economic adjustment of the immigrant becomes apparent with the first work undertaken in his behalf. Ignorant of our language, of the country, and of the American standard of wages, and compelled by his poverty to secure immediate employment, the immigrant is especially defenseless when he offers himself in the labor market. And at no time does he need disinterested guidance and help more than in securing his first work. Yet, he is dependent in most cases upon the private employment agent; and he becomes, because of his ignorance and his necessities, a great temptation to an honest agent and a great opportunity to an unscrupulous one.

For this reason, an investigation of the Chicago labor agencies was made by the Immigrants' Protective League in order to determine what kinds of work may be obtained through these agencies by the immigrant man or woman, in what ways they are exploited, and what changes in the laws are necessary to reduce such exploitation to a minimum.[1] In the course of the investigation 178 agencies were investigated, and 110 of them were found to make a specialty of placing foreigners.

---
[1] A report of this investigation was published in the *American Journal of Sociology*, XIV: 289-305, "The Chicago Employment Agency and the Immigrant Worker," Grace Abbott.

Finding a First "Job"

Since all the agencies in the neighborhood of any of Chicago's foreign colonies were visited and also those in the downtown district, it is believed that all those which handle immigrants in any large numbers were covered in the investigation.

As the industrial problems and difficulties of the immigrant man and woman are quite different, their relation to the employment agent must be separately considered. According to the Annual Report of the Commissioner-General of Immigration, the number of men and boys was almost twice the number of women and girls admitted as immigrants to the United States during the year ending June 30, 1914.[2] This proportion is the usual one. The relative number of women who enter industrial life is still smaller; for of the women admitted, a considerable number are coming to their husbands and will be employed only in their own households.

The foreign women who do not go into domestic service are, in New England, employed in the largest numbers in the cotton and woolen mills and in the shoe factories; in Chicago and other cities with a similar industrial organization, they are found in the various sewing trades, in the twine factories, as coremakers in foundries, in the stockyards, the tobacco factories, the market gardens, and in many other occupations in or near the city.

Work of this sort is usually secured by application at the factory and not through employment agencies The following table shows the extent of this practice in Chicago.

[2] See p. 42; 798,747 males and 419,733 females were admitted.

The Immigrant and the Community

	Agencies Supplying Women Only	Agencies Supplying both Men and Women	Total
Number of agencies offering housework	28	..	28
Number of agencies offering hotel or restaurant work.....	18	17	35
Number of agencies offering factory work	4	5	9
	50	22	72
Agencies counted twice........	17	1	18
Total number of agencies..	33	21	54

The immigrant girl usually pays the agent less than $2, in contrast, as will be shown later, with the immigrant man, who usually pays from $3 to $14. The work offered her is almost without exception hotel or housework; so the small army of foreign girls at work in the Stockyards and at the various clothing trades in the city must secure their positions through other means. Since the Jewish and the Italian girls will not go into service, the largest numbers of women placed by the private employment agents are Poles, Bohemians, Slovaks, and Lithuanians. For this reason the immigrant "intelligence offices" are usually found in the neighborhood of these colonies. The restaurant or hotel work offered the immigrant girl means dishwashing or cleaning, for which she is paid from $16 to $25 a month with board; for housework she can get from $16 to $25 a month with board and room.

Finding a First "Job"

Migratory workers among the women are much fewer than among the men, still they are not unknown. Every year large numbers of women are sent by employment agents to work in the summer hotels. They return to the city with the end of the season. Many are sent out from Chicago to hotels and restaurants as far away as the Pacific coast on six months' contracts which provide for transportation back to Chicago at the end of that time. During good years the agents can without much difficulty place these women again on their return to the city. During periods of business depression, however, they become a part of the "unemployment problem."

The opportunity for the moral exploitation of the immigrant girl by the employment agent is apparent; and occasionally unmistakable evidence is found of actual coöperation between the agent and the keeper of the house of prostitution. For example, a Roumanian and a Hungarian-Jewish girl, both under eighteen years of age, applied to a Russian-Jewish employment agency for work in the summer of 1914. The agency license was in the name of an illiterate old woman, but the agency was actually conducted by her married daughter. These girls had been told by the woman that there was no work for them; but as they were leaving the room, they were stopped by her husband, who promised them easy jobs entertaining men that would pay from $25 to $50 a week. This amount was so large that they did not believe him and told the story to a park policeman who spoke Yiddish. He advised swearing out a warrant for the man. This was done; but when the case was called, it was continued and the man released on a $25 bond. This action on the

The Immigrant and the Community

part of the court convinced the officer that political influence was being used in behalf of the man, and he asked the coöperation of the Immigrants' Protective League. Efforts to locate the man were unsuccessful; the Inspector of Private Employment Agencies thought it was useless to take any action against the agency; and the judge, seemingly satisfied with the rôle he had played, forfeited the bond and dismissed the case.

The Chicago Vice Commission [3] (1911) found 13 out of 28 employment agents willing to supply servants to a supposedly immoral place, in violation of the employment agency law. Four of these agencies, however, said that they would send a woman but not a girl; and three others thought the law was not designed to protect colored women and offered to supply them, with apparently no fear that the law would be used for the protection of the Negro girl.

In the investigation made by the United States Immigration Commission,[4] 17 out of 22 licensed agents were found to be willing to furnish girls for work in an alleged "sporting house." This investigation also revealed the fact that one half of the Immigrant Homes, supposedly operated for the protection of girls, actually supplied girls to the Commission's investigators for work of the same kind.

In most cases the employment agent who places women is herself a woman, her office is also her kitchen or her parlor, and the place is usually dirty and almost without exception unbusinesslike. The experience of the Immi-

[3] See their report, entitled "The Social Evil in Chicago," pp. 218-20.
[4] See *Reports of the U. S. Immigration Commission,* Vol. 37, p. 142.

Finding a First "Job"

grants' Protective League has been that the commonest offense of the agent is a dangerous disregard of the character of the places to which she sends a girl rather than a commercial connivance in the girl's ruin.

With the immigrant man, however, the industrial situation is often more difficult. He finds himself greatly handicapped when he tries to obtain work. In the first place, because of his ignorance of English and his consequent inability to give or to receive direction, he cannot be used without an interpreter, and interpreters can be profitably employed only when large groups of immigrants work together. Such groups are employed by the foundries, at the Stockyards, in mines, or railroad, car-line, and building construction, in ice and lumber camps, and in other similar kinds of work. Much of this is seasonal work and is located at a great distance from the city. For example, a large number of men are needed for a few months or weeks to harvest Dakota crops, to build a railroad in Wyoming or Arkansas, to harvest ice in Minnesota, to pick Michigan berries, or to work in the oyster beds of Maryland.

That the labor agencies are mainly concerned in meeting the demand for this class of laborers is indicated by the figures in the table on page 32, showing the kinds of work offered by the labor agencies covered in the investigation of Chicago Employment Agencies.

According to this table, 52 out of 77 agencies offered the immigrant what they described as "gang work." This gang work is usually construction work at a distance from the city The "city jobs" that the agent offers are usually jobs wrecking buildings, cleaning in

The Immigrant and the Community

Type of Work Offered	Agencies Supplying Men Only	Agencies Supplying both Men and Women	Total
"Gang work"	49	3	52
Restaurant or hotel work	2	15	17
Factory work	2	6	8
City jobs	8	..	8
	61	24	85
Number of agencies counted twice	5	3	8
Total number agencies	56	21	77

office buildings, or odd jobs on the railroads. It seemed most significant that the investigation showed that the only kind of work offered by 68 per cent. of the agencies handling immigrants was at a distance approximating a hundred to a thousand miles from Chicago.

Those who work on the railroads of the country — grading the roadbed, laying ties and rails, ballasting with gravel and crushed stone, ditching, and doing general track work — constitute the largest single group of these migratory laborers.

The subcommittee on Immigration of the Mayor's Commission on Unemployment (Chicago),[5] which reported in March, 1914, submitted to the principal railroads that enter Chicago certain questions with regard to this class of labor. The following information was obtained:

"These railroads estimated that about one third of the

[5] See p. 69, "Railroad Gangs," by Grace Abbott, Chairman of Sub-Committee on Immigration.

Finding a First "Job"

men employed for this work are 'hoboes'— the Irish, English, and American survivals of the time when all this work was done by English-speaking immigrants or native Americans. The others are 'foreigners'— Italians, Poles, Greeks, Bulgarians, Croatians, Russians, and others from southern and eastern Europe. The 'hoboes' are not only old hands at this work, but they are familiar with the ugliest aspects of American life in every city in the country. Most of the 'foreigners,' on the other hand, are having their first experience in industrial life in America, are ignorant of English, of the extent of the country, and of how a man may 'beat his way' from place to place and avoid arrest.

"Construction work lasts from six to eight months, beginning as soon as the weather permits, in March or April, and lasting until the work is finished or until the cold weather brings it to a close, in November or December.

"The number of men required for this work is difficult to determine. Eight railroads in answer to this question, replied that they tried to keep 11,414 men at work during the season. One of the railroads, whose gangs required 4593 men, estimated that twelve or fifteen times that number had to be sent out; another railroad reported twenty men sent out for every job; another ten; one wrote that it was impossible to say, because 'men were shipped out constantly from Chicago.' The total number of shipment must therefore reach several hundred thousand — how many men are involved, the railroad records do not show. About 75 per cent of the number, the railroads estimated, are secured from the Chicago labor

The Immigrant and the Community

market and return to Chicago for the winter. The other 25 per cent. come from St. Louis, Kansas City, Omaha, and other smaller centers.

"They are employed for this kind of work not as individuals but in groups of thirty or more, and are sent in charge of an 'interpreter' who acts as 'straw boss' to parts of the country of which they are entirely ignorant

"The wages of the 'hoboes' and 'foreigners' are usually the same — during the past season (1913) from $1.80 to $2 a day, two years ago $1.25 to $1.60 a day. In every other respect the two groups are so different that they must be considered separately.

"The 'hoboes,' or 'white' laborers as the men are sometimes called, very often ship out with no intention of going to work. The payment of an employment agency fee gets a man much more comfortably and safely to Minneapolis, Billings, Denver, or even California than 'beating his way.' 'Hoboes' who go to work at the place to which they are shipped usually stay only ten or fourteen days. They sleep in the freight-car bunks that the railroad provides free of charge, pay the commissary company $4 or $5 a week for wretched board, and four or five prices for tobacco, gloves, shirts, and other supplies Liquor, too, is sometimes sold in the camp for exhorbitant prices.

"Bad as the food, the sleeping quarters, and the wages are, these are no longer the reasons why the 'hoboes' drift from camp to camp, back to the city, out to the harvest field for a few days, on the road again, and finally to the city in November with about $30 in money.

Finding a First "Job"

Here they frequent the five-and ten-cent lodging houses and the 'barrel shops' of the hobo districts and are hungry, cold, and wretched during January, February, and March.

"The 'hobo' is physically and morally what his work and living conditions have made him. Demoralizing as any kind of temporary work is, this construction work at a distance from cities or towns is much worse than that which comes with the rush season in city factories and shops. The freight-car or shack bunks are usually unspeakably dirty, the food is wretched, the work is hard, and the hours long. Separated from their families and from society in general, without normal, wholesome recreation, the men are the easy victims of vice. Many of the Irish, English, and American laborers of a generation ago, forced by the necessities of our industrial system into becoming homeless workmen employed for six or eight months a year, have become diseased and are now incapable of the self-restraint that is necessary for regular employment. . . .

"With the 'foreigners' the case is quite different. The testimony of all the railroads consulted is that, unless the whole gang leave because they do not like the work or the camp or for some causes which, according to the railroad 'cannot be ascertained,' they stay until the work is over or the season closes. There is little of the restless, irresponsible drifting back and forth that characterizes the hobo group."

These men secure their work through private employment agencies, and it is customary for each road to depend upon some one agency to supply its gangs. In his

The Immigrant and the Community

dealings with these agencies, the immigrant usually suffers in one of three ways: (1) he is overcharged for the services rendered; (2) the work obtained is not as represented by the agent either in character, permanency, or remuneration; (3) he fails to get work, or the work lasts only a few days, leaving him stranded at a great distance from the city labor markets.

In Illinois the maximum "registration fee" that the employment agent may charge is fixed by statute at two dollars. This term is not defined by the law; but it is interpreted by the Attorney-General, as it would undoubtedly be by the courts, as in no way limiting the right of private contract. This means that an agent may charge any amount for a particular job; and as the registration system is practically never used by agents supplying unskilled workers, the statutory provision is no protection to the immigrant. An investigator who represented himself to be a man who collected "gangs" was told frankly, "We charge all we can get."

Fees are higher when the applicant is unable to speak English. In several cases the investigator was offered the same job for two or three dollars less than was demanded of the man who was ignorant of our language. For this reason it is impossible to say with any accuracy what fees are charged, but the table on page 37 gives the fees charged the investigators sent out by the Immigrants' Protective League.

The fees vary greatly with the season and with the amount of work that is being done. In the early spring, when all the men are eager to get out, fees as high as ten, fifteen, or even twenty dollars are the rule. In the

Finding a First "Job"

Fees Charged	Number of Agencies
$0 50 to $1 00	..
$1 00 to $2 00	13
$2 00 to $3 00	..
$3.00 to $5.00	23
$6 00 to $10.00	12
$11 00 to $14 00	3
Per cent. of wages	..
	51
Fees not reported	8
Total number of agencies	59

summer, when gangs are hard to fill, free shipments are common.

The agent promises a "steady job" even when he is speaking of work that from its very nature cannot last more than a few weeks or a month or two. The wage promised is usually less than two dollars a day. All things considered, then, it seems very clear that the service rendered is not worth the price paid, and yet the men who pay out of their small, hard-earned savings know of no other way by which they can get this work.

In many cases the fee includes railroad fare, but the value of the railroad ticket is difficult to determine. The agent always gets reduced rates or, when the work is in connection with a railroad, the men are shipped free. How much is railroad fare and how much the agent's fee does not appear on the receipts which the men receive. Division of fees with the railroad bosses or employment superintendents, although contrary to law, is undoubtedly often demanded. Fourteen agents interviewed in the course of an investigation made in Chicago

The Immigrant and the Community

said that they had arrangements of this sort with contractors. An agent who sent fifty Bulgarians to work near Springfield claimed that one half of the six-dollar fee was railroad fare. The men failed to get work; and in a hearing before the Commissioners of Labor the fact was brought out that $150 had gone, not to the railroad company, but to the company's contractors.

The "industrial graft" of factory and construction foremen should be spoken of in this connection. Sometimes a present, more frequently a sum of money, is exacted of the immigrant workman before he can get a job, or a payment to his foreman is required or expected if he is to keep his job or secure a promotion. A recent report — "Job Selling in Industrial Establishments in Ohio"[6] — of an investigation made in connection with the enforcement of the Ohio employment agency law by the Department of Investigation and Statistics of the Industrial Commission of Ohio, gives the payments frequently exacted by foremen from immigrants and the methods of collection that they used.

Chicago courts usually hold that the payment of fees of this sort to a foreman does not constitute a violation of the Illinois Employment Agency Law, and so recognizes this as a form of "honest graft." In Massachusetts[7] the practice is specifically prohibited by statute, but the law affords the men little protection because, unless they are organized, it is usually quite impossible for the one who is bold enough to make the complaint to get corrob-

[6] *See Report No. 24, Department of Investigation and Statistics,* The Industrial Commission of Ohio.
[7] *Report of the Massachusetts Commission on Immigration,* House Document No. 2300, p. 40.

Finding a First "Job"

orating evidence. If the job is a good one or if poor jobs are hard to get, the men regard it as the part of wisdom to pay and keep quiet.

Most employers are, of course, opposed to this practice on the part of their foremen, although they make little effort to put the employment and the dismissal of the men on such a basis as effectually to prevent it. Occasionally, however, this very ugly kind of exploitation is traced to a man very high in authority. For example, a young Greek brought to the office of the Immigrants' Protective League a receipt for $100, which he said he had paid to secure a job in a large manufacturing establishment in one of Chicago's industrial suburbs, and asked if we could get back the money. It seemed incredible that payment of such a sum had been exacted, and we feared the man had been robbed by some one who represented himself to be an official of the company. However, we presented the facts, as the man had reported them, to the superintendent, whose name was signed on the receipt. By return mail, we received a check from the superintendent for $100 and the explanation that the payment was made not to the company but to him personally, and, to quote his words, " the money was on a real estate proposition and if he don't care to go through with it, the amount is so small that I don't care to go any further with him." The receipt did not show this; and the man had never heard anything about the land, nor had any of the others who subsequently brought similar receipts to the League.

It has been said that the fees charged by the employment agents are large even if work which lasts

The Immigrant and the Community

a few weeks or months is secured on the terms promised, but too often this is not the case. Several cases that have come to the attention of the League will illustrate the extremely temporary character of the jobs purchased in this way. In 1908 a railroad was building from Searcy, in north-central Arkansas, to Leslie, which is about ninety miles farther west. Great numbers of men were sent that year from Chicago to Leslie to work on this road. One group was made up of Hungarians — fifty-three men and two women. The women, one of whom had a baby, were employed to act as cooks for the gang. These men and women were shipped out in April of that year by a Chicago agent, through a St. Louis agent. They paid the Chicago agent $14 each and were promised steady work at $1.40 a day. According to the story of the men, this is what happened: When they reached Leslie, they were told that the work was twenty-five miles from that point. They walked the twenty-five miles, but the foreman laughed at the "gang" and said that he had no work for any such number. He finally put to work fifteen men and the woman who was unencumbered with the baby. The rest were told that there would be work for them later on; but as they were without any money or food, they could not stay. They started to walk back to Chicago, where more such jobs are always to be had! At the end of the third day the woman and baby gave out, and the men pooled their money and sent them home on the railroad. Then the men scattered in the hope of finding work on the way. Two of them were shot by the police in St. Louis for attempting to board a train.

Such was the story that one of the men told an investi-

Finding a First "Job"

gator in answer to a question whether the agency which shipped them out was a good place to get jobs. It was told solely as a warning to a fellow-workman. And since it seemed as if it must be true, an effort was made to have the fees that had been paid the agent refunded. The agent denied that the men were not offered work; and in attempting to learn the facts, the League came to appreciate how helpless the immigrant is who has risked all his money to "get a job" and is sent to a remote and isolated part of the country where no one understands his language or cares about his difficulties. Although letters were written to various people with regard to these Hungarians, the League was unable to learn anything definite. The contractor wrote that, though his men were moved on from one place to another, they were all eventually offered work which some of them refused because they objected to being separated. This the men denied, but at such a distance from Searcy they were unable to prove their story.

The League found, however, another agent who, although he had shipped about five hundred men to Searcy during the winter, said, "You cannot get men to go there now because other agents sent too many men and they did not get jobs." A third agent offered thirty jobs a week at Leslie for $15 apiece after the contractor had assured the League that "the work was finished a few weeks ago."

Similar hardships were encountered by ten Polish laborers who lived in the same house on the West Side of Chicago and were sent to Wyoming in the winter to work in a lumber camp. They paid an agent $10 each

The Immigrant and the Community

for the jobs they were promised. When they were put off the train in Wyoming, they found no work of the character described but were given work for a short time on the railroad. When they were "laid off," they started to walk back to Chicago. One of the men, a bright young fellow of twenty two, froze his foot. With no money to pay a doctor for treatment, he thought the only thing he could do was to keep walking on. When he finally reached Chicago, blood-poisoning had set in, and it was necessary to amputate the foot. Although crippled for life, he felt not so much resentment against the agent who sent him, as shame that he should have been so ignorant of the climate of Wyoming and humiliation that he should have proved such an easy victim. This is often pathetically true in cases of immigrant exploitation. The men are ashamed to tell their story. "Every one cheats a greenhorn," they say; and sometimes they want to conceal from those who are anxious to help them, what they consider a reflection on their own intelligence.

The economic waste that results from such methods of distribution should be evident. The Massachusetts Commission on Immigration [8] found that the methods by which men were sent to the Maine lumber camps in the autumn and early winter of 1913 afforded a good illustration of the wastefulness of the system. During the preceding summer, many men had gone into Maine from Canada to work on an extension of the Grand Trunk Railroad. When the railroad camps were closed at the end of the season, these men were available for work in

[8] See *Report of Massachusetts Commission on Immigration,* House Document No 2300, p 41

Finding a First "Job"

the woods. The New York, Boston, and Bangor agencies, which working together had supplied the lumber men in previous years, paid no attention to an overstocked labor market in Bangor. More men were sent from New York and Boston to be laid off in a short time, and their places taken by other men in order that the fees might be collected by agents.

It is practically impossible for any of these men to get work when they get away from the city without first returning to the central market. There may be work near the place where they are stranded in Maine, Wyoming, Arkansas, or Nebraska, but they have no means of knowing where or how it is to be found. Unable to speak English and with no funds to live on temporarily, they are afraid to go farther in search of work. It is little to be wondered at that they are homesick and discouraged and anxious to get back to their friends in the city.

Few of us could deal successfully with men as expert in practices of exploitation as are most of the employment agents, and men who know nothing of our language, who cannot give accurate accounts of where they have been because of their ignorance of the country, who do not understand what is told them when they reach their place of destination, are easy victims. The agent, on the other hand, takes few chances when he sends these men out to jobs that do not exist, because they are so defenseless.

The report made by the Immigrants' Protective League after its investigation into the relation of the immigrant to the Chicago employment agency pointed

The Immigrant and the Community

out that certain changes in the Illinois law regulating employment agencies would prevent some of the abuses from which the immigrant suffered. But it also pointed out that such changes would reach only the surface of the trouble. This was (1) because the opportunities of cheating the immigrant are too great for the average man, anxious to make money, to withstand; and (2) because even if honest, the private agent is interested only in the collection of fees, and not in so distributing labor as to serve the larger interests of the community and to make the largest possible use of such intelligence and skill as the immigrant possesses. Following the League's investigation of 1909, the employment agency law was amended and strengthened. But during times of economic depression, when jobs are hard to secure, the immigrant has continued to suffer from misrepresentation and fraud.

It is sometimes hard to get judges to appreciate the far-reaching effect of these violations of the law. For example, in the spring of 1914 a Greek who has a candy store in Chicago offered to get work for a group of forty-two Albanians on the Pennsylvania Station, on which the newspapers reported work was about to begin, if they paid him $10 each. Most of the men had been out of work all winter and did not have any money; but their credit was still good and twenty five of them borrowed the money from the proprietor of an oriental bakery, and an old man from the group staked ten others. The Greek admitted receiving the money but said that his failure to secure work for the men was due to the fact that a man whom he represented and who had influence

Finding a First "Job"

with the Pennsylvania management and who could have placed the men had run off with the money. The Albanians appealed to the Immigrants' Protective League, and some time was spent in investigating the case. The evidence was turned over to the State Inspector of Employment Agencies, and the Greek was arrested for conducting an employment agency without a license. When it came to trial five of the Albanians were heard and made very good witnesses; and the State Inspector of Employment Agencies brought out the fact that the Greek had once been a licensed agent and had applied for a new license two days before he took this money, so that he was thoroughly familiar with the law. The judge before whom the case was tried dismissed it on the ground that the Greek could not be said to be running an employment agency without a license when he had no employment agency sign on his store. This decision was made worse by the judge's statement from the bench that he could not believe the Albanians anyway since they were Mohammedans and did not know the meaning of an oath.

The defendants find that the easiest way to beat these cases when they are taken into court is to continue them, as the men are compelled to ship out to work at the first opportunity. How easily this method is used was illustrated in the case of nine Roumanians and twenty-two Armenians who paid an Italian agent, the former $10 each and the latter $12 each, for work in Ottawa, Illinois. They were sent to Ottawa on May 10, 1914, and returned on May 13, after the Chief of Police of Ottawa had telegraphed to the Inspector of Employment Agencies

The Immigrant and the Community

that there was no work for them. A warrant was taken out, and the case was heard for the first time on May 23, and was continued to May 25, then transferred to the criminal branch and set for June 10. In the meantime the Roumanians had found work outside of the city. All the men were in the city during the winter; by March all but two of the Armenians were out of reach and the Roumanians were in Indiana. Although repeated efforts were made to speed up the court machinery, the case was not finally settled until the spring of 1916, when the men were repaid in part. Civil action in these cases is usually fruitless, as most agents have no property and the bond they give is only $500. The claims against this agent amounted to over $1500.

When the agencies have an interstate business, state regulation and inspection breaks down completely. The Report of the Massachusetts Immigration Commission [9] tells of several Russians who were picked up by a runner in Boston and piloted to an employment office. Here they were promised work in the woods as sawyers, and the agreement was made that the transportation and office fees were to be deducted from their wages.

These men were given a receipt calling for work as sawyers in Kineo, Maine, but they were sent to Calumet, Michigan, and put to work in the copper mines. The trouble which led to the strike in those mines had already begun, and the Russians were regarded as strike-breakers from the time of their arrival at the mines. They were not allowed to take their clothes when they tried to leave, probably because they were regarded as being in debt to

[9] P 43

Finding a First "Job"

the company for the expensive railroad journey from Boston to Calumet. They finally reached Chicago and asked the Russian-speaking officer of the Immigrants' Protective League to explain why they were sent to the mines instead of to the woods. They still had the card of the Boston agent showing that they were to be given work as sawyers at Kineo, Maine

They knew that they had been deceived and that they had unwittingly offended their fellow-workers by going to Calumet. They knew that the boarding boss had kept their clothes when they came to the conclusion that they must leave. By staying a few days in a place they had worked their way back to Chicago, and they hoped to be able to get back to their Russian friends in West Hanover, Massachusetts. Massachusetts was quite powerless to extend the protection of its laws to either Michigan or Illinois, while the latter States could not reach an offender against a Massachusetts statute.

Federal regulation of these agencies is, of course, needed; but for the real prevention of the evils, state or city employment agencies clearing through a national agency are necessary. These public agencies should together undertake comprehensive studies of the labor market; give especial attention to the casual labor problem; and, after placing the individual man or woman in the individual job, should develop a follow-up system, so that subsequent placements shall be increasingly efficient.

None of the public agencies as at present organized have been able to do much in the placement of the non-English speaking immigrant. For his own protection as well as for the protection of the American workman, the immi-

The Immigrant and the Community

grant is not allowed to enter the United States under an agreement to work. This is done in order that he may not be brought here as a strike-breaker, and because his ignorance of American standards places him at too great a disadvantage in entering into any labor contract from so great a distance. When, for the same reasons, the need of directing and assisting the immigrant in securing employment is urged, there is a tendency on the part of the public official to take the position that the claims of the immigrant are being pressed in opposition to those of the native born

It is as important to the community as to the immigrant that he should receive the prevailing rate of wages; that he work under decent conditions at a trade which will offer him the largest future earning capacity; and that he is not sent out to jobs which do not exist, or for a few weeks' work to an already oversupplied labor market.

If this is to be done, the advice and help of a disinterested public agency is necessary. Public agencies have made very substantial progress during the last two years. Since the great depression of 1914-15 set men thinking about the problem of unemployment, there has been a wider appreciation on the part of the public of the service that might be rendered, and a more effective demand that they be separated from politics and placed on a really efficient basis. The employment work recently begun by the United States Department of Labor, under the supervision of the local inspectors of immigration, gives promise of demonstrating the need of a really adequate national labor exchange. But without inter-

Finding a First "Job"

preters and an understanding of the problem that the non-English speaking immigrant faces, the public agency cannot rescue him from the private agent who exploits and misdirects him. And it will still be necessary for private social agencies to assist in making the public agencies available for the immigrant.

Frequently, quite regardless of his previous education or trade training, it is assumed that a person who cannot speak English must of necessity be an unskilled laborer. For example, a young Italian who had been a stone mason in Tuscany had worked during his first year in the United States as a porter in a saloon. Had he applied at an employment bureau, only his American experience would have been considered. And yet it is quite evident that what he needed to do was to join the masons' union and to follow his trade. But he was somewhat in debt because he had found it impossible to support his family on the $9 a week which he was receiving, and in consequence he did not have the money to pay the union fees. After arrangements for him to join were made with the union, a loan of a part of the fee was secured. Through the union, the man was given a job at $6 a day, so that he was soon able to pay off his other debts and the loan which had been secured for him.

A similar case was that of a Pole who had worked for three years as an engine repair man in Europe He had worked during the two and one-half years he had been in the United States in a restaurant as porter, bus boy, kitchen helper, and sandwich man. When he came to the Employment Department of the Immigrants' Protective League, he was questioned about his education and

The Immigrant and the Community

industrial experience in Europe, and the suggestion was made that he go back to his old trade. He said that he had been hoping for that kind of job ever since he came, but had not supposed that it was possible to get one. By explaining in English, as he himself was not able to do, what his European experience had been, the League was able to get him the chance to demonstrate that he could do skilled work in a railroad repair shop.

A different but an equally important question is how to find suitable "jobs" for the young immigrants who have had no trade training abroad. Among the new-comers, there are large numbers of boys and girls between sixteen and twenty years of age who are having their first industrial experience in the United States Even more than the native-born children, because their ignorance is greater, they need to be guided into jobs where there is some chance of advancement.

There is a great demand on the part of the public that the public agency undertake to act as an "intelligence office" There are, however, many serious problems in this connection, especially in finding housework for the girls. Girls are not always morally safe in what are often described to us as "good homes." As the mistresses of the better homes want girls who can speak English and furnish references, the most desirable places are usually not open to the immigrant.

German and Scandinavian girls, because they are known to be excellent servants and because servants are difficult to secure, can often get good places although they are ignorant of the language. This is coming to be true of the Bohemian and Slovak girls, about one half of

Finding a First "Job"

whom go into domestic service. But in placing any of these, exercise of the greatest care is necessary

One Swedish girl wrote asking "whether when the man in the house treats his housemaid very badly there is anything she can do when she had no witnesses?" This girl was convinced that an appeal to her employer would have resulted in her instant dismissal and charges would have made it impossible for her to get a good position; while if she left without explanation a reference would also be refused her. It was possible for us to get around this difficulty, but the danger in placing girls was emphasized in this and other similar instances.

Apart from this difficulty, housework is often nothing more than a blind-alley job; and it is extremely difficult to learn as much about the conditions under which this work is performed as can be learned about industrial establishments. When an untrained girl takes a place where the work is hard and the pay low, she should be transferred as soon as she has served her apprenticeship to a place where the organization of the work requires more skill and less physical strength and where the pay is higher. This sort of change can be made only when the placing agency is familiar with the households to which its girls are sent and with the progress which the girl is making The girl whose ability points to other employment should be discovered.

As the public is very eager that the immigrant girl should always be satisfied with domestic service, so there are very large numbers of people who think the immigrant men should do farm work. Here, as in domestic service, the work is quite unstandardized in the length of

The Immigrant and the Community

the working day and in the worker's lack of control of his leisure; but, unlike domestic work, it does not pay so much as can be secured in other occupations.

Of the immigrants admitted in 1914, 288,053 gave their occupation in Europe as farm laborers and 14,442 as farmers — over 42 per cent. of all men and boys over fourteen who were admitted that year. Among the Italians, Poles, Lithuanians, and Russians, the percentage was much higher. Many of the "farm laborers" belonged to the "landless" peasant class at home, while in other instances the immigrant who is described as a farm laborer worked on his father's farm and at his father's death would inherit a share of his small holdings. When these immigrants come, they are without the capital necessary for independent farming.

The impracticability of sending groups of immigrants to a general region in which farm labor is temporarily needed has been demonstrated. For example, in the summer of 1914, the Kansas State Bureau of Labor sent out an appeal for 42,000 farm hands. It was given much publicity by the United States Department of Labor. As it was a summer of great distress because of unemployment, the temptation to send at once some of the many who came daily asking the League for work was very great. But a letter of inquiry was sent asking for names and addresses of farmers who needed men, and explaining that men could be sent if the necessary specific information was given The reply was that the harvest lasted about one week in a place and that it would probably not be a wise plan for the immigrants to come, as there was no way by which they could be informed of

Finding a First "Job"

other openings after they had finished the first job. Many commercial agents sent large numbers of men during that season. It was not long, however, before complaints began to come in from some of the people who made this expensive and useless trip. Some of the men arrived in Kansas without funds, and had to walk or beat their way back.

A typical case was that of ninety-nine Roumanians who were sent by a Cleveland employment agent to whom each of them paid $18. They arrived in Topeka and found no work They stayed two nights and a day in the railroad station, and then as there was no work available, twenty two of them started to walk back to Cleveland, begging their way and getting what jobs they could. Each day some one had to drop out, sick or too weak with hunger to walk farther. Three reached Chicago utterly exhausted. A group of Russians who paid $18 each to a steamship agent in Chicago had a similar experience.

During the past year the Federal Bureau of Distribution has placed a large number of farm laborers, and it is hoped that in a few years this supply will be really organized by the Federal Government. Something might then be done in the placement of peasant colonies on land.

It would seem to be unnecessary to continue to bring forward evidence that organization of the employment market by public employment agencies is needed in the United States. We have the experience of England, of Germany, and of Austria to guide us, and a history of fraud, exploitation, and needless suffering in the United

The Immigrant and the Community

States to urge us on. It ought to be unnecessary also to reiterate that these agencies must be businesslike and free from political control. It should also be unnecessary to point out that they should have interpreters competent to handle the various immigrants who constitute so large a part of the labor supply and who as they come might be so easily directed into those occupations and industries which are not overcrowded or declining, to the advantage of themselves and of the community. It is no longer necessary to discuss this question academically. We should be making strides every year in working out the practical difficulties connected with the proper reorganization of our employment market.

CHAPTER III

THE SPECIAL PROBLEMS OF THE IMMIGRANT GIRL

FEW American women realize that in the past five years more than half a million immigrant girls have come to the United States to make their own way, to help the fathers and mothers they have left at home, and to see that their younger sisters and brothers are given some of the opportunities which poverty and isolation denied to them.

The nationality and the numbers of the young unmarried women, which the reports of the Commissioner-General of Immigration show have come to the United States during the five years from July 1, 1910, to June 30, 1915, are given in the table on page 56.

These numbers cannot but fail to be impressive. More than one half a million non-English-speaking girls and women under thirty years of age came during the five-year period, which included one year of the war (1915), and in consequence one year of greatly decreased immigration. Of this number more than a hundred thousand were Polish, and more than 84,000 of these Polish girls were under twenty-one years of age. Most American women have never heard of the Ruthenians, the representatives of the Ukrainians, who come from eastern Galicia and Hungary, and yet here are 23,101 of them under twenty-one years of age coming to the United

The Immigrant and the Community

Nationality	14 to 21 years of age	Ages 22 to 29 years of age	Total 14 to 29 years of age
ENGLISH SPEAKING			
English, Scotch, Welsh..	19,828	25,230	45,058
Irish	32,069	21,652	53,721
Total	51,897	46,882	98,779
NON-ENGLISH SPEAKING			
Bohemian and Moravian	5,489	2,285	7,774
Croatian and Slovenian	10,215	4,576	14,791
Dutch and Flemish	2,500	1,979	4,479
Finnish	6,886	4,313	11,199
French	6,566	4,481	11,047
German	31,214	17,843	49,057
Greek	4,894	2,622	7,516
Hebrew	65,866	14,691	80,557
Italian	50,832	23,262	74,094
Lithuanian	14,793	5,800	20,593
Magyar	13,364	3,608	16,972
Polish	84,633	17,043	101,676
Portuguese	3,931	1,472	5,403
Roumanian	1,389	872	2,261
Russian	6,177	2,479	8,656
Ruthenian	23,101	3,648	26,749
Scandinavian	22,385	15,806	38,191
Slovak	15,666	2,583	18,249
Syrian	2,495	591	3,086
All others	14,267	8,583	22,850
Total	386,663	138,537	525,200

States — more than the number of the Scandinavian girls whom we know so well.

As one thinks of this great stream of Polish, Russian, Jewish, Italian, Ruthenian, Lithuanian, and all the other girls who have been coming from the country districts

Problems of the Immigrant Girl

of southern and eastern Europe, one wonders how they had the courage to undertake this excursion into the unknown. Several years ago, while studying the districts in Galicia, in northern Hungary, and in Croatia, from which so many girls have come to the United States, I kept asking myself and those whom I met this one question. A professor in the Polish University of Lemberg, which Americans have learned since the war began is the capital of Galicia and the center of a large Polish and a larger Ruthenian population, told me that the first thing I needed to understand in any study of emigration from this region was that the peasants did not go because they needed work; there was plenty of work for them there; he knew landlords whose crops were rotting in the ground because the men and women of the neighborhood had all gone to America. It was a fever that was running through the entire peasantry, he explained. They went to the United States as he might go to the next street.

A few days later, I visited the region he had described to me. It was in the autumn, when the principal food of the peasantry — potatoes and cabbages — was being stored away for use during the long winter. On the largest estate of the neighborhood I looked in amazement at a potato field on which there were so many people working that they almost touched elbows as they moved across the field. Guided by the priest, I visited all the types of houses in the village — the poorest as well as the best. At first one felt the appeal of the picturesque, for the fields were gay with the bright, peasant costumes of the girls, and the low, thatched-roof cottages had been

The Immigrant and the Community

freshly whitewashed and had flowers in the queer little windows.

But there was nothing picturesque about the dirt floors, the absence of chimneys and furniture, and the long distance that all the water had to be carried. When it was dark, most of the population gathered in the village square, where the girls were paid about twenty-five cents for their day's work. I followed them into the little church for the vesper service; and, as I looked at the patient, tired faces of these girls, I understood why it was that they could not start for America until letters had come bringing them tickets from the Galician village to the city in the United States where a brother or sister or a friend is already established. I understood, too, why, when the tickets came, they would start, without hesitating at the dangers they might meet on the journey or the possibility that failure might await them at the other end.

A little to the west of this village there was another where economic conditions were much better. There was a sugar factory, a distillery, a big dairy; and the great landlord of the neighborhood had a beautifully kept estate and farms, which employed many peasants.

The houses, too, were better. There were wooden floors, chimneys, more tiled and fewer thatched roofs; and there were fruit trees round each house. Instead of the small, dirty, and poorly furnished elementary school of the first village, there were a kindergarten and a gymnasium in addition to an elementary school. In this neighborhood there were organizations of peasant men and women for the promotion of more scientific

Problems of the Immigrant Girl

farming. In a domestic science class there were about thirty girls of high school age learning sewing, cooking, laundry work, and something of the farm industries. When they were asked how many of them had girl friends in America, the hands went up all round the room, and then in response to the question how many were coming themselves, and again how many were coming to Chicago, there were still many hands It was not economic necessity that was sending them. I came, however, to understand why they, too, desired to try life in America.

Forced labor was abolished in Austria in 1848; but it was not until 1867 and 1869 that the right of the peasant to divide his land was made general, so that serfdom remained, in a sense, until that time. As I talked with the landlords of the neighborhood, I found that, like the Southern white man in his attitude toward the Negro, they were indulgently tolerant of the faults of the peasantry but were convinced that these faults were due to the fact that the peasants were a quite different order of human beings from themselves. They laughed at us for taking the peasants so seriously and imagining we could make ladies and gentlemen of them. The peasants, they were sure, were all "spoiled" by an American experience. The older peasants are themselves sometimes equally conservative in their devotion to the old social order; so the ambitious young peasant has the opposition of his own class as well as the class prejudice of those above him to overcome.

Whether or not it is completely reasoned out by the peasant who undertakes the journey, this class feeling is

The Immigrant and the Community

an important cause of emigration. It is much simpler to break entirely with the past, to abandon the picturesque costume, the little farm, the dependence on the landlord of the neighborhood, and to stake everything on a possible success in America than to try to break down the century-old social barriers of the village. In other words, it was the fact that apparently nothing could change either for themselves or for their children, which sent many of these women from Austria and Hungary to America.

But many things have changed since then. Galicia, which had known black poverty and suffering for many years, and Western Russia, from which so many Poles, Lithuanians, White and Little Russians and Russian Jews have emigrated to the United States, have been crossed and recrossed by the armies of the Czar and the Kaiser. Houses, villages, and forests have been destroyed. Communication with American friends has been interrupted, and neither money nor tickets have been received for more than two years now. It needs only sympathy, not the gift of prophecy, for us to realize that with the end of the war many of the people who came to the United States from that region and who have left behind them parents, or children, or sisters and brothers, will return to see whether they have lived through all the misery and the suffering which have come to them. That some of these returned immigrants will stay to share with their family the suffering involved in rebuilding the homes and villages, is probable But that many of them will return, bringing their sisters and daughters to the United States, seems quite certain.

Problems of the Immigrant Girl

Whether or not immigration as a whole increases at the end of the war, there will undoubtedly be larger numbers of young unmarried women emigrating from eastern Europe to the United States. It is, therefore, important for us to consider the peculiar problems of the immigrant girl in order that those who have suffered so much in Europe may be prevented from further unnecessary suffering here.

During the years from 1910 to 1915 the Immigrants' Protective League received from the ports of entry the names of 26,909 women and girls who came alone from Europe to Chicago. These girls were visited as soon after their arrival as possible by visitors of the League who spoke the language of the girls and were prepared to help them in adjusting themselves to their Chicago environment. By far the largest number who have been coming to Chicago, as to the United States, are Polish, and it may be assumed that the needs which were discovered in the visits made to these immigrant girls of Chicago are typical of the needs of the girls who have come to other cities and industrial towns.

The foreign-born girls face no simple situation when here in the United States they become self-supporting and self-directing. Most of them begin their new life indebted to a relative or a friend who has paid for the steamship ticket that brought them here. To the nervous apprehensions about her ability to repay so large an obligation is added the general bewilderment every girl feels who is experiencing life in a city and as part of a great industry for the first time.

Many of those who come are so young that their only

The Immigrant and the Community

work at home had been to watch the sheep and the cattle in the fields or on the mountain slopes from sunrise to sunset. Others worked side by side with the men in the harvest fields or in the factories. Some of them were hod-carriers and toiled up the ladders with the heavy brick or stone which the masons — always men — laid.

How far they have taken the places of the men in industry during the war, we do not know; and how much of what they have sacrificed and suffered will have improved the position of the women, we shall not know for several years Although they worked side by side with the men before the war, they were never in any sense regarded as the equals of the men with whom and for whom they toiled. The belief in the inferiority of women was deep rooted, and it takes an optimist to believe that two years of militarism will result in materially improving the condition of these peasant women. In those districts in which there were no schools, or in others in which the term was very short, or where the number of those allowed to attend was limited, as among the Jews in Russia, illiteracy was much more common among the women than among the men. In the past two years the educational movement in these regions will have moved backward instead of forward.

The immigrant girls do not realize their handicaps, and usually begin work in the United States without any of the doubts and anxious fears which many of us have for them. Being young, they believe that the world must hold something good in store for them. In the faith that America feels kindly toward them they expect to find here among us that happy future to which all girls

Problems of the Immigrant Girl

look forward. And in this expectation these young foreign women and girls undertake the great American adventure.

Those of us who can remember our own great expectations as we left college and the anxious fears of that first year of our "independence" can, perhaps, understand the greater crisis which the immigrant girl faces in her first year in the United States.

Most of them are, at first, homesick and disappointed. The streets of the city are not always broad and beautiful, and life not always gay and bright as they had hoped it would be. On the contrary, the experience of the Russian-Jewish girl who came to a cousin on Liberty Street in Chicago is not unusual. A returned immigrant translated to her the word "Liberty," and she imagined that she was coming to live on an avenue which would symbolize all that one bearing that precious name should. But she found her cousin living in a rear house on a short, narrow, unpaved, dirty street. The houses on Liberty Street are as poor as any Chicago knows, and there is no place where poverty seems more intimate and its ugliness more inevitable. After a short experience in a tailor shop, she had to give up the struggle. She did not live long enough to know anything about the United States except the disappointment of Liberty Street.

Sometimes it seems to the peasant girls as if they had exchanged the green fields and woods and the long, quiet winters for a hideous round of noise, heat, and bitter cold.

For the Polish girls, the change is often very sudden Most of those who come to Chicago are young girls, and

The Immigrant and the Community

many of them have no near relatives to help them through their difficulties. Out of 2013 who arrived in Chicago during a period of eighteen months and were visited by the Immigrants' Protective League, 1107 were between the ages of sixteen and twenty, 751 between twenty and thirty years of age. Only 81 had parents in this country, and 626 came to cousins or friends. Sometimes these "friends" have never known the girls at home. When they were discussing their journey to America, some one in the village suggested that they could stay during the first few weeks after they arrived with a brother, cousin, or friend of the speaker who was living in the United States. In such cases, and often too when the girl comes to an uncle or an aunt of her own, as soon as she gets her first job and finds a place to board, all feeling of responsibility on the part of the relatives or friends is ended For example, one girl of seventeen came to an uncle on the North Side of Chicago He took her to the Stockyards neighborhood, some twelve miles away, found her work and a place to board, and then regarded his duty to his niece as fully performed. When the girl was in the most serious trouble, six months later, she had no idea where he lived and had no one to turn to for advice or help.

More than one half of the Polish girls visited did farm work at home, one eighth were servants, while some had followed one of the sewing trades, and a few were clerks, factory workers, and teachers In Chicago, about one fifth of them work in hotels, restaurants, or hospitals, scrubbing or washing dishes for ten hours a day. Before the enactment of the Ten-Hour Law for Women, they

Problems of the Immigrant Girl

worked often as long as fifteen hours a day. They were given in payment from four to seven dollars a week and two meals a day.

One hundred and eleven of the 2013 referred to were already at work in the Stockyards when they were visited by the League's representatives, and practically all the others who came to that neighborhood and were not yet employed expected to get work at the Yards in a short time. One hundred and ten found employment as servants, eighty one were at work in laundries, sixty seven in tobacco factories, while the remainder were working in the corerooms of foundries, in the dusty twine mills of a harvester company, and in the tin can factories, where so many girls lose their fingers in the inadequately guarded machinery. In fact the Polish girls are found doing almost every kind of heavy or disagreeable work in Chicago. Because they are large and strong looking, there is a popular belief that they can do work which would be physically too heavy for others. But the belief is based on ignorance of what it costs the Polish girls to do these tasks.

How many of them give way under the strain of long hours, bad living conditions, and the confused excitement which comes with their new environment, few people realize. The tragedy of this physical breakdown was illustrated one summer when the service of the Immigrants' Protective League were asked on behalf of a young Polish girl. Although she seemed entirely well when she came and had been passed by the examining doctors at Ellis Island, she had developed tuberculosis after a few months of factory work in Chicago. She was

The Immigrant and the Community

taken to the County Hospital and soon learned that she had no chance of recovery. She was most wretchedly homesick when the visitor for the League saw her at the hospital. She had only a cousin in this country, who could not come to see her because it was the season of overtime work in his trade and the County Hospital was many miles away. She was unable to talk to those around her and found it impossible to eat the strange American food given her, and, worst of all, she realized that all her girlish plans to earn money, send for her mother, and marry well were to come to nothing. Polish food which we were able to procure for her did not comfort her, however, for she wanted only one thing — to be sent back home so that she might die with her mother. In this, too, she was disappointed, for although she improved somewhat when she learned that she was to be deported, she died alone at sea.

The Lithuanian girls, who come from the country districts near Kovno and Wilna, and the Ruthenian and the Little Russian girls, who come from near Lemberg in Austria and across the Russian boundary to the south of Kiev, and the White Russian and Great Russian peasant girls, who have just begun to come from Central and Northern Russia, confront much the same problem. Like the Polish girls, more than one half of them have done farm work at home, and in Chicago they, too, find employment principally in the hotels and restaurants, at the heavier factory work, and in the Stockyards, although all these nationalities are also represented in the sewing trades and in domestic service

With the Bohemians and Slovaks, the industrial move-

Problems of the Immigrant Girl

ment is different. About one half of them have done housework at home, and in Chicago about the same proportion still do housework and the others find employment at tailoring, in the restaurants, laundries, and factories.

The Bohemian or Slovak girls who have worked in English-speaking families are, of course, more Americanized than those who have lived among their own people and worked in a factory. Still, the immigrant girl in the latter situation is usually safer than in the former. A too rapid Americanization is dangerous, and the girl who leaves her own people and eats strange American food, learns a new language, and gives up her old country clothes and manners, often wrongly concludes that all her old-world ideals are to be abandoned and that in America she is to live under a very different moral code from the one her mother taught her.

Of the Jewish women and girls who came during the same period, 613 were Russian. Most of them were unmarried and under twenty-five years of age. Four hundred and twelve had followed one of the sewing trades at home, and in Chicago the great majority are also employed at tailoring or dressmaking. But whatever their industrial experience in Russia may have been, the Jewish girls have never known the large, crowded workshop and the pace which piece work always demands in the United States. Probably 90 per cent. of them come on prepaid tickets and they all expect to repay this loan and be able soon to send for some relative or friend

The Jewish girls come expecting to make America their

The Immigrant and the Community

permanent home, and they are, therefore, eager to learn English and to become Americanized. They attend night school more regularly than the girls of any other nationality, and in a year they usually make rapid progress if they are strong enough to keep up the day and evening work.

There is much greater diversity in the ages of the Italian girls who come than of the others. They seldom come unaccompanied by their mothers. The work they prefer is home finishing, but they do all kinds of home work, most often cracking nuts and making artificial flowers — until state regulation compels them to break reluctantly with their traditions and follow the work to the factory. The Italian girl, because of jealous parental supervision, is less frequently in trouble than are the girls of other nationalities, but this supervision means that she cannot attend night school or take part in the American recreations of her neighborhood, and that she must marry young so that, before her father dies, she will have a husband to protect her virtue. These traditions, which cannot live when the girl goes to the American factory, often make the Italian girl's adjustment to her American social environment a difficult family problem.

The conditions under which most of these immigrant girls must live are far from satisfactory. While many of them come to relatives or friends who can give them the care and protection they need, many of them must live among strangers upon whom they have no claim. Because more men than women emigrate to this country, the families with whom they live usually have, in addition to the girl, three or four men lodgers. The Immi-

Problems of the Immigrant Girl

grants' Protective League has found in its visits to the newly arrived immigrant girls that about one half of the Polish, Lithuanian, Slovak, and Russian girls who come to live with relatives find themselves one more in a group of boarders. Sometimes all the other boarders are men, and the girl innocently does not see that because of the congestion and the consequent lack of privacy and of the restraints which privacy exercises, she is quite unprotected against herself and the people with whom she lives. The following examples of boarding conditions which are all too common among the Polish girls may help to explain the difficulties which are met.

A nineteen-year-old girl, without relatives in Chicago, was found living with a man and his wife, who have in their three-room flat four men and three other women boarders. This girl paid two dollars a month for her part of a room — the usual price. It is customary for each boarder to select and pay for his or her own food, which is usually cooked by the landlady. The landlady is not often paid for her work, but whatever is left belongs to her and this supplies the family needs for the most part. Another eighteen-year-old girl and a friend live with a family of four in a four-room flat where there are six men and four women boarders. Occasionally a group of women rent rooms and live together. Five Polish girls, all under twenty, were found living in two rooms. They all worked in factories and each one did some part of their simple housekeeping.

The Lithuanians have no safer conditions. One girl lived with a married cousin who had a four-room flat in which she accommodated six men and two women board-

The Immigrant and the Community

ers. The girl and the other boarders all worked in the Stockyards. Another Lithuanian girl of twenty, who cleans street cars at night, boards in a four-room flat which houses, in addition to the four members of the family, five men and one other woman boarder. These conditions are frequently met.

Immigrant men sometimes live in non-family groups, using the ordinary flat building which is so ill adapted for group housekeeping This mode of living is generally regarded as so demoralizing to the men that it cannot be recommended as a way out of the lodging difficulty unless buildings especially constructed for that purpose are provided. In this kind of overcrowding, which every housing investigation shows to be common, the lack of privacy and of the restraints which privacy brings may be, with the complete absence of evil intent on the part of either the man or the girl, the sole cause of her ruin. There are also cases where, under some special strain or excitement, as for example, after a wedding or some other celebration, when liquor has been freely used, the moral barriers are broken down. This occurs most frequently in the homes that are overcrowded, and where, in consequence, an easy familiarity has been developed.

These living conditions follow inevitably from the fact that large numbers of young men and smaller but still large numbers of young women are coming into our industrial neighborhoods where no lodging provisions are made for them. The " company-owned boarding house " cannot be looked to as the solution of this problem. For long and often bitter experience has convinced employers, employees, and the interested public that it is undesirable

Problems of the Immigrant Girl

to combine the functions of employer and landlord. It is true that the employers might provide the buildings and allow them to be controlled by an independent body of trustees, so that the workers could not be evicted in cases of industrial disputes or feel that they were too completely under the tutelage of their employers during normal times.

The solution usually suggested for these conditions is a good housing law vigorously enforced. But this will not meet the social need. The enforcement of decent housing standards will reduce the overcrowding, but it will still leave the immigrant girl open to a kind of temptation to which no girl should be exposed. It will leave the non-family groups of men with no social relationships, so that abnormal vice will almost surely develop among them. Municipal building, the final remedy, will probably not be undertaken until we have gone much further in accepting the simpler propositions for municipal ownership. Private philanthropy should, in the meantime, experiment with lodging houses for these men and women so that we could learn the best type to build. Such building would also perform the valuable purpose of calling attention to the needs of these large groups of young men and women and so make ready for a real solution.

There are many explanations for the fact that the immigrant girls sometimes become unmarried mothers. There is the greater helplessness which is due to their ignorance of English; there is also the more dangerous environment in which they live, for it is near an immigrant or colored neighborhood that disreputable dance

The Immigrant and the Community

halls and hotels are usually tolerated. Moreover, their recreational needs are less understood than those of the native-born American, and the break with the old-world traditions has left them with fewer standards of discrimination.

At home, the girls have been accustomed to out-of-door dances and sports. In Chicago, when Saturday night comes, the demand for some sort of excitement after a hard and uneventful week, has become too strong to be ignored. But the danger is that because of her physical and nervous exhaustion and her demand for acute sense stimulation, the girl will become an easy victim for the unscrupulous. The neighboring saloon keeper, alert to the business side of her needs, is constantly seeking to attract her to the dance hall which he conducts in the rear of his saloon. At its best, such a dance adds to the nervous demoralization which began with the girl's overfatigue. At its worst, it leaves her disgraced and ruined. An extension of Chicago's admirable system of parks and playgrounds or a wider use of the public schools while helpful, is not enough to meet this situation. For these girls must first be given sufficient leisure to enable them to enjoy the wholesome recreation and opportunities for self-advancement which the city is offering them. This, they are not able to do after ten hours of scrubbing or coremaking six days in a week.

Sometimes the girl is not morally safe in her place of work. The Polish girls who work in restaurants seem to be in special danger. They usually resist at first, but often in the end find themselves unfortified against the combination of force and persuasion which is exerted

Problems of the Immigrant Girl

sometimes against them by the restaurant keeper or a fellow employee. This occurs most frequently in the Greek restaurants, in which, usually, only one girl is employed and there is, in consequence, not the protection which a group always affords. Many of the proprietors of the Greek restaurants are men whose families have not yet joined them in the United States or who have few opportunities to marry, as the number of Greek girls in the United States is small. These men have, in consequence, no normal social relationships.

But it is not always a restaurant employee. American foremen in factories sometimes abuse a power which is more absolute than any man should have the right to exercise over others, and on threat of dismissal the girl submits to familiarities which if they do not ruin her cannot fail to break down her self-respect. One does not need to be told how serious the situation is when a young immigrant girl explains that she has learned how to " get on with the boss " and " take care of herself " at the same time.

Occasionally a girl who has preferred housework in the belief that it would give her a " good home " is ruined by some man in the family for whom she has worked. One young Bohemian girl comes to my mind in this connection. She had had a very hard life at home where a drunken and brutal father's control had been followed by that of a brother no more considerate. She came to America before she was twenty, expecting to earn enough to send for her mother so that the old woman might spend her last years free from the sort of abuse she suffered at home. The fulfilment of this dream was delayed

The Immigrant and the Community

by the great misfortune that came to the girl, although her dream did in fact eventually come true. With a courage that humbled those of us who listened, she explained that she must have a good job so that she could support her baby and bring her mother to America. During the years that we watched her in her successful struggle to accomplish this great task, we realized that although, as the girl mourns, the baby "has n't got a name" it has at least a good mother.

Promise of marriage may, of course, be a factor in cases of the betrayal of American girls, and the foreign girl, whose village experience has not prepared her for the easy way in which men can disappear in the United States, is more easily victimized through her affections.

A study of the pathetic stories of the betrayal or the weakness of these girls makes it clear that the prevention of delinquency among immigrant girls presents no entirely new or indeed unusual problems. It is the same story of the desire for affection, together with loneliness, lack of knowledge of herself, and long hours of hard, monotonous work. The difference between the temptations which meet the American country girl who comes to the city and those of the immigrant girl, is in the main, one of degree and not of kind.

Those who see race differences as the explanation of all social facts have attempted to discover whether the girls of one nationality more than those of another "go wrong." Statistics on this subject are generally unreliable, especially when in their interpretation no account is taken of general population statistics, the length of time that the nationality has been coming to the United

Problems of the Immigrant Girl

States, and the peculiar temptations to which, because of employment, environment, or prejudice, the girls of a particular nationality are subjected.

Much more important, however, than the relative numbers of girls of the various nationalities who " go wrong " is the question whether any girl has suffered in this way when such suffering could have been prevented.

Much official attention has been given to the means of preventing immoral women and girls from coming into this country. Stirred by the stories that oriental women were being brought into the United States under contract for immoral purposes, Congress passed an Act in 1873 aimed especially at breaking up this "trade." The Immigration Law of 1903 excluded " prostitutes and persons who procure or attempt to bring in prostitutes or women for the purpose of prostitution." The language of the law was made more inclusive in 1907 [1] Those entering in violation of this law were made deportable if their presence in the country was discovered within three years after their coming. In 1910, in accordance with the agreement reached at the Paris Conference on the suppression of the " White Slave Traffic " of 1904 and in part as a result of the investigation of the United States Immigration Commission, a further act was passed making it a felony " to persuade, induce, or coerce " any girl or woman to come to the United States for any immoral purpose or to assist in its being done, and making it a misdemeanor to " keep, maintain, control, support,

[1] It provides that "prostitutes or women or girls coming into the United States for the purpose of prostitution, or for other immoral purposes; persons who procure or attempt to bring in prostitutes or women or girls for the purpose of prostitution or for any other immoral purpose" are to be excluded.

The Immigrant and the Community

or harbor in any place used for immoral purposes any girl or woman who has been in the United States less than three years." [2] These provisions, it is apparent, are intended primarily to reach those who profit from the illegal earnings of the girls. The Immigration Law was also amended the same year so that any alien girl or woman who is an inmate of a house of prostitution or is employed in any place frequented by prostitutes, may be deported regardless of the length of time she has been in the United States.[3]

These laws applied the double standard of morality in the tests for exclusion and deportation The man who profits by the social evil or who brings a girl into the country for immoral purposes is subject to punishment, but the man who is himself immoral is not regarded as an "undesirable" immigrant.

In so far as the Immigration Law breaks up the trade in women, in so far as it sends back home girls whose mothers and friends are in Europe and whose reformation, in consequence, will be more probable in Europe than in the United States, we can feel that the law is both useful and humane. But in its enforcement, it often means that we deny girls who have made some serious mistake at home the chance which they need to begin a new life here in the United States. For example, a few years ago, a young Austrian whose military service was uncompleted could not, therefore, marry the girl with whom he had lived and who was about to become a mother. They came to the United States that they might marry and their child be legitimate. The man was ad-

[2] Act of June 25, 1910, 36 United States Statutes, 825.
[3] Act of March 26, 1910.

Problems of the Immigrant Girl

mitted but the girl was excluded. She was unmarried and her condition apparent, and as a matter of routine ruling she was denied admission. The young man had no relatives in this country. He was coming to Chicago because his one acquaintance in the United States lived in Chicago. He was overwhelmed by the excluding decision and told his story to the first sympathetic listener he met in Chicago. Special appeals from Chicago women resulted in reversing the decision. The woman was admitted and married on the day of her arrival in Chicago. And most people would probably agree that the moral level of the United States is not raised by the kind of harshness in judging others which an excluding decision such as this one showed.

Under this law, it is also possible to deport girls who are not citizens, although they have been in the United States since they were little children, whose ruin has been accomplished here, whose parents and all those who might help them back into an honest life are in the United States. Some Russian-Jewish girls, under exactly these circumstances, were recommended for deportation. Added to the family separation, these girls were ordered returned to a country in which religious prejudice made their outlook the more uncertain. In such cases, the United States was merely insuring that the girls would continue their immoral life by sending them away from any possible sources of help to live in what was to them, in spite of their citizenship, an alien country. And after these girls had been banished, could any one feel that the country was safer when the men and the conditions responsible for their ruin were left here in the United

The Immigrant and the Community

States — a menace to other girls, both immigrant and American?

There is no reason to feel that the moral health of the country will be promoted by special severity in dealing with the immigrant girl who has gone wrong From the standpoint of the welfare of the community, attention could be much more profitably directed toward helping her to meet the difficulties she now encounters in the United States

For this reason, it is to be regretted that the administration of the immigration law is so entirely in the hands of men The women in the Immigration Service are " matrons "— the cross between a housekeeper and a chaperon who is rapidly disappearing in the best public and private institutions. Without the same pay as inspectors, these matrons are not expected to measure up with the men in intelligence and ability, although they often do. But they have, largely for these reasons, not been able to make much impression on the " Service " and have not secured the adoption of standards of comfort and consideration which trained women could institute in a place like Ellis Island, where so many thousands of women and children are detained each year.

Investigation of girls on charges of immorality should be made by women inspectors. Anonymous reports are investigated by the Department, and it often means serious injury to the reputation of a respectable girl to have a man inspector call to " investigate " her

A woman's department has recently been organized in the Immigration Service, but there are no indications that these old traditions about the position of women in

Problems of the Immigrant Girl

the Service are to be abolished The " presence " of a woman in an Immigration Station is sentimentally supposed to give protection, but any practical person knows that ability, training, and resourcefulness on the part of women officials are necessary if they are to render the services which the immigrant women and girls really need.

The same measures have not been taken by private as well as public agencies to safeguard the immigrant that have been taken to protect the American girl. Boarding clubs, which are among the first kindly expressions of interest in the American girl, have not, except in a very few instances, been provided for the immigrant. Agencies which are trying to help girls who have made some misstep have usually not felt it necessary to employ women able to speak the language of the immigrant or to understand her social traditions

The immigrant girl has a long and hard road to travel. She suffers from the industrial and legal discriminations which are the common lot of working women In addition, she must overcome the stupid race prejudice which leads many Americans to conclude that she suffers less from shame and humiliation than do other women and girls. Without trade training and with little education, as a rule, she begins at the bottom industrially, where, if the wages of the men are low, the wages of the girls are still lower.

And yet, in this struggle in which they are so handicapped, these girls are winning little by little — often at a terrible cost to their health and, in consequence, to the health of the children they will bear in the future. There

The Immigrant and the Community

are many who are moved only by this danger to the future generations. But for the girls of this generation, we should ask more leisure, better pay, better homes, and more sympathy before they are too old and broken to enjoy the fruits of their toil and of their eager sacrifices.

CHAPTER IV

PROTECTION AGAINST EXPLOITATION

COMING out of a great modern cotton factory in the Slovak district of Northwestern Hungary some years ago, I saw a woman threshing her grain after the primitive method women used a thousand years ago. The cotton factory was equipped with improved machinery and devices for purifying the air. Struck by the industrial contrast of the well-organized and up-to-date factory and the woman pounding out her grain, I stopped with my friends to talk to her and was told that her daughter worked in the neighboring factory and that the daughter's husband had died of pneumonia in a public hospital in Chicago. This had been a great tragedy, because she and her daughter were to have joined him in America. Now, she said, they had nothing to which they could look forward. Seeing that we were touched by her grief and by her faith that America was to have meant so much to her, she went on to tell how seriously handicapped they had been since his death because remittances no longer came from America and they had had to pay his funeral expenses She and her daughter had already sent $100, but she said she had to send $200 more because " funerals, like everything else in America, are expensive." The local official through whom they had sent their savings and who had the name of the undertaker was not in town that day, so that I was unable to

The Immigrant and the Community

get it. But when I remembered how undertakers are sometimes given privileges and favors by our public institutions, I felt sure this undertaker had never given a man who was poor and without friends in America a $300 funeral. It was, indeed, more probable that he had been buried by the county. I was ashamed that there in Hungary as in the United States I should meet evidence that exploitation which could so easily be prevented was yet so easily perpetrated.

The petty frauds which are practised on the immigrant by those who meet him and recognize that his ignorance of the language and of the country will enable them to deceive and defraud him, cannot be altogether prevented; but certain general practices could be so controlled as to make these losses much less frequent. Those which the immigrant suffers at the hands of the immigrant banker could, for example, be greatly reduced. This is a matter of very real importance; for, while the deposits made in these banks are small, a considerable volume of business is done in the transmission of money abroad

The immigrant rarely comes to the United States quite free from all responsibility and obligations toward those he has left behind him. While much is said about the desirability of family immigration, it still remains true that the careful husband and father will precede his wife and family, find out whether he can or cannot "make a go of it," and have a home ready for them upon their arrival. Thousands of immigrants do this every year; and until the family reaches the United States, some part of the weekly wage, however small, must be sent to the

Protection Against Exploitation

children and their mother in Europe, and something must be saved for the purchase of the steamship tickets which will bring them to America. Many of the young unmarried men and women, too, count as a part of their cost of living the money that they send back to their old fathers and mothers or to the younger members of the family. They, too, frequently purchase the steamship tickets which bring a brother or a sister or the old parents to America.

This was as true in the days of the "older immigration" as it is to-day. One writer reports that by 1868, the Irish immigrants had sent back to Ireland 24,000,000 pounds sterling. This went, he says, to pay for passages to America, to support the old parents, or to help the younger sister or brother. He speaks especially of the contributions of the girls, saying that "the great ambition of the Irish girl is to send 'something' to her people as soon as possible after she has landed in America; and in innumerable instances the first tidings of her arrival in the New World are accompanied with a remittance, the fruits of her first earnings."[1]

Now, as then, the remittances that travel from the United States to Europe represent much sacrifice and family devotion. And one of the tragedies that has come with the war is the fact that it has often been impossible to reach those who have for years been entirely dependent on their relatives in America.

Because this saving and sending of money is so uniformly done by all immigrants, every foreign neighborhood has its "immigrant banks." The smallest of these

[1] John F. Maguire, *The Irish in America*, pp. 313-315.

The Immigrant and the Community

have few of the characteristics of the state or national banks or of the private banks, as Americans know them. As there is no regulation of private banks in Illinois, these " immigrant banks " have been subject to no supervision or restrictions of any kind. In 1913 an effort was made to find out how many of these " immigrant banks " there were in Chicago and to learn something of their business methods and the number of their depositors. At that time, 127 such Chicago " banks " were visited by the investigators of the Immigrants' Protective League. Certain districts of the city were well covered in the inquiry — the Italian quarters of the North, South and West sides, the Polish districts of the Northwest side, the Bohemian settlement near West Eighteenth Street, and the Stockyards neighborhood. Allowing for the fact that the great immigrant communities in South Chicago, Burnside, Pullman, and other parts of Chicago were not covered in this enumeration, it was estimated that there were probably more than two hundred such bankers in Chicago. The nationality of the 127 Chicago bankers visited was as follows: Italian 55, German 22, Polish 16, Bohemian 14, Slovak 6, Jewish (Russian and German) 6, Russian 3, American 3, and Hungarian 2

The patrons of these banks were seldom exclusively of a single nationality but were found to be Italian, Bohemian, Polish, Slovak, Croatian, Russian, German, and Hungarian A German banker on Eighteenth Street, for example, does business with all these nationalities except the Italian.

The principal business is the transmission of money abroad. The deposits for safekeeping made by recently

Protection Against Exploitation

arrived immigrants are usually intended for the purchase of a steamship ticket for relatives who have been left behind.

Of the Italian bankers visited, 5 did not receive money for safekeeping, 35 were steamship agents, and 15 labor agents; 11 "banks" were in grocery stores, 4 in drug stores, 2 in saloons, one in a barber shop, and one in a real estate office. In the Slavic neighborhoods, the "bank" is usually a real estate office and steamship ticket agency as well as a bank, but this is not always the case. Two Slovak bankers and a German one on Chicago Avenue were found to be the presidents of Mutual Benefit Associations; and the private accounts of the bankers, the depositors, and the Mutual Benefit Association were not separated. One Hungarian banker was also a tailor; a Polish one was a druggist; several of these bankers were lawyers; one was a grocer; and one Russian Jew found it possible to be both banker and plumber.

The financial risks which the immigrant takes in dealing with these banks are: (1) that his money is often intrusted to irresponsible persons with the attendant risk of loss through dishonesty or carelessness; and (2) that the private bankers, although honest, are not controlled as are state or national banks as to the kind of investments they make with the money deposited with them. If their business speculations fail, as they often do, they are unable to meet their obligations to the depositors. Many of these "bankers" are quite inexperienced in business methods and know little about what constitutes "safe investments." This second danger is chiefly incidental to the business of the safekeeping of moneys.

The Immigrant and the Community

The temptation to dishonesty, however, is particularly great in transmitting money to foreign countries. The immigrant bankers usually send money abroad through reputable banks, express companies, and foreign exchange bankers, and have in their offices the blanks of the bank or company through whom they transmit, but this affords no protection for the purchaser of the money order because only the name of the " banker " appears on the receipt given him, and the bank or express company never assumes any responsibility until the " banker " pays in the money together with the name and address of the person to whom it is to be forwarded. For this reason, companies place their blanks in the hands of " bankers " without requiring any bonds, although inquiry is usually made as to the honesty of the banker. If he absconds and it is discovered that he has failed to transmit money given to him to send abroad and has taken with him the small savings of the newly arrived immigrant, there is no legal redress when there are, as often happens, no " resources " beyond a little office furniture. Even if the banker can be found, a criminal prosecution usually fails and a civil one is made difficult because the principal witnesses are in Europe. The total as well as the individual amounts lost are relatively small; but they are, nevertheless, proportionately very great to those who lose them. After some of the disappearances, suit is not even instituted The matter is reported to the police, some effort is made to locate the man, and then nothing more is done

A single case will illustrate the way in which many immigrant men and women are victimized. A young

Protection Against Exploitation

Croatian who was only twenty-two years old opened a bank near the Croatian and Bohemian settlements in Chicago after two years' residence in this country. It was very easy to have his "bank" made a sub-postal station and thus give the immigrant the impression that the United States Government stood behind all the receipts that were issued. The sub-postal station was eventually withdrawn because a check given by the banker to the Government was not honored. This precipitated a run on the bank. People began to hear that money which they had sent home had never been received. One Croatian supposed he had sent $1600, the savings of a life of hard work, by post-office money order. He had, however, been given an order on a bank in Croatia, which was not honored because the "banker" had never carried an account with any bank in Croatia. A criminal prosecution was begun on this and several other similar complaints; but they were dismissed because letters, cablegrams, or affidavits declaring that money which Chicago Croatians had intrusted to the "banker" to send to Europe had not been received could not be accepted as evidence in a criminal prosecution. In most cases the amount sent is comparatively small, and word that it has not been received is slow in coming; and, when protest is made to the banker, he says that it was delayed but has been sent; and the man waits to hear again, perhaps leaves the city and does not know what to do. If sufficiently pressed, the "banker" usually sends the money after having had the use of it for a considerable period of time.

During the winter of 1914 and 1915, when unemploy-

The Immigrant and the Community

ment resulted in great suffering and when the little savings were so sorely needed, the number of these bank failures was especially large.

One immigrant bank that defrauded all its depositors was conducted by a Russian who had been in the United States six years. He had worked for three years in a factory in St. Louis and then came to Chicago to open a bank. He made a practice of transmitting money and of selling steamship tickets, which because he was not an authorized agent he bought from another private banker on the Northwest side, now also an absconder. As a means of getting business, he wrote Russian letters for those who were illiterate, and assured every one that he had many friends among the American manufacturers with whom he would get them good jobs.

In the late summer of 1914 this Russian banker disappeared. Most of his depositors were Little Russians who, like himself, came from the Province of Kiev. One was a young fellow, seventeen years old, who earned $10 a week in a tin can factory; he had $45 on deposit and had given the banker $28 to send to his mother, but she had never received it. Another man, a laborer who was earning $1.75 a day and had been in the United States one year, had $60 on deposit. Another man who had been in this country two years and was persuaded by the banker to send his savings, $250, to Europe, lost everything. The bank had no discoverable assets. There was not even a safe — nothing except a few pieces of cheap office furniture.

That year there were other failures — a Greek and two Italian banks which had very much larger numbers

Protection Against Exploitation

of depositors — as well as others whose liabilities were small. It was a time of great suffering because of unemployment, and many immigrant families had to be helped that winter who had always before been self-supporting. It is impossible to say how much of the increased dependency was due to the loss through the failure of immigrant banks of the small savings that would have tided families over the winter. With a number of families and of single men, this was clearly the case.

But private bankers have also "disappeared" since the period of business depression ended. One failure, which attracted much public attention, came during the summer of 1916, and more than a thousand depositors — practically all of them Russian peasants who have been in this country less than three years — found to their amazement that the banking laws did not cover the institution which was in their midst. When they collected in crowds at the closed doors, the police beat them back with their clubs, a very sad expression of the organized authority of the community.

The immigrant banker is usually, as has been said, a steamship ticket agent, and irregularities are occasionally practised in this connection. One combination banker and steamship ticket agent had Polish and Ruthenian depositors. The Immigrants' Protective League had several claims against him which he was paying in instalments, when a telegram came from the New York Bureau of Industries and Immigration that a Ruthenian and his family who were returning to Europe were stranded in New York with fraudulent steamship tickets which they had purchased from this banker. They were

The Immigrant and the Community

issued on the Bryde Line, a Gulf to Norway line, but called for passage on a Holland-American boat. The banker promised us that he would refund the money as soon as the tickets arrived, but by that time he had disappeared. He was eventually located in Racine, Wisconsin, doing a similar business; was arrested, convicted, and placed on probation on his promise to repay the claims filed against him.

It would be quite incorrect to give the impression that all the two hundred or more immigrant bankers in Chicago are either dishonest or careless or unbusinesslike in their methods. The view taken by many that the immigrant banker is necessary, is equally incorrect. It is true that the American banks have not met the needs of the immigrant. They are usually without clerks who can speak the foreign languages, are unwilling to keep open at hours when the immigrant can do his banking, and are generally impatient of him and his needs. But in recent years, American bankers have begun to see that his business is worth securing, and self-interest may make them more considerate. But there is no reason for sentimentalizing about the services that the immigrant banker performs. In a few cases, he may be a public-spirited leader and interpreter of his people and his bank may be a neighborhood center of information and general helpfulness. In too many cases, however, the reverse is true; and it is a part of the "banker's" business policy to develop among his countryman an undesirable dependence upon himself, by conducting what is often a bureau of misinformation. In Boston he meets the immigrants at the docks and takes them to

Protection Against Exploitation

the bank, and gives them his business cards and envelopes before he sends them to their relatives or friends; should the immigrant be detained by the inspector, he prepares, often very badly and for a high price, the affidavits of their relatives and promises to arrange through his friend "the senator" for their admission; he gets them jobs, and furnishes an interpreter, a lawyer, and a bondsman should they be in trouble, for with all such persons and with many others he has shrewdly established connections. But whatever services the immigrant banker does or does not perform in addition to those that relate to banking, they cannot be considered as an excuse for the lack of supervision that at present jeopardizes the savings intrusted to him.

Discussion with the foreign exchange bankers and express companies through whom these bankers usually send the money they receive for transmission to Europe, confirms the opinion that reasonable regulations would be something of a hardship to some of the honest bankers. But, knowing the evils of the present system, they agree that there is absolutely no other way to protect the poor against the kind of abuses which now exist. The whole responsibility for honest dealing under great temptation is now placed on the immigrant banker. That he does not yield more frequently is perhaps the surprising thing. All the reasons which can be offered for the careful protection of the deposits in savings banks apply with special force to the institutions we are now considering.

The present system is, moreover, in the long run really profitable only to the express and steamship companies,

The Immigrant and the Community

whose business is undoubtedly stimulated by the activity of the greater numbers who are thus engaged in urging the immigrants to send their money abroad or to begin to save toward the purchase of steamship tickets.

The failures that occur are always made the basis of an appeal to the immigrant to send his money to the government banks at home. Following the failure of the banks which had many Russian depositors in Chicago, the Russian Consul distributed circulars calling attention to the fact that the Consulates have in effect been made branches of the Government Savings Bank of Russia, so that money can be deposited and withdrawn and interest collected at the Consulate.

It was hoped that the Postal Savings Bank would take the place of these unregulated private banks A very large per cent. of the depositors are estimated by the postmasters to be recently arrived foreign born. But the post office does not advertise the facilities it offers; and it is, in consequence, not well known and cannot compete with the aggressive banker who is constantly soliciting the immigrant's business, has clerks who speak his language and welcome him day or night, Sundays or holidays. Regulation of all these bankers is therefore the only means of protecting the depositors.

Some regulation of "immigrant" banks has been attempted in a few States — first in Massachusetts and later in New York, New Jersey, Ohio, and Pennsylvania. In all these States except New Jersey, there is no regulation of private banking, and the laws referred to have been carefully phrased, so that they reach only what are known as the "immigrant banks." New Jersey has, in

Protection Against Exploitation

addition to its general regulation of private banking, a law passed in 1907, which requires those engaged in the transmission of money abroad to be licensed by the State and in order to prevent the kind of practices described requires that money received for transmission shall be sent within five days from its receipt, placing the initial burden of proving that it has been sent upon the banker instead of on the transmitter. This statute has been copied in Pennsylvania and New York.

In these States a license is required, and there is a minimum of inspection and supervision by the State Bank Commissioner or Inspector. But in these States, too, immigrant savings are inadequately protected. The very fact that the requirements of the law are so much less than is required for state and national banks means that the deposits cannot be properly secured. In Massachusetts the amount of the bond is fixed by the Bank Commissioner and is uniformly low. For example, one Italian banker in Lawrence who disappeared had been allowed to furnish a personal bond of $1000. The Massachusetts Immigration Commission found that one man had reported claims against this banker amounting to $960 and that another had given him $700 to send abroad, which was never sent.

Illinois is in the section of the United States in which regulation of all banks is favored, and the guaranteeing of deposits has been successfully tried in a few of the neighboring States. Regulation of immigrant banks is given no hearing because the demand for regulation of all kinds of banking is general. And so the immigrants in Illinois will apparently not be given the kind of pro-

The Immigrant and the Community

tection they have in the States just referred to, and it may be possible for some years to come for men who cannot afford to go into the grocery business to open a " bank."

The immigrant does not know of the national and state banks, which are regulated, so that in using the neighborhood places he cannot be said to have " chosen " with full knowledge and at his own peril the unregulated bank, as it is sometimes assumed that the American does. But most Americans do not understand the risk they are running, and here, as in so many other situations, the immigrants' need of protection is not so different in kind as it is greater in degree.

The New York Bureau of Industries and Immigration has found that the notaries public are quick to take advantage of the difference in the standing of the notary here and abroad. In many foreign countries to become a notary a man must have been trained for judicial service, and the title is a guarantee of learning and authority. In the United States the notary performs for the most part merely clerical services, and he is not appealed to for legal advice. The immigrant requires the services of a notary in the renunciation of allegiance to his own country, in securing exemption from military service, in the acknowledgment of deeds and other papers which are to be sent to Europe, and in making affidavits promising support, which must be sent to the relatives in Austria or Italy who are coming to join him in America To execute these papers properly, a knowledge of Italian, Russian, Austrian, or other law and of the United States Immigration Law is necessary. Many of

Protection Against Exploitation

these notaries advertise to do much more than take acknowledgments of deeds and other instruments, although they are usually entirely without the training even for this service. A Polish notary advertised in a Boston paper as follows: "I make legal documents approved by consuls; am interpreter in court in the Polish and Russian languages; attend to cases of accidents, loss of life, and recover on old cases. Whoever is arrested, I try to release him. I do not serve capitalists, only working people. Whoever is in misfortune let him come to me. Advice given free"[2] A newly arrived immigrant might conclude on reading such a statement that this notary is an officer appointed by the State to look after the interests of the Polish and Russian working men of Boston. Similarly, a Magyar notary in Chicago advertises that he has the "only expert law and notary public office in Chicago where you can call confidently on every question because of my past six years' experience and also innumerable letters of appreciation; furthermore, thousands of carefully and honestly finished cases give guarantee of all this." This man is not a lawyer, and is quite ignorant of ordinary business methods.

In the United States, no questions are ever asked regarding a man's qualifications for a notary, and signers of a petition for a license usually think the signing of it a matter of little importance.

Another form of exploitation that could be prevented is in connection with the sale of farm lands. This business offers an excellent opportunity for taking advantage

[2] *Report of Massachusetts Commission on Immigration*, Chap. VIII, p. 190.

The Immigrant and the Community

of the immigrant's ignorance of the extent of the country and of social and climatic conditions. Most of the immigrants when they come are without the capital necessary for independent farming. Moreover, many of them, especially those who have lived under the landlord system of Southern Italy and Russia, feel that the farm means poverty and suffering, and that a weekly wage in the city or town is the road to the things they hope America is to give them. Many of them find this to be the case. But many others find factory work an unhappy and unhealthy substitute for farm work, and the weekly wage not possessed of the purchasing power they anticipated. They are eager to return to the land. For many of these, the safest route would be by first serving an apprenticeship as a farm hand. How inadequately the demand and supply of farm labor is organized has already been illustrated.[3]

But there are many who have saved some money toward the purchase of a farm. The interest of the United States lies entirely in their accomplishing this object. Dr. G. E. Di Palma Castiglione, who was for several years connected with the Italian Immigrant Aid Society of New York and more recently with the Immigration Department of the Italian government, has pointed out that "the Italian peasant, who has had centuries of experience in tilling the land, who understands all kinds of cultivation, who is not only expert in viniculture, but also in the culture of all the vegetables and fruits of his new country, is using but the minimum part of his productive habits, i.e., his physical force"

[3] See Chapter II.

Protection Against Exploitation

when he becomes a laborer in the city, and all his technical qualities are, in consequence, "lost both to himself and to the country which harbors him." [4] This is equally true of some other nationalities. Mr. W. W. Husband, Special Immigration Inspector, after a study of Russian immigration, reported that the Russian could be directed to the land instead of to industrial centers.[5] Russian immigration has, of course, almost ceased since the war, but it is generally agreed by those familiar with conditions in Russia that peasant immigration from that country will greatly increase in the future; and in the words of Mr. Husband, it "affords the best opportunity for developing a movement to the land since the Scandinavians so largely settled the North Central States a generation or more ago."

Sometimes the foreign born who have accumulated a little capital and are eager to get on a farm are persuaded by the immigrant bankers that their chances of success are greater if they return to Europe, and so they undertake to purchase at $250 to $400 an acre European land which has been worked, carefully and scientifically, it is true, for many generations. That they will accumulate sufficient capital to make this venture successful is very doubtful. Many who have tried it have failed and returned to the United States to take up their old life in the factory.

Those who desire to purchase land in this country are entirely without the kind of information which would

---

[4] "Italian Immigration into the United States," *American Journal of Sociology*, Vol XI, p 200.
[5] *Annual Report of the Commissioner-General of Immigration,* 1914, p. 401

The Immigrant and the Community

enable them to act wisely. Unscrupulous land agents canvass the immigrant neighborhoods of every city telling in glowing terms of the amount that can be realized on farms in Florida, Texas, and Colorado. They distribute illustrated folders describing the possibilities of securing a home and independence in Marconiville or Sobieski, or Kossuthville. The name of their national leader is intended to lessen the fear of failure which they might have in a new venture and also to suggest to them that this new settlement which they are invited to join will be like the friendly village which was the center of the farm life at home. Many of the propositions are *bona fide*. But the agent is usually interested only in his commission which is a part of the first payment, and so he frequently persuades the immigrants to leave the city long before they have sufficient funds to give them even a reasonable chance of success. In such cases, the men become discouraged, give up their payments, lose all that they have invested, and return to the city to discourage all those who are eager to get away from the city.

Sometimes men are promised an opportunity to work, for example, in a sawmill during the winter, and so keep themselves until their farming is on a paying basis. A Russian who had been here three years had managed to save $400. He wanted to get on a farm and was persuaded to make an initial payment of $115. He was promised employment in a lumber mill and thought this assured him a livelihood. He built himself a house on the farm with lumber furnished him by the company, moved his family and furniture from Chicago, and spent

Protection Against Exploitation

the first summer clearing stumps from a part of the land. But he was given no work during the winter, and spring found him indebted both to the company store and to his neighbors; so he concluded there was nothing for him to do but return to Chicago, defeated. Then the company attached his furniture; so he came back without anything.

Some of the companies conduct what is in effect a lottery. One such company had a large tract of land, which it proposed to divide into 5000 smaller tracts of from 10 to 160 acres. An orchard company was organized and shares issued. Every man who paid $15 to the company was given a contract for this amount which entitled him either to a tract of land or to stock in the orchard company. The drawing which decided what each purchaser was to receive was, in order " to comply with the federal law," an auction at which, by mutual agreement, no one was to bid more than the $15 already paid for the contract. This company has recently gone into bankruptcy. The petition for the appointment of a receiver gives the names of no less than 15,000 persons who have paid in sums ranging from $10 to $100.

Sometimes the title given is not good. Several Bohemians who joined in a colonization project in Louisiana complain that they were given nothing at all to show for what purpose the money they had paid into the company was to be used.

In several States the " Blue Sky Laws " prevent some of these frauds. But neither the Blue Sky Laws nor the prosecution of land sharks will meet this situation. Before any far-reaching change in the agricultural situa-

The Immigrant and the Community

tion in the United States can be made, much needs to be done. There are, for example, large holdings of farm land in the United States which will have to be broken up if the farmers of the future are to be farm owners; the rural credit system, which is, as yet, in the initial stages of experimentation, must be extended to include the prospective purchaser and not remain, as at present, a source of help only to the man already established on a farm; more irrigation projects must be undertaken; the question of cheaper marketing of farm products must also be solved. But pending the working out of such thorough-going reform measures, some unnecessary failures could be prevented by a relatively small expenditure of money.

The Massachusetts Commission recommends as a first step in the protection of the native or the immigrant city worker who wants to make farming his occupation that a scientific "exploration" of the farm lands of the various States be made by the States. If the information thus secured were open to prospective purchasers, the American would be able to protect himself against many of the frauds from which he now suffers. For the immigrant, much more is necessary. The information secured in such an exploration must be passed on to him by some disinterested person who speaks his language and with whom he comes in contact in other ways; some one who can give him in terms of his own experience the information the State or the nation has about the particular piece of land he is considering purchasing and where he should go to have the title investigated Such a person attached to a State Board or Commission of

Protection Against Exploitation

Immigration or to the Division of Information and Distribution of the United States Immigration Bureau would enable many of those who are willing to put hard work and eager intelligence into their farming experiment to succeed where they now fail and return to the city to discourage others by the story of their misfortunes.

To protect the immigrant against exploitation and unnecessary loss, he need not be treated like a child, as though he were a ward of the State, incapable of making his own decisions and of abiding by the consequences which flow from his own best judgment. For without a reasonable opportunity to know the facts, he cannot be said to be guided by his own judgment.

Moreover, we have departed very far from the theory that every man must act at his own peril, and the State is beginning to protect us in those transactions in which we cannot reasonably be expected to protect ourselves But the State cannot give this protection to those who, because of their ignorance of the country, are most in need of it, unless our complex population is considered in framing laws and, what is even more important, in the administration of the laws which are enacted.

The usefulness of a state or city bureau which will take up cases of exploitation and give disinterested advice and assistance to immigrants has been demonstrated by the New York Bureau of Industries and Immigration, which was established in 1911, and also by the California Commission on Immigration and Housing and the Cleveland Immigration Office, which were more recently established.

The last annual report of the New York Bureau

The Immigrant and the Community

records 3482 complaints and 2571 requests for information received during the year. In 1915, the California Commission received 2906 complaints and 1402 requests for information and advice.

The Massachusetts Commission on Immigration recommended a State Board of Immigration which should be authorized to maintain offices to which immigrants should be encouraged to go for disinterested advice and information; to establish a clearing house of information useful to the immigrant; to investigate complaints of exploitation with a view to their adjustment, and the recommendation of measures by which such frauds may be prevented; and the accumulation of information with regard to the immigrant population, so that expert advice may be at the disposal of interested public and private agencies.

The powers given under the New York and California laws are much more sweeping; and there is in consequence, especially in New York, an overlapping of the Bureau's power with long-established offices and boards which has made it both impossible and even undesirable that the Bureau should do what it is directed to undertake by law. In both States, the principal usefulness has been along lines covered by the Massachusetts recommendations. Such bureaus or commissions are a necessity in every State in which there is a large non-English speaking population.

In the new charter adopted by the City of Cleveland in the spring of 1913, provision was made for a city immigration office in the Division of Employment of the

Protection Against Exploitation

Department of Public Welfare. The Cleveland office has had very inadequate support, but the immigrant population has appreciated the city's offer of disinterested help. Within a period of two years, the office handled 1542 complaints and applications. In Chicago, the Immigrants' Protective League, a private organization, received 3258 complaints and applications for advice in the year 1915. These complaints are singularly alike in New York, Chicago, Cleveland, and San Francisco Many of them are easily adjusted. Others indicate well-developed systems of exploitation, and new legislation is sometimes found necessary.

Federal bureaus of information would be even more effective than state or city ones and could be developed in connection with the labor exchanges which have been opened under the Bureau of Immigration.

The United States should have realized long ago that it is of much more than passing importance that the immigrant have some one, other than those who seek to profit at his expense, to whom he may go and who will speak to him in a language he understands and will listen patiently and sympathetically to the story of his difficulties. The immigrant cannot be adequately guided by an American who does not understand the sources of the difficulties which arise during the period of his adjustment; nor can he be helped by friends who have only recently come themselves and who are, in consequence, not qualified to interpret American life. It is only through a public organization created to meet these needs that the civic, social, and educational resources of

The Immigrant and the Community

the community will be made available for those who are most in need of them. It is only in this spirit of helpful understanding that a public program of Americanization will have the cooperation of the foreign born.

CHAPTER V

THE IMMIGRANT IN THE COURTS

THE first conscious contact of the immigrant with our laws comes in most cases with his first experience in the courts, and his respect not only for our judicial system but for the Government as a whole is largely determined by the treatment he receives at that time. Much has been said and written about the "immigrant and crime." But whenever any set of facts have been assembled on this subject, they have been studied solely with a view to determining whether or not all immigrants or some particular "brand" of immigrants should not be excluded on the ground that they are "filling our prisons and jails" Very few have asked whether we are helping to make certain temptations easy or difficult for immigrants to resist; whether we are giving them the opportunity they should have to protect themselves against the criminals in their own midst; and whether, when accused of crime, they are given the kind of trial that will give them confidence in the American judicial system.

The relation of immigration to crime should be considered with a view to determining:

1. Whether the volume of crime in the United States is disproportionately increased by immigration, and whether, in consequence, if crime is to be reduced, immigration must be reduced.

The Immigrant and the Community

2. Whether the kinds of crime committed and the temptations that lead to these crimes differ in the case of the immigrant and of the native born of native parentage. For if this be true, any program for crime prevention must be adjusted to meet the differences which are the result of race or early environment.

3. Whether the foreign born are given the same opportunities to secure justice as are the native born.

The rights of aliens are usually guaranteed in treaties made by the United States; but the fact that under our division of authority such rights must be enforced by the States gives rise to difficult and complicated situations in the civil as well as the criminal field. These questions which grow out of our federal form of government are not here discussed.

It might be said at the outset that sufficient evidence is not available for the complete verification or denial of any one of the propositions enumerated But the various sources of information indicate the needs that should receive serious consideration. In considering the volume of crime among the foreign born, it is necessary as a preliminary step to call attention to what is at present being done through our immigration laws to prevent criminals from coming to the United States from other countries.

At present, those aliens "who have been convicted of or admit having committed a felony or other crime or misdemeanor involving moral turpitude"[1] are debarred from entering the United States. The obvious difficulty in the enforcement of this law is that, except in unusual

[1] United States Immigration Act of February 20, 1907, Section 2.

The Immigrant in the Courts

instances, the United States has no advance information regarding the character of immigrants; and admission of guilt cannot be expected from the really criminal. The exclusion of the immigrant rests with administrative officers — the so-called " Board of Review " composed of inspectors — with the right of appeal to the Secretary of Labor.

The Immigration Act does not place upon the applicant for admission the burden of proving that he does not belong to this or any of the other excluded classes; but inasmuch as the courts have held that there is no testimony which it will hold necessary or insufficient to warrant the findings of the Inspectors,[2] and since the immigrant is not allowed counsel at his hearings, the rights usually guaranteed the accused are not accorded the immigrant in the determination that he is excludable as a criminal. As a result, the immigrant is often denied admission on evidence which a court would not accept as establishing the fact that he had been convicted of a crime.

Those who are admitted but who are found within a period of three years[3] to have belonged to one of the excluded classes are liable to deportation. At the hearing in these cases, which is also before an officer in the immigration service, the alien is allowed to inspect all the evidence on which the warrant for his deportation was issued and to have counsel at his hearing, so that deportation is usually a more difficult process than exclusion. The nationality of those debarred and deported as criminals for every one thousand admitted

[2] See case of U. S ex rel. Barlin v Rodgers et al., 191 Federal 970.
[3] The Law of 1917 (Sec. 19) makes this a five year period.

The Immigrant and the Community

during the year ending June 30, 1914, is given in the following table: [4]

Nationality	De-barred	De-ported	Number Deported and Debarred for Every 1000 Admitted
African	20	1	2.5
Bohemian and Moravian	2	1	.3
Croatian and Slovenian	14	2	.4
English	67	36	2.0
Finnish	7	2	.7
French	37	9	2.5
German	63	22	1.1
Greek	17	14	.7
Hebrew	35	3	.3
Irish	25	9	1.0
Italian (North)	26	2	.6
Italian (South)	197	12	.8
Lithuanian	3	—	.1
Magyar	51	8	1.3
Polish	42	2	.4
Roumanian	32	1	1.4
Russian	20	2	.5
Ruthenian	18	1	.5
Scandinavian	8	11	.5
Scotch	15	5	1.1
Slovak	16	1	.7
All others	40	13	.5
Total	755	157	.8

This table shows that so far as the records of the immigration service are concerned a larger per cent. of criminals are found among the immigrants from western Europe than among those from southern and eastern

[4] *Annual Report of the Commissioner-General of Immigration*, 1914, pp. 105 and 108.

The Immigrant in the Courts

Europe, but that the numbers excluded are relatively very small for all nationalities.

It is generally believed, however, that debarring and deporting criminals from the United States under the present law has made the general emigration of European criminals impossible, although the individual offender occasionally succeeds in passing inspection.

Suggestions for further precautions against the admission of criminals are made from time to time. The one which was approved by the United States Immigration Commission [5] and has received serious consideration is that every applicant for admission shall be required to present a certificate showing that he has not had a criminal record and is not under observation as a dangerous or suspicious character by the police in the country from which he comes. That political offenses, with which Americans generally sympathize, would make it impossible for many to secure such certificates is the objection which has defeated that plan. The suggestion that American investigators determine the personal and family history of each immigrant before emigration, which has been made by some eugenists [6] as the only safe method of insuring a pure racial stock, has not been considered practicable.

Owing to the fact that our criminal records do not give the race, the birth-place, and birth-place of the parents of the defendant, and other facts regarding his social status, it is still impossible to discuss with complete accuracy the question whether the immigrants

[5] *Reports of the Immigration Commission*, Vol 2, p 221.
[6] C. B. Davenport, *Heredity in Relation to Eugenics*, pp. 222–223.

The Immigrant and the Community

have increased, disproportionately to their numbers, the volume of crime in the United States. A considerable body of evidence is, however, available on this subject.

The *Reports of the United States Immigration Commission*[7] say that "no satisfactory evidence has yet been produced to show that immigration has resulted in an increase of crime disproportionate to the increase in the adult population. Such comparable statistics of crime and population as it has been possible to obtain indicate that immigrants are less prone to commit crime than are native Americans." According to the special report of the United States Census on *Prisoners and Juvenile Delinquents in Institutions, 1904*,[8] "it is evident that the popular belief that the foreign born are filling the prisons has little foundation in fact. It would seem, however, that they are slightly more prone than the native whites to commit minor offenses." The New York Commission on Immigration[9] also found that "there is no evidence to prove that the aliens who have been in this country less than five years are more likely to commit crimes than are citizens of the same sex and age" The *Report of the Massachusetts Commission on Immigration* (1914)[10] showed a disproportionate amount of crime among the foreign born, but that "of these foreign-born offenders, the number of those who come from English-speaking countries is disproportionately large, as they constitute 34 6 per cent. of all those committed to penal institutions."

The most recent analysis of the racial status of those

[7] Vol. 36, *Immigration and Crime*, p 1.
[8] Pp 18-19, 40-41.
[9] *Report* (1909), p 20
[10] See p. 101.

The Immigrant in the Courts

among us who are arrested and convicted of crimes and misdemeanors is contained in the *Report of the Chicago Council Committee on Crime,* which was submitted to the Council in March, 1915. As Chicago's immigrant population is fairly typical of other large industrial centers, the findings of this committee have national as well as local significance. The popular belief that immigration is a cause of crime, according to this Report, is "largely due to a comfortable theory that we are superior to the people of Europe, and to a desire to shift the responsibility for our shortcomings onto other people." [11] The Chicago figures, however, show that we are not entitled to enjoy this comfortable feeling, " for, comparing the distribution of arrests with the distribution of the population over fifteen years of age, it appears that the Americans, both white and colored, have a larger percentage of arrests than their proportion of the population entitles them to have, while the immigrant, who forms 46.7 per cent. of the population, furnishes only 35.3 per cent. of the arrests. Comparing the convictions with the population, the Americans, both white and colored, make a still more unfavorable showing; that is, 59 4 per cent. of those convicted were Americans (white), while their percentage of the population over fifteen years of age was only 50.9 per cent., whereas the immigrants, who formed 46.7 per cent. of the population, were only 33.4 per cent. of those convicted." [12] Commenting on this, the Report says that in convictions for both felonies and misdemeanors [13] " the various

[11] See p. 59
[12] *Report of the Chicago Council Committee on Crime,* p 52.
[13] *Ibid,* p. 56.

The Immigrant and the Community

foreign groups show almost uniformly a smaller percentage of convictions than their proportion of the population entitles them to have." "The Italians show an excess of one tenth of 1 per cent. in convictions, and this is surely so small as to be negligible. And the Greeks, who form .6 per cent. of the population, form 1.8 per cent. of the arrests and 2.2 per cent. of the convictions. That is, the Greeks have 1.2 per cent. of the arrests and 1.6 per cent. of the convictions in excess of the percentage justified by their proportion of the population."

The following table taken from the same report [14] shows the nativity of male persons arrested and convicted for felonies and misdemeanors:

A. NATIVITY OF MALE PERSONS ARRESTED AND CONVICTED FOR FELONIES, 1913

Nativity	Arrests No.	Arrests Per cent.	Convictions No.	Convictions Per cent.	Per cent. Distribution of Male Population of Chicago 21 Years and Over
American					
White	5,756	56.3	2,241	56.9	43.1
Colored	882	8.6	354	9.0	2.6
Foreign	3,599	35.1	1,344	34.1	54.3
Austrian	401	3.9	158	4.0	11.2
English	166	1.6	79	2.0	5.2
French	22	.2	10	.3	....
German	815	8.0	366	9.3	12.6
Greek	139	1.4	29	.7	.6
Hollanders	19	.2	8	.2	.7
Irish	186	1.8	98	2.5	4.4
Italian	392	3.8	108	2.7	3.2
Russian	1,027	10.0	331	8.4	8.5
Scandinavian	214	2.1	93	2.4	6.7
Other	218	2.1	64	1.6	1.2
Total	10,237	100.0	3,939	100.0	100.0

[14] *Report of the Chicago Council Committee on Crime*, p. 56.

The Immigrant in the Courts

B. NATIVITY OF MALE PERSONS ARRESTED AND CONVICTED FOR MISDEMEANORS, 1913

Nativity	Arrests		Convictions		Per cent. Distribution of Male Population of Chicago 21 Years and Over
	No.	Per cent.	No.	Per cent.	
American					
White	50,999	58.5	23,656	59.6	43.1
Colored	4,741	5.4	2,179	5.5	2.6
Foreign	31,416	36.1	13,855	34.9	54.3
Austrian	3,282	3.8	1,492	3.8	11.2
English	1,240	1.4	537	1.3	5.2
French	181	.2	90	.2	....
German	6,942	8.0	2,977	7.5	12.6
Greek	1,592	1.8	947	2.4	.6
Hollanders	209	.3	115	.3	.7
Irish	2,354	2.7	901	2.3	4.4
Italian	2,972	3.4	1,333	3.4	3.2
Russian	7,519	8.6	3,314	8.3	8.5
Scandinavian	2,857	3.3	1,330	3.3	6.7
Other	2,268	2.6	819	2.1	1.2
Total	87,156	100.0	39,690	100.0	100.0

"In these tables which have been compiled separately for felonies and misdemeanors it appears that the offenses of the Greeks are largely misdemeanors. That is, .7 per cent. of the felony convictions were Greek. This apparent excess of 'crime' among the Greeks is undoubtedly due to the fact that the Greeks are largely engaged in the peddling business, and violations of ordinances would undoubtedly bring them to court often." [15]

These quotations have been given at some length

[15] *Report of the Chicago Council Committee on Crime,* p. 56.

The Immigrant and the Community

because it is considered important to show that our real problem does not lie in the disproportionate amount of crime for which the immigrant is responsible, but in the possible reduction or prevention of crime among the immigrants as among Americans.

To determine what measures would tend to accomplish this or how those measures that have been generally accepted as promoting this end may be adapted to the needs of the immigrant population, it is necessary (1) to know the kinds of crimes usually committed by the various national groups, and (2) to understand their social, environmental, and racial characteristics. Until proper records are kept by the courts and penal institutions, it will be impossible to determine the first of these. The United States Immigration Commission made "the central feature" of their investigation of crime the determination of how "the criminality of the immigrant differs from that of the native."[16] The material available or secured by the Commission was, however, very meager; and no attempt was made to discover to what extent apparent tendencies on the part of certain races to commit certain kinds of crime were the result of local conditions rather than of race.

Much further investigation on this subject is obviously necessary, and until we have a satisfactory collection of criminal statistics in this country no safe conclusions can be drawn as to the relative degree of criminality in various races. In the meantime it is possible on the basis of such material as is now available for a city to make important experiments in crime prevention by an

[16] Vol. 36, p. 12.

The Immigrant in the Courts

intelligent use of its educational and social institutions. The Chicago figures, showing an excess not in serious crimes but in the number of misdemeanors committed by the immigrant, are suggestive of immediate need of instruction regarding the many ordinances of which he is wholly ignorant.

The Massachusetts Commission on Immigration [17] called attention to the fact that " in so far as a lack of proper recreation and provisions for social intercourse tends to result in immorality among young men and women of all nationalities, it is especially serious in the case of non-family groups of young foreign men and young immigrant women whose needs the American community has much greater difficulty in understanding. The lack of proper social life, together with the absence of the old forms of social control, is undoubtedly responsible for much of the very serious and often unnatural moral delinquency which is found in non-family groups of single men." A program for crime prevention must take into consideration the needs and the prejudices of such groups.

To formulate such a program means nothing more than recognizing the fact that the population of the United States is and always has been a cosmopolitan one and that such plans as are adopted should be designed to meet the needs, not of a homogeneous but of a cosmopolitan population.

Misdemeanors are frequently committed by immigrants in entire ignorance of the law, because of an adherence to peasant customs which, innocent in a rural

[17] *Report of the Massachusetts Commission on Immigration*, p. 104

The Immigrant and the Community

district, are dangerous in the city and have therefore been prohibited. The release from old restraints which has come with that breaking away from old traditions which inevitably follows emigration, results in some cases in a moral confusion which assistance in adjustment to their new environment could prevent. If such facts are properly considered, the initial breaking of the law can be prevented in many cases by the expenditure of a relatively small amount of money and forethought.

This does not mean that the immigrant population is to be dealt with as a group outside of the community life. It does mean that, if we are to reduce the temptation to commit crime, plans should be made after consideration of the customs and language differences of the various elements in its population and of their ignorance of American law. If this is not done, such reforms as are undertaken will not meet the needs of the people of the community. Ignoring these differences sometimes leads an entire colony to conclude what is unfortunately not always untrue, that there is a double standard of law enforcement — one for the American and another for the immigrant.

In so far as the fear of punishment acts as a deterrent of crime, it is dependent upon the conviction in the minds of the people that the law is surely and uniformly administered It is, moreover, not fear so much as confidence in the fairness of the courts that prevents men from settling their private differences by an illegal taking of the law into their own hands.

It is, therefore, important to inquire whether in his arrest, trial, and commitment, the foreign born is denied

The Immigrant in the Courts

any of the safeguards that protect the American born, and whether the complaint of the foreign born is heard with the same consideration as that of the native born.

In Chicago, 57 per cent. of all the cases disposed of by the criminal branches of the Municipal Court in 1913 were discharged.[18] As the Report of the Chicago Council Committee points out, there are two possible explanations of this: (1) "A large number of innocent persons are arrested and are in consequence discharged without conviction; or (2) a large number of persons who are legitimately arrested and who should be convicted are being released because of some defect in our prosecuting machinery."[19] In either case the result is the greatest confusion in the mind of the immigrant as to what is and what is not unlawful in the United States.

Arrests are frequently made either because a policeman fails to understand a man or because the man does not understand the officer and so fails to obey orders. As there are no interpreters at the courts, so there are no interpreters at the police stations; and without any further examination the man is locked up. The following case is one of many that illustrate the way in which the immigrant suffers in this connection. A Polish woman went to the station to ask an officer to protect her and her children against her drunken and brutal husband. She was much excited. The officer thought that "something was the matter with the woman" and locked her up. Fortunately, the Polish investigator for the Immigrants' Protective League discovered her, and she was sent with an officer to the rescue of the children.

[18] *Report of the Chicago Council Committee on Crime*, p 42
[19] *Ibid*, p. 31.

The Immigrant and the Community

The Central Howard Association of Chicago reports the case of a German sailor who missed his boat and was left stranded without money or clothes. A bystander advised him to apply to an officer who would give him a place to work at fifty cents a day until the boat came back. He applied to the officer, was locked up, and fined $15 and costs. When released, he expected to receive $15 and was amazed when he was handed five cents for carfare.

The Chicago police force is constantly charged with corruption and inefficiency. A few years ago we had a series of bomb explosions that did considerable damage to property. Thirty-six bombs were thrown; and the police did nothing except arrest "suspects," who were subsequently discharged. The police first explained that the bombs were the result of a "gamblers' war" and then attributed them to "labor troubles." But whether the police department did or did not know by whom the bombs were "planted," no satisfactory public explanation of the explosions was ever made.

There is the same scandalous situation with regard to the so-called "Black Hand" outrages. One of the Chicago papers reported forty-five murders in seven months which the police charged to the Black Hand. The police method of preventing crime of this sort is as unintelligent as it is unjust. On one occasion following several "outrages," the police arrested quite at random fifty Italians in one neighborhood. The men were all fined one dollar and costs for disorderly conduct, and the inspector thought that this would frighten the colony into behaving. Instead, the arrest and conviction of men

The Immigrant in the Courts

known to be innocent was teaching disregard rather than respect for the law.

Prominent Italians and the leading Italian newspapers have tried to interest themselves in this situation. Most of these believe that, although there is probably a Black-Hand organization, very little of the murder, bomb-throwing, blackmailing, and kidnapping charged to such a society are really committed by its members; and hold to the theory that a band of criminals are operating under police protection and that the police are covering up their failure to arrest the offenders to the satisfaction of the American public by attributing them to Italian Black-Hand organizations. These Italians refuse to believe that the police cannot discover the Italian perpetrators of the small per cent. of these crimes which they hold the Black Hand really commits. This seems a reasonable theory, because such woeful police incompetence, as the situation would otherwise argue, seems impossible.

The Italian consulate employed a man for a time to investigate every Black-Hand case reported in the newspapers. Out of the first thirty investigated, there was only one which could not be explained on some theory other than that it was committed by the Black Hand. The result of all this is that the Italian suffers at every turn. He is not protected against the criminal inside or outside of his own ranks; and the general public grows increasingly indignant, not at the police but at all the Italians.

The immigrant, because of his friendlessness and his ignorance of English, is an easy victim of any form of police corruption or violence. This should be a matter

The Immigrant and the Community

of serious concern to the American public, because the foreigner does not understand that the American usually reasons that allowances must be made for the American police; and a dangerous disrespect for American law is liable to result.

During the autumn of 1915, when a strike of many thousand clothing workers was in progress and many arrests were being made in consequence, an inspector of jails discovered a Russian in the Maxwell Street Police Station who seemed thoroughly respectable and in great distress. He had not been booked; and as he was unable to speak English, the Immigrants' Protective League was asked to send some one to see what could be done for him. Investigation showed that the man was a small shopkeeper who lived in a neighborhood where housing conditions are notoriously bad. A fellow-Russian, in attempting to pay a visit to a neighbor the evening before, had had a very bad fall through the broken floor of a rickety porch. As his injuries seemed serious, the police ambulance was called by a Russian-speaking clerk in a near-by drug store. The small shopkeeper accompanied the injured man to the hospital, was asked and gave his name and address, and returned home. A few hours later he was aroused from sleep and taken to the police station by two officers. He was kept for twenty hours in one of the underground cells which has an open sewer, without any explanation as to why he had been arrested. By that time the police had discovered that he was not, as they supposed, "a striker who had assaulted and seriously injured some man merely because he wanted to work." Investigation before arrest had seemed entirely

The Immigrant in the Courts

unnecessary to the police, and the officers seemed wholly unconcerned over what this man and his wife had suffered because of their own illegal acts.

One of the Hull-House residents tells of an officer who ordered a man to get off a garbage can on which he was sitting. He did not understand English and so did not obey. The officer shot and killed the man. Although this occurred some years ago, in a recent visit in the immediate neighborhood it was found that these people believed American law permitted that kind of arbitrary punishment on the part of the police, and had little feeling of respect for it in consequence. Murders not unlike this are committed by plain-clothes men every year. In the spring of 1916 two Chicago officers entered a house where some boys were playing dice, and with drawn revolvers demanded that the boys throw up their hands. There were four of the boys, and the oldest, an undersized Slovenian lad, was fifteen years old. At a distance of about one pace from this boy, one of the officers shot and killed him. This and similar public murders may go unnoticed by the general public as they go unprosecuted by our official prosecutors, but it is to be expected that the neighborhood will reach dangerous conclusions about American law

We have a saying that it is better to let one hundred guilty men escape than to punish one innocent man; but the police do not hold to that theory and sometimes, in effect, take into their own hands the making and executing of laws. The relationship between such criminal conduct on the part of the police and the general increase of crime should be carefully considered.

The Immigrant and the Community

The kind of prejudice against the stranger that means a denial of justice is less frequently met with in the courts in larger centers, where the population is cosmopolitan, than in small cities and towns. Even in the great centers, however, evidence is not lacking that judges and juries are sometimes easily convinced that a foreigner, especially one from eastern Europe, is probably guilty of any crime with which he is charged. The indiscriminate and unfounded generalization as to racial traits and differences, which are often so thoughtlessly made, contribute to such prejudice. Much more common is the belief that the foreigner feels disgrace less keenly than the American or that his social position is already so low that he does not suffer much from arrest or conviction Because of this belief, he is often committed on evidence on which an American would be dismissed.

For example, some years ago a German-Hungarian girl who was in the Bridewell was reported to the local inspector of the United States Immigration Service for deportation. Investigation showed that she had come to this country with her foster-parents. She secured housework through a newspaper advertisement with a family who overworked her and then dismissed her without paying her. In the meantime, her foster-father had died; and the mother returned to Europe, unable to communicate with the girl before going. The girl could speak no English, did not know how to find another job, and had great difficulty in finding the family with whom she and her parents had stayed when they first came to Chicago. After an exhausting search, the former landlady was discovered, but she refused to take the girl in

The Immigrant in the Courts

because she had no money; so she slept out of doors a night or two, looking for work in the daytime. For this she was reported to the police, was arrested, and sent to the Bridewell, as the judge and the police explained, because "she had no friends and needed cleaning up." Her release was secured as soon as these facts were learned by the Immigrants' Protective League. Housework was found for her and she proved faithful in her work. She has been in no trouble since that time, but she has always considered that the officer of the League who suddenly appeared to rescue her from her terrible fate deserved to be consulted before she made any important decision. And so, in subsequent years she came back to the League when she was sick and wanted to consult a doctor; when some money that she had sent to Hungary was not received; when she wanted to open a savings account at a bank; in 1915 to ask the League to find out the character of the man whom she wanted to marry and who was at that time conducting an employment agency in West Virginia; and then, after marriage, to hold her bank book, which showed a balance of $500, until she had learned by experience whether her husband was going to allow her some measure of economic independence.

Although the injustice of the court secured a friend for this friendless girl, it was only by chance that she did not serve out the sentence so unjustly given her. Even if she had not been deported, she would have been released, discouraged and embittered by the punishment the community had visited on her because she was for the moment homeless and poor. Complete ignorance on

The Immigrant and the Community

the part of the court of the social resources of the city and the belief that the girl would not mind going to a jail "because she had no friends and needed cleaning up" rather than actual unkindness, were the faults of the judge. The League has known other cases in which the court refused to apply the American standard of what is regarded as humiliating, in the case of a man or woman from eastern Europe.

The municipal or police courts are the courts which to the immigrant serve as object lessons in American justice or injustice. Police judges and justices of the peace have frequently been known grossly to abuse their power for their own financial or political objects, and the worst possible lesson has been learned by the immigrant in his first conscious contact with American law. While these practices are still common in smaller industrial communities, they are no longer possible in the reorganized municipal courts in our larger cities. But an intelligent and impartial judge alone is not sufficient to guarantee the non-English-speaking immigrant a fair trial.

Lack of proper interpreters often prevents the immigrant from securing justice. To know in advance the offense with which he is charged so that he may summon witnesses and employ counsel in his behalf, to be confronted with the witnesses against him, and to have an opportunity to relate his own story, are, in theory, the rights guaranteed every accused person; but because of his ignorance of English, they are often denied the immigrant. Cases in which the charge was not understood have come to the attention of the Immigrants' Protective League. For example, a policeman in the employ of a

The Immigrant in the Courts

railroad company arrested a Polish man who was trespassing on the elevated tracks. No interpreter could be found in the courtroom, but as there seemed to be no question that he had been trespassing he was sent to the House of Correction. Not only was he given no chance to tell the court his story, but the charge was not explained to him. It was assumed that he knew that he had committed a misdemeanor when he walked along the elevated track and would understand the reason for his arrest. But such an assumption is, in this and many other cases, unwarranted.

The significance of signing a jury waiver usually goes unexplained also. It is probable that even the English-speaking people who sign these waivers often do not understand just what they are doing. It is doubtful if the foreigner ever does. He is handed a paper that he signs as a matter of course, without having its contents translated. While a trial without jury may be equally fair, nevertheless a jury trial is a recognized safeguard of the accused; and the foreigner should have an explanation of this fact.

The Massachusetts Commission on Immigration [20] found that there were no official interpreters employed in any of the courts of Boston except the central municipal courts. Men who spoke Italian, Polish, Greek, and other foreign languages were found to make a practice of hanging about the courts in the hope of being called as interpreters, and the judges usually called the same ones day after day. Some of these interpreters were given a very simple test of their ability to

[20] *Report of the Massachusetts Commission on Immigration,* p 108.

The Immigrant and the Community

understand the language they were interpreting in the courts. Most of them revealed their incompetence at once. For example, one man who was regularly employed to interpret Polish and Lithuanian in the South Boston Court was asked to translate from a Polish newspaper a paragraph which translated reads as follows:

> Rochester, N. Y.—Frank Zgodzinoki, sixteen years of age, was arrested for stealing coal from the New York Central Railroad Yard. During the hearing of the case it was learned that the boy was sent by his mother to get coal. The boy was discharged, but the judge threatened to send his mother to jail if she taught the boy to steal.

After reading and rereading and having it read to him, the "interpreter" was able to make out the following:

> Rochester, N. Y.—There was arrested 16 March Francis Zgodzinoki for — something about the mother. I understand some the mother was arrested in some affairs. Central President, that is New York Central.

The man realized his inability to translate it and offered various excuses; he said, for example, that questions are asked in court in a "quite different way entirely"; that "when the man comes upon the stand to testify we know what he is going to say"; and that in important cases the judge allowed him to use a dictionary. Another interpreter who claimed to speak and to understand Polish, although he was not able to read it, was sure he could translate this same paragraph if it were read to him. This was done and he translated sentence by sentence as follows:

> It was arrested about sixteen years ago a man by the name of Francisco Zgodzinoki. The charge was larceny of the New York Central He was tried and acquitted. His mother sent a boy. He was asked the question whether he was going to teach the children to steal.[21]

[21] *Report of the Massachusetts Commission on Immigration*, p. 109.

The Immigrant in the Courts

In Chicago, except in the Juvenile Court, there are no interpreters whose competency, honesty, and impartiality have been officially tested. In canvassing the situation at one time the Immigrants' Protective League found that in five of the criminal branches of the Municipal Court, court officials (usually clerks) were used; in eight, policemen occasionally interpreted; in two, the police did all the interpreting; five courts depended largely upon people they "picked up in the courtroom"; one sometimes called in a neighbor of the accused; in one the prosecuting attorney translated; and in three we were told that sometimes interpreters were not obtainable, in which cases they "got along the best they could." In one branch of the Municipal Court the bailiff said that he very often thought that the judge's finding would be different if the defendant were able to state his side of the case; and that he sometimes felt convinced that innocent men were "sent up." In another court, the clerk said that it was only in the case of Italians that there was any difficulty in getting interpreters, and in these cases "we do the best we can without." When asked if that was not rather hard on the Italians, he answered casually, "Well, we don't have very many of those cases."

In the Court of Domestic Relations, where the foreign girl so often appears with her baby in her arms as the complainant against the man who has deceived her, there are no interpreters. During a morning in that court one not infrequently hears the clerk call out, "Is there any one here who speaks Lithuanian? or Italian? or Polish?" And a casual bystander, who is picked up in the crowd

The Immigrant and the Community

in this way, is accepted by the court as a competent interpreter

These interpreters are frequently runners for lawyers and make a practice of collecting fees that are shared by both. The Juvenile Protective Association of Chicago reports the case of a young unmarried Lithuanian girl who was having great difficulty in supporting herself and her illegitimate child. She got together seventy dollars that an interpreter who hangs about the court to which she was directed demanded of her. The interpreter secured a lawyer for her, and the father of the child was ordered by the court to pay the girl $250. The interpreter kept $50 of this, and the girl went back to Russia, where she would have to support herself, her baby, and her old mother.

Such methods of selecting interpreters result only in injustice. In the first place, there is no real test of competence. A Bohemian interprets for Poles, Slovaks, Croatians, Servians, and Russians. He may, of course, be able to do this. In most cases, however, although he can understand something of what is being said because of the similarity of the languages, he does not appreciate the finer distinctions that are so important in a trial. There is also no guarantee of honesty and impartiality. A police officer, and especially one that has had anything to do with a man's arrest, should never interpret for him. Neither should the prosecuting attorney nor a relative of the defendant or complainant be used as interpreters They may be honest, but they cannot be impartial. A change in the emphasis alone may make a great difference in the mind of the judge.

The Immigrant in the Courts

Sometimes an interpreter acquires a reputation for misinterpretation on behalf of the party by whom he is employed It was said, for example, to be impossible to convict an Italian who employed a certain shrewd midwife in Chicago as his interpreter. This was known throughout the Italian colony long before it was suspected by prosecuting attorneys. She is now generally known and is not allowed to interpret. A man may, however, be honest and intelligent and also a good linguist, and still be a poor court interpreter. Languages rarely fit into each other with nice precision, and legal language is especially difficult. A special faculty for interpretation is needed and also a highly developed social sense to perform this very important service

To correct these abuses, official interpreters, who are salaried officers of the court and who are appointed only after a thorough test of their competence by civil service examination, are needed. It is also important that these official interpreters should belong to a central bureau from which they could be summoned when needed

Whether a man who is charged with an offense is adjudged guilty depends all too often on the kind of lawyer he has to defend him. The immigrant has no lawyer upon whom he is in the habit of calling; so when he is in trouble, one is usually secured by the following methods, which indicate the type of lawyer likely to be found

1. Through a saloon-keeper or "immigrant" banker.[22] If an immigrant gets into trouble, he usually appeals to the saloon-keeper or banker, who are persons of prestige

[22] See Chapter IV, p. 91

and power in every foreign colony. A lawyer is then recommended. He is likely to be the lawyer who will pay the highest percentage of his prospective fee to the saloon-keeper or banker, and is rarely a man of any ability or standing Nevertheless, care is taken to secure a lawyer who does something in the last resort, lest people will not apply to the saloon-keeper or banker in the future.

2. Through the police. That the police sometimes recommend lawyers on a percentage agreement, there can be no doubt. In one case an investigator for the Immigrants' Protective League talked with an officer at one of the Municipal Courts about the case of an Italian who had had a man arrested for assault. The officer explained that as the Italian did not know how to present his case, the officer had asked for a continuance for him, and said he expected the man to "come across" with $5 or $10. The investigator said that he would look up a lawyer for the man. To this the officer replied that he was going to recommend some one but that he was willing to "go in" for the investigator's lawyer, if they both "got something."

3. Through personal solicitation by the attorney. This is the method usually employed with men who are held awaiting trial at the County Jail in Chicago. The names of all the prisoners brought in during the preceding twenty-four hours are posted in the jail every morning. About twenty-five lawyers of the lowest grade, both in honesty and ability, go over these lists every morning and solicit the patronage of the prisoners. The posting of these lists is a comparatively recent innovation. Before it was done, there were frequent complaints

The Immigrant in the Courts

that the guards sold the names to certain lawyers, who thus got a monopoly of the business. The "reform" has evidently given the same class of lawyers an equal chance at the prisoners, but has afforded the latter no additional protection. The most successful of the lawyers who hang about the courts offering their services to the immigrant who is arrested are able to communicate with him in his own language and are therefore able to deceive him.

4. The recommendation of fellow prisoners. Lawyers very often make an arrangement with the prisoners at the County Jail to recommend them to their fellow prisoners and also to "tip them off" as to which prisoners have money or relatives who will employ an attorney. The warden of the County Jail says that prisoners often make quite an income from the commissions they receive for this service.

The kinds of misrepresentation from which the immigrant suffers at the hands of the lawyer whom he usually secures in one of these ways might be summarized as follows:

1. The prisoner expects the lawyer that he has employed to secure bail for him. The most frequent way in which these lawyers deceive their clients is by promising to secure bondsmen or "put them on the street," as the saying goes at the County Jail The prisoner pays the lawyer whatever he has, in the hope of immediate release. When the prisoner complains to the jailer of the failure of the lawyer to fulfil his agreement, the only receipt he can show is for a retainer's fee; and the lawyer, of course, denies having promised to secure bail.

The Immigrant and the Community

2. After the acceptance of a fee, the lawyer fails to appear at the trial. In one quite typical case a lawyer received $90 from the sister of a German who was held in jail awaiting trial. The sister understood that the lawyer was to secure bail and to defend the man. He did neither, and the man was convicted. When the case was reported to the Bar Association, the lawyer went to the court and asked for a modification of the sentence. In another case a lawyer promised a man who was accused of theft and awaiting trial, to defend him for $25. Thinking he was signing an agreement to this effect, the prisoner signed an order authorizing the "lawyer" to receive the money the police had taken from him at the time of his arrest — $63. Having secured this, the lawyer did not appear again. The man was quite without friends, did not speak English, and did not know the name of the lawyer. He wrote to a visitor of the United Charities, with whom he had spoken quite by accident in the courtroom. She reported the case to the Immigrants' Protective League. The lawyer's name was not difficult to learn; and, as both the Immigrants' Protective League and the Legal Aid Society had other cases against him, it was possible to have him disbarred It is not necessary to point out that disbarment is a wholly inadequate remedy for evils of this sort.

3. Another practice of dishonest lawyers is to have the trial delayed by securing "continuances" in order to collect money from the relatives or friends of the prisoner. The following case illustrates the method employed. A Pole, who was arrested for forgery, was supplied by a saloon-keeper with an attorney. The man's

The Immigrant in the Courts

wife paid $25 as retainer's fee, and later $30, $10, and $2 in instalments. The case came up several times; and, as the lawyer failed to appear, the Legal Aid Society took up the matter, and told the attorney that unless he came to court on a certain day to defend the man they would get along without him. He finally did appear. The man was found not guilty. He had been in jail from December 24 to February 17. The lawyer afterwards tried to collect an additional fee of $33, as the fee agreed upon had been $100. His reason for delaying the trial was that he wanted to collect $30 in addition to the $100 fee agreed upon and thought the only way to do this was to keep the man in jail. Cases are often continued, so that men are kept in jail for eight or nine months, only because the attorney fears he may have difficulty in collecting his fee after the trial. During this time the families of the prisoners are making every effort to secure the money, and they suffer with him the disgrace of his imprisonment. For even if the accused should be declared innocent, the stigma of his long imprisonment is almost as great as if he had been found guilty.

4. Sometimes the lawyer appears, but makes little or no attempt at defense. The type of lawyer that seeks out the immigrant who is in trouble does not usually care anything for his professional reputation. He usually is not keen enough to make a good criminal lawyer; and so after he has collected all the money he can he does as little work as possible. A case in point is that of a young Italian who was arrested for murder. A lawyer visited him in jail, and said he would guarantee for a thousand dollars to "put him on the street." The

The Immigrant and the Community

man wrote home to Italy, and his mother sold her farm and sent him the money. When the case came up for trial, the man was given a life sentence. There may be some doubt as to the man's innocence, but there is no doubt whatever that his lawyer defended him in an utterly incompetent way. Both the judge and the state's attorney expressed disgust at the way the attorney had conducted the case. This same lawyer, when asked afterwards why he had not appealed the case, said he felt convinced of the man's guilt, and thought that if the case were tried again there was little doubt but that the man would get a death sentence. He later offered to appeal the case, however, for an additional $300. Shortly after this the uncle of the defendant came to this country with $500 to see if he could do anything further about the matter. He kept paying small sums, $10, $25, $50, to different lawyers to look into the case for him. Most of them, after investigation, offered to take it up for $300 or $400. He finally accepted the offer of one who promised to see it through the Supreme Court, if necessary, for $200. After getting the money, this lawyer allowed the time for appeal to elapse without doing anything. When he learned that an organization was interested in the case he returned all but $30. Other lawyers wrote to this Italian, one of whom said that he had heard of the case through the clerk of the court and had become interested in it. It is hard to say just how many had a share of his $500. At any rate, when it was gone, the man went back to Italy without having accomplished anything.

Efforts to drive these lawyers out of jails and courts,

The Immigrant in the Courts

particularly in foreign neighborhoods where no interpreters are employed, are sure to be unsuccessful. Until the community undertakes to see that the accused are not unjustly punished as well as that the guilty do not escape punishment, the trouble into which the poor and the inexperienced fall will continue to be the great opportunity for the "shyster" lawyer. All those who have seen the immigrant in court must be convinced that because of his peculiar helplessness a public defender is especially needed for the non-English-speaking immigrant who is accused of crime.

Professional bondsmen are denied access to the men awaiting trial, and they are therefore compelled to work through the relatives or the lawyers. Lawyers are eager to secure for themselves, all the money that the accused man has, and so usually refuse to share with a bondsman except when they have an "understanding" with him. The bondsmen find the relatives difficult to deal with, for they are likely to turn to the local saloon-keeper or "banker." Often these men themselves go bail, being very well paid for this as well as for all the other services they render the immigrant.

In one case in Chicago we found evidence that the bondsmen, lawyer, and policeman had for their mutual profit secured the arrest of a man. It needs a corrupt judge to make such a combination really effective, and the municipal judges have not been the type of men who would lend themselves to the petty exploitation that police judges sometimes practice.

It should be possible entirely to do away with the evils connected with this system of securing bondsmen, by

The Immigrant and the Community

arranging to have a reliable bonding company notified by the police. But in many cases the professional bondsmen have friends high in political favor with whom they have an informal business partnership, and so the system still flourishes.

Our system of sentencing a man who is unable to pay the fine imposed upon him by the court, which system " virtually sends men to jail because of their poverty, is not only unjust, but demoralizing to the individual and costly to the State." [23] The recently arrived immigrant who perhaps through ignorance violates a city ordinance is, because he is poor and without well-to-do friends, compelled to suffer a punishment that was not designed for his offense, and in consequence runs the risk of the kind of demoralization that too frequently comes from contact with jails and prisons. While the immigrant for reasons which are well known is often unable to pay a fine during at least the early part of his residence in the United States, he belongs more frequently than other offenders to those who in their first crimes or misdemeanors, have stumbled rather than fallen. They can, therefore, be reclaimed if the proper treatment is prescribed.

The system of paying fines in instalments under the supervision of a probation office would, it is believed, prevent the petty offender from becoming a confirmed criminal, and so actually reduce the number of serious crimes committed by the foreign born. With more speedy trials, dependence on the professional bondsmen would be reduced; and the man who wants to be decent

[23] *Report of the Chicago Council Committee on Crime*, p. 43.

The Immigrant in the Courts

would be less frequently compelled to place himself under obligation for his release to the worst element of a neighborhood.

We have seen that from the statistics available it is impossible to prove that any of the immigrant races are especially prone to commit crime, but that in any general program for crime prevention special consideration should be given to the prevention of crime in the various groups. The injustices which the immigrant sometimes suffers are most frequently due to their ignorance of English and lack of proper interpreters Because of this, too, they suffer more than does the American at the hands of "runners," professional bondsmen, and "shyster" lawyers, who are permitted to hang about the courts. The system of requiring men unable to pay fines to "work it out" and of holding in jail those unable to give bail, in effect, penalizes poverty. As the recent immigrant is usually poor, the accused immigrant appreciates to the full the law's delays as he waits in jail for his trial.

Correction of many of these abuses and injustices has been urged by those interested in the reform of our criminal procedure. The peculiar helplessness of the immigrant, as well as the especial importance of having his first conscious contact with our legal machinery impress him with its justice and efficiency, makes the adoption of these reforms peculiarly urgent.

CHAPTER VI

THE IMMIGRANT AND THE PUBLIC HEALTH

SOME years ago a young sanitary engineer read a paper at one of the National Conferences of Charities and Correction which was based on a study of typhoid fever he had made in Pittsburgh. He had found that epidemics of typhoid usually begin in the immigrant districts and spread from there to other parts of the city. His explanation of this was that the immigrant is accustomed to a purer water supply at home and therefore succumbs more quickly to the diseases of impure water than does the native American, who represents a sort of survival of the fittest in the struggle with the typhoid germ. His conclusion was that some entrance test should be worked out which would enable the United States, in the interest of the public health, to exclude all those who are likely to become victims of an impure water supply.

This is too frequently the attitude of mind that the American brings to any set of facts relating to the immigrant. He wants to know at once if new evidence has not been discovered to show that additional restrictions of immigration are needed. Obviously, if this young sanitary engineer's explanation of the causes of epidemics of fever in Pittsburgh were correct, the very large foreign population of Pittsburgh constituted an additional reason why the city should provide all its peo-

The Immigrant and the Public Health

ple with pure water. It may have been that, when the young man thought of the political reasons why pure water could not be secured, he was convinced that the only way to keep down the number of cases of typhoid fever was to restrict in some way the number of people coming to Pittsburgh, and he saw no way of doing this except through an amendment of the immigration laws.

As a matter of fact, Pittsburgh solved her typhoid problem by installing a filter system, which reduced the typhoid death-rate in a single year from 125 to 45 per hundred thousand; and the rate has since fallen much lower. It is scarcely necessary to point out the fact that the elimination of typhoid rather than the restriction of immigration was the more desirable solution.

There are, as this story indicates, two aspects of the public health problem that are to be considered in connection with immigration: first, the protection of the United States against the coming of those whose physical or mental condition would be a menace to the present or future health of the United States; second, the raising, or some would say the maintaining, of our present standard of health and sanitation among the foreign as well as the American born in the United States. The first duty clearly belongs to the Federal Government; the second would, in general, be the duty of the local community.

Under the present law, those immigrants who are " afflicted with tuberculosis or with a loathsome or dangerous contagious disease," the idiots, imbeciles, and feeble-minded persons, the epileptic and the insane, and those not otherwise excludable who are certified by the ex-

The Immigrant and the Community

amining surgeon as having such mental or physical defects as may affect their ability to earn a livelihood, are denied admission [1] at our ports of entry. The enforcement of the Immigration Law is in charge of the Bureau of Immigration under the Department of Labor, but the medical examinations on which these exclusions are based are made by the United States Public Health and Marine Hospital Service, which is a bureau under the Treasury Department.

It is, of course, impossible to give a complete medical examination to every immigrant who arrives. Such an interference with the traveling public is justified only when some epidemic renders the delay imperative. Trachoma, a contagious disease of the eyes, and such skin diseases as favus, are the contagious diseases with which the immigrant is most frequently afflicted; and every arrival is carefully examined for these afflictions. The eyelids of each one are turned back as he embarks by the steamship doctor and again at the port of arrival by the United States examining doctors, and the scalp and hands are examined for evidence of a skin disease If the doctor sees signs of the presence of any other disease, the immigrant is taken out of the line and "marked for special examination," and as much time as is necessary for proper diagnosis is then taken. While mistakes are sometimes made, the examining doctors become quite expert in detecting signs of disease.

The number of persons excluded because of physical or mental defect or contagious disease during the period from 1910 to 1915 are shown in the table on page 141.

[1] 34 Stat. L. pt. 1, p. 898, Sec. 2

The Immigrant and the Public Health

NUMBER OF PERSONS EXCLUDED BECAUSE OF PHYSICAL OR MENTAL DEFECT OR CONTAGIOUS DISEASE DURING THE PERIOD FROM 1910 TO 1915

Causes of Exclusion	1910	1911	1912	1913	1914	1915
Loathsome or dangerous contagious disease	3,123	2,831	1,733	2,562	3,253	1,701
Tuberculosis (non-contagious)	5	15	15	2	4	1
Mental or physical defect which may affect ability to earn livelihood	312	3,055	2,288	4,208	6,537	955
Idiots, imbeciles, and feebleminded	181	164	164	555	1,077	335
Insane and epileptics	198	144	133	198	197	128
Total number excluded for causes enumerated	3,819	6,209	4,333	7,525	11,068	3,120
Total number immigrants admitted	1,041,570	878,587	838,172	1,197,892	1,218,480	326,700

The Immigrant and the Community

The cost of the medical inspection service is heavy; and the numbers excluded are, as the table on page 141 shows, very small compared with the number admitted. For example, in 1913, taking the year before the war, 1,197,892 immigrants were admitted and in addition to the 7525 excluded because of physical and mental defects 12,413 were denied admission on other grounds. It cost $2,575,000 to maintain the immigration service for that year, and practically all that expenditure of two and one-half million dollars was made in order that less than 20,000 persons who were deemed undesirable could be separated from more than a million who were admitted to the United States. Those who realize what this money would have done if expended in behalf of the immigrants who are admitted think of the costliness of this exclusion with some impatience But we are reminded that these exclusions, although few as compared with the number admitted, are supposed to prevent diseased and defective persons from undertaking the journey. Moreover, the fines that the law [2] imposes on the steamship companies for bringing to the United States persons so afflicted, if the existence of the disease or defect could have been discovered by a competent medical examination at the time of embarkation, have compelled the steamship companies to provide medical inspection at the ports of embarkation. As a result, many who would be excluded by the United States if they came to our ports are refused sailings by the steamship companies.

Little more can be done by the United States to make the exclusion of the diseased and defective more certain

[2] 34 Stat. L. pt. 1, p. 898, Sec 9

The Immigrant and the Public Health

except to increase the number of examining surgeons. As medical science advances, diseases not now classified as contagious may be added to the list as they have been in the past. As better mental tests are worked out, more of the subnormal will be discovered. To return to Europe an immigrant who has broken his connections at home works a very serious hardship; and this should, therefore, be done only on unmistakable evidence.

As for the second problem — that of maintaining or raising the standards of health and sanitation among the foreign born — much that is curiously prejudiced has been written and said. The *Report of the Council of Hygiene and Public Health of the Citizens' Association of New York upon the Sanitary Condition of the City*, which was made in 1865, is most interesting in this connection. The city was divided into twenty-nine inspection districts for the purpose of a comprehensive health survey. Each district was assigned to a doctor who was to make such a "thorough and systematic sanitary inspection" as would form "the basis of sanitary reform."

One doctor who covered an East End district inhabited largely by German and Irish immigrants reported [3] "decaying vegetable and animal refuse" uncollected from the gutters of the streets, sewers often choked, houses "generally out of repair," outhouses located in the yards in close proximity to the houses and the water supply, *only* ten or twelve slaughter houses in the district but these "always to be found in filthy condition" He found 110 cases of "typhus and typhoid fevers" and 176

[3] *Report of the Council of Hygiene and Public Health of the Citizens' Association of New York* (1865), pp. 165-170.

The Immigrant and the Community

of diarrhea, principally among the children. The remedies which occurred to him seemed difficult to administer because the Germans and the Irish were, he reported, " so ignorant, so degraded, so careless of their own best interests, present or future " that to obtain their coöperation in "any scheme of hygienic amelioration which would involve a change of habit, abandonment of vice, sacrifice of comfort, or the increasing of expense" seemed almost impossible.

He considered the immigrants a " fruitful cause of the propagation of disease," but found himself unable to say " in what way or in what manner the wafting of the many diseases which always are their companions, can be better guarded against than at present," and he wondered if the usefulness of the immigrant counterbalances the evils that accompany him. His conclusion was that " medical missionaries may effect the sanitary conversion of these hardened sinners," and recommended " the distribution of tracts upon matters connected with the public health."

This doctor was connected with a dispensary in a district in which the poor German and Irish immigrants of that day lived. They were making their way in spite of the kind of municipal neglect which he described and for which as a citizen he felt no sense of responsibility, while he found time to congratulate himself and the city that he had come through this dangerous contact with the Germans and the Irish without infection or personal contamination

The remedies suggested by most of the doctors took somewhat better account of the social, economic, and

The Immigrant and the Public Health

political diseases in their districts than did this one. But they generally found that the " German old clothes man " and the " Irish rag picker " explained, in part at least, the insanitary conditions of their districts.

There is the same tendency to-day as in 1865 to regard racial differences as the explanation of the infant mortality rate in a poor Polish or Italian district. It is always much easier to blame the immigrant than to face the economic and political causes that are really responsible.

It is probably true that, even if the immigrant creates no new problems in public health, he complicates existing problems. It is only these " complications " that can be considered here. Much educational work is being done among Americans in order to make them appreciate the importance of the new public health creed, which has been formulated on the basis of recent advances in preventive medicine. It is, of course, very difficult to explain to people who speak little English the precautions that must be taken in order to prevent disease. The fact that they come in the main from rural districts and live in congested neighborhoods in our cities makes their need of health education the greater. Much has been done in recent years by some city health departments to meet this need. Putting leaflets, speeches, and moving picture legends into twelve or fifteen languages is not always enough for the spreading of this public health gospel. Public health nurses able to speak the language of the people are much more useful in helping them to solve the problem of healthful living under great disadvantages.

Sometimes the traditions and the prejudices of our im-

The Immigrant and the Community

migrant population must be consulted in determining an important health policy. An admirable illustration of this necessity may be found in the question of what should be our state and city policy with regard to the practice of midwifery.

The question of training and supervision of midwives has such an important bearing on our efforts to reduce infant mortality, unnecessary blindness, and the needless invalidity of mothers and babies, that a somewhat detailed discussion of the midwife and her practice seems profitable. It will, moreover, illustrate the immigrant aspects of public health problems.

It is estimated that 40 per cent. of all births in the United States are attended by midwives. In New York the estimate is 39.2 per cent., in St. Louis 75 per cent., in Wisconsin as a whole 50 per cent. While the figures of Chicago have not been officially published, from examination of the books of the county clerk it appears that during 1913, 19,713 births were registered by midwives, as compared with 19,729 registered by physicians. According to these figures, approximately 50 per cent. of all births registered were attended by midwives.

Discussion of what shall be done to protect the mothers and the babies from the untrained and therefore careless, dirty, and dangerous midwife, has divided the laymen and doctors into two opposing camps in recent years. But in the discussion, little consideration has been given to the attitude of mind of foreign women with regard to their treatment at the time of childbirth.

While midwives are commonly used by the poorer people of England and were relied upon by American

The Immigrant and the Public Health

women in the colonial period and in the early part of the nineteenth century, they are little used at the present time by women of native parentage. Those who are interested in securing the best obstetrical care only for American women of native stock can devote their attention to the elimination of the ignorant and poorly trained doctor. But more than this must be done if the immigrant woman is to be protected against the ignorant and untrained midwife, for it is not because she believes that the doctors are poorly trained that she insists on the midwife

The immigrant preference for the midwife is due in part to the very different position that she occupies in Europe. There, good schools of midwifery are numerous; and in most countries the midwives who are licensed are carefully supervised by the state. In the United States quite the reverse is true. A difference of this sort is always a difficult thing to make clear. The women are quite as likely to conclude that because we do not use midwives American women do not know how competent they are, as to follow our argument that because they are less competent American women prefer a doctor. But this difficulty is not so insurmountable as the prejudice against the assistance of a man during childbirth, a prejudice so deep that it is only when a physician is urged as a matter of life and death that his attendance will be tolerated by the patient or excused by her circle of friends. That this prejudice will undoubtedly disappear with longer residence in this country may be true; but other women are constantly arriving with the same prejudice, so that its consequence must be faced

The Immigrant and the Community

as, in a sense, a permanent obstacle to the use of the physician.

In order that the subject might be more clearly brought before the authorities and the thinking public in Chicago, the Immigrants' Protective League undertook in 1914 an investigation into the subject of the use and qualifications of midwives in that city.[4]

The names and addresses of the midwives and the number of births each had reported during three months of 1913 were copied from the records of the county clerk as a working list. One hundred and eighty-two schedules were then secured from a number of midwives whose names were on this list and from others who were found in the various foreign neighborhoods in the course of the investigation The schedule included information as to the general education and training of the midwife, the condition of her bag, her house, and person, and also as to the number, nature, and care of the cases diagnosed as abnormal in 1913, the number of examinations made during labor, the treatment of the third stage of labor, the number of lacerations and by whom repaired, the measures taken to prevent *ophthalmia neonatorum,* and a number of other questions that gave the investigator an opportunity to judge what in general are the Chicago midwife's standards of care and treatment and whether she is overstepping the bounds of her profession.

Because of the way in which records of licenses issued by the Illinois State Board of Health are kept, the number of midwives practising in Chicago could only be estimated. In the 1914 city directory 432 were

[4] The report of this investigation was published in the *American Journal of Sociology,* Vol XX, pp. 684-699.

The Immigrant and the Public Health

listed; 475 registered births during the three months that were covered in the examination of the books of the county clerk. That there are many, both licensed and unlicensed, who do not register births is unquestionable. A number of those from whom schedules were obtained said that they never registered births because it was not worth the trouble. While the licensed midwives are probably not any more remiss than doctors in this particular, those who are unlicensed either do not register the births or register them through some doctor with whom they have a friendly understanding It has been noted that 19,713 out of 39,442 births registered were registered by midwives. This probably means that more than half the births in the city are attended by midwives, which is an increase over the year 1908, when only 47 per cent. of the registered births were reported by midwives.[5]

It is not uncommon for a midwife to have a very extensive practice, though there is naturally much difference in this respect. Three of the Italian women said that during 1913 they attended 600 births. During the three months covered by the examination of the county clerk's records 71 midwives registered fewer than 50 births, 345 registered from 50 to 100, and 41 registered from 101 to 150.

The seriousness of the problem is measured, of course, by the extent of their practice in connection with their lack of training For in some countries, notably Denmark, where the midwives attend a very much larger per cent. of all births than they do in the United States, the

[5] *Journal of the American Medical Association*, Vol. L, No. 17, p. 1346.

infant mortality rate is lower and the relative amount of unnecessary invalidism among mothers less than with us.

Examining and licensing are regarded as the first steps in a proper control of midwifery. In Illinois, midwives are licensed by the state Board of Health under the provisions of the Medical Practice Act of 1899.[6] They are required to take a written examination in physiology, hygiene and antisepsis, anatomy, and care of the mother and child. Candidates for licenses are not required to have either a general education or any training for midwifery. For a medical practitioner the State fixes the standard of general education and medical training that are prerequisites for a medical degree and requires an examination in addition. There is a growing demand for the standardization of the nursing profession by means of registering those whose training meets certain requirements and allowing only those so registered to use the degree R. N. (Registered Nurse). But in the case of a midwife, merely passing a theoretical examination is all that is required. It is not surprising, therefore, to find that the only preparation which is considered necessary by women who expect to be midwives is to secure some one familiar with the type of questions usually asked to coach them for the examination. During the few weeks or months when answers are being hastily memorized, their only concern is whether they will be able to remember this undigested mass of information when they take the examination.

How many of those who are practising have undergone even this test cannot be ascertained. Seven from

[6] *Illinois Revised Statutes,* Chap. 91, sec. 6.

The Immigrant and the Public Health

whom schedules were obtained said they were practising without being licensed, ten others were unable to produce their licenses. They gave many kinds of excuses, and each promised to send the next day the number of her license, but none did so, and the investigator was convinced that none of them had passed the examination required by law. The records of the county clerk were searched for several of these, and they were not found on the books. One woman reported that she practised with the "permission" of the doctor with whom she was studying on condition that she took two other women from the "school" with her. Two others were "authorized" by a doctor to put out their signs on condition that they called the doctor to assist them. As there is no provision for the supervision or investigation of midwives by the state Board of Health, it is to be expected that even the present law, inadequate as it is, will not be enforced.

A knowledge of English is not necessary for those desiring to take the examination. Translators may be provided by the applicants, and in practice these are usually the doctors who have trained the candidates. The translators are seated at one end of the examination room, and the monitors employed by the state Board of Health take the translations of the questions to the applicant. The official translator employed by the State translates the answers into English, and the papers are then graded.

Out of the 182 midwives from whom schedules were secured in Chicago, 57 were graduates of European schools of midwifery. These may be assumed to be fairly well trained. The remaining 125 had had only the most ridiculously inadequate training. Most of them had had very little general education. Fifty said that they had never gone beyond the fourth grade, and ninety one others had not gone beyond the eighth. One was illiterate, several could read and write only with the greatest difficulty. Their professional training had been equally unsatisfactory

There are in Chicago no schools of midwifery worthy of the name. One doctor who "trained" fourteen of the midwives from whom schedules were received gives one or two hours' instruction five days a week, for six months. The only requirement for admission to this school is ability to read and write and the ability to pay the money for tuition — $100. The school is held in the physician's office, which was found to be dirty and confused. At the first interview with him, the doctor was found to have been drinking, so that he was not able to talk coherently. Another physician with whom twenty seven of those from whom schedules were obtained had prepared for the examination calls himself and his office a "College of Midwifery." Instruction, he reports, is by lecture, text-book, manikin, and skeleton. Students are not required to witness any definite number of deliveries, but are taken with him to witness them as often as possible. One Polish midwife, who reported that she attended 138 births in 1913, had never been to school at all before she began to study midwifery. She had learned to read a little at home, and during her nine months' preparation for the examination in midwifery she learned to write. She did not, during training, attend a single birth. How much of the theoretical work

The Immigrant and the Public Health

which she was given in lectures could be understood by a mind so untrained can be imagined. After five years of practice, she was unfamiliar with the names of the solutions she used, and said that she relied in case of emergency upon the drug stores for advice. She diagnosed as abnormal thirty-five cases in 1913. She said that she often treated such cases and made it a habit to repair lacerations unless they were quite serious.

Another midwife who finished the fourth grade at school attended thirty-five "lectures" in preparation for her examination. She had witnessed no births during training, and explained quite simply that when she was called to her first case she was very much frightened, but "God helped her and the birth was very easy." An illiterate Italian midwife, who was herself untidy in appearance and whose bag was very dirty, explained that she "used old methods but always had good luck." A Polish midwife who finished the third grade in school paid $150 for a nine months' lecture course with a local physician. She has herself had twelve children. Five of them died. She considered that this personal experience which she has had was of the greatest professional value. Her husband was found to be sick with tuberculosis, so that when visited she felt the need of extending greatly her practice.

Because the examination is entirely theoretical, graduates of reputable European schools of midwifery with years of experience often find it more difficult to pass than the ignorant woman who has never witnessed a delivery but has been carefully coached for the questions in advance of the examination. One woman with such train-

The Immigrant and the Community

ing and experience has taken six examinations and has spent over $300 for fees and for interpreters, and has not yet secured a license. She has applied again and again to social agencies, asking if there is not some good school that she can attend in order to learn "American" methods, which she feels sure are not properly taught by the doctors who are conducting schools of midwifery in her neighborhood. To her these doctors seem poorly trained themselves, careless in their habits, and often vulgar in speech

Some of the midwives who are intelligent and well trained are unfortunately not in the habit of taking the precautions that they know to be necessary for surgical cleanliness. That is probably in part due to the fact that they are no longer subject to the supervision to which they had been accustomed in Europe, and in even greater part to the fact that the standard of midwifery is so low in this country. Because of the professional prejudice against her, a midwife would not feel free to call a good doctor in case of a complication; and therefore the well-trained midwives are soon demoralized by the doctors with whom they come in contact as well as by the American trained midwives whom they know.

To many of the midwives surgical cleanliness is entirely unknown. This was indicated, among other things, by the condition of their bags. Twenty one of the bags inspected were found to be dirty, while fifty four could be called only fairly clean. Under such circumstances, the care of normal cases is dangerous, and the willingness to undertake abnormal ones is alarming Seventy one said quite frankly that they themselves

The Immigrant and the Public Health

treated cases which they diagnosed as abnormal, but that when these proved to be very serious they called in a doctor. Many of the women had pills and instruments in their bags, although the use of either constitutes a violation of the Medical Practice Act for which they may be fined. One who had instruments explained that she charged $15 extra whenever an operation of any sort was necessary. Some complained of prosecution for such practice, maintaining that they had been falsely accused.

In the course of the investigation, evidence of criminal practice was forced on the attention of the investigators, and many midwives reported their competitors as willing to perform abortions. No attempt was made to verify these stories or to secure any evidence as to the extent of this criminal practice among them for the reason that it is believed to have little or no relation to the problem of the education or training of the midwife. While perhaps more dangerous to the woman, it is no more criminal for the ignorant midwife to perform illegal operations than for the well-trained doctor. At any rate, this is not in any sense an immigrant problem.

The general standard of care given by the midwife may be indicated by the precautions taken to prevent blindness through *ophthalmia neonatorum*. The use of a solution of nitrate of silver is now regarded as a simple protection against this disease, and its use should never be omitted. Of the midwives interviewed, only ten said they used it in every case; eighteen others said if the baby's eyes were "inflamed," "red" or "sore" they used nitrate of silver; ninety eight said they always used boracic acid, while four others said they used boracic acid only in cases of inflamed eyes; fifteen used other solutions; and twenty five used water. One woman reported that her treatment for either " red spots on the face " or " red eyes " was to rub them with the mother's placenta for two or three days. Another said she used the mother's milk, which is in fact rather commonly regarded as a cure by ignorant people. Several of the midwives knew they should use nitrate of silver in every case, but said they were "afraid to"— meaning that they feared prosecution for the illegal use of drugs.

With more than 50 per cent. of the births of Chicago attended by these women who are for the most part quite untrained, infant mortality, preventable blindness, and cases of serious invalidism or of deaths of mothers are greatly increased. As has been said, there is a difference of opinion as to the steps necessary to lessen these evils. It is admitted by every one that the midwife with all her faults is not responsible for as many deaths as the ignorant doctor who refuses to recognize his limitations.[7] It is also generally agreed that the midwife, however well trained and supervised, can never furnish the best standard of obstetrical care. This can be given only by the doctor who has been well trained in obstetrics. There are, however, very few such doctors; and there is a general agreement that much greater emphasis must be given to the teaching of obstetrics in medical colleges. But there is much difference of opinion as to whether the training and supervision of midwives

[7] Dr J. Whitridge Williams, " Midwifery," *American Association for Study and Prevention of Infant Mortality, Transactions of the Second Annual Meeting,* p 192

The Immigrant and the Public Health

should be regarded as any part of a program for providing better care for all mothers.

The argument against the midwife is, briefly, that she is of course not a doctor, and that a well-trained doctor to attend every woman during childbirth is the ideal toward which we should direct our efforts. Any attempt to train midwives, say those holding this view, means that clinical opportunities which are needed for medical students will be given to these women.

Those who oppose the training and the supervision of midwives are generally persuaded that the midwife's patients are too poor to pay a doctor, and their remedy for the difficulty is the elimination of the midwife through the establishment and extension of medical charities — hospitals and dispensaries.[8]

It is at this point that the fundamental error is made. In most cases the immigrant woman, as has already been pointed out, employs a midwife, not only because she finds the midwife cheaper than a doctor, but because she prefers a midwife to a doctor who is a man. Social workers who have tried to persuade a woman of this type to accept dispensary care can give much testimony on this subject. The case of the Polish woman who was dependent upon charity because of the illness of her husband and who refused to have a doctor attend her, even when she was threatened with the withdrawal of all relief, is not unique. In her case the neighbors, although themselves poor, contributed toward the payment of a midwife in order that the woman should not be

[8] Dr. Charles Edward Ziegler, "The Elimination of the Midwife," *American Association for Study and Prevention of Infant Mortality, Transactions of the Third Annual Meeting*, pp. 231-32.

The Immigrant and the Community

made to suffer the "shame" which the society had suggested to her.

It is unnecessary to point out that little by little, especially when there are some women physicians on the staff, the dispensaries gain the confidence of the women in spite of this social taboo. Among the Russian Jews of Chicago, in whose neighborhood dispensary service was first organized in that city, much progress has been made. But although the work of lying-in dispensaries has been much extended in recent years and an increasingly effective and sympathetic force of visiting and infant-welfare nurses who coöperate with the dispensaries in the effort to supplant the midwife is now available, the percentage of births attended by midwives has increased in Chicago. All of this is, of course, an argument for more dispensary service; but to those who are considering the welfare of the women of to-day and of twenty or fifty years hence, it seems also an argument for making some effort to raise the present standard of midwifery.

The physicians and the laymen who believe that the midwives should be trained, licensed, and supervised do not believe obstetrics to be an unimportant branch of medicine. They do not hope to make a doctor out of a midwife. They do believe that it is immediately necessary to train the midwife so that she will be clean and careful in the care of normal cases, so that she will be able to bathe and care for the mother and baby, and, what is equally important, teach the mother the care of herself and her baby better than a doctor is able to do.[9]

[9] The Children's Bureau has published an interesting study of infant mortality, the results of a field study in Johnstown, Pennsylvania, in

The Immigrant and the Public Health

Illinois, it has been said, has taken the first step necessary for regulating the midwife. The law recognizes midwives and authorizes them to practise if they have passed the examination given by the state Board of Health. How inadequate this step is has already been shown. Very little more has been done in any other place in the United States.[10]

Since 1907 the department of health of the city of New York has had the power to adopt rules and regulations governing the practice of midwifery in that city.[11] Under this authority rules have been adopted requiring (1) that permits to practise midwifery must be renewed each year; (2) that the applicant for such a permit must be twenty-one years of age, must be able to read and write, must constantly show evidence of habits of cleanliness, and must present a diploma or certificate showing that she is a graduate of a school for midwives which is approved by the state Department of Health.[12] The last requirement was, however, waived in the case of all those who had been previously authorized to practise midwifery by the board.[13] The only approved school is the one conducted in connection with Bellevue Hospital, which is the only good school of midwifery in the United States.

which the discussion of attendance at birth confirms the conclusion based on the Chicago conditions. See U. S. Department of Labor, *Children's Bureau Publication No. 9* (Infant Mortality Series No 3).

[10] See Carolyn C Van Blarcom, *The Midwife in England*, pp 15–18.

[11] *Laws of 1907,* Chap. 432.

[12] Rule 3 adopted by the Board of Health of the Department of Health of the City of New York, October 14, 1913, to take effect January 1, 1914

[13] *Ibid.* Before the adoption of this rule, the applicant must have attended under the instruction of a licensed physician at least twenty cases of childbirth.

The Immigrant and the Community

The Department of Health in New York City has also adopted rules governing the practice of the midwife. These include an enumeration of the conditions under which a physician must be summoned, the equipment the midwife must carry with her, and the solutions she should use. The enforcement of these rules is under the direction of the director of child hygiene. In 1915 the inspections were made by five medical inspectors and nine nurses, and on the basis of their reports as to whether the rules of the department are being followed, the permits of the midwives are renewed or revoked. New York City has thus the beginning of a system that will, if developed, do much to improve the standard of midwifery.

New York State has in the past lagged far behind New York City, although the problem was relatively more important in the smaller localities because of the absence of medical charities. In November, 1914, however, the New York State Board of Health, in accordance with the authority to amend the sanitary code given it in 1912, adopted regulations which will raise the standard very much These regulations are practically the same as those in New York City except that applicants, although not graduates of a recognized school for midwives, may secure a license if they are able to present evidence of having "attended, under the instruction of a duly licensed and registered physician, not less than fifteen cases of labor and have had the care of at least fifteen mothers and newborn infants."[14] With this system of annual licensing, if intelligent and sympathetic

[14] *Sanitary Code,* New York, Chap. 4.

The Immigrant and the Public Health

supervision is provided, much will be accomplished in New York.

As representing the other point of view, Massachusetts deserves some special consideration. Quite by intention and not by neglect as in many States, the midwife in Massachusetts is omitted from the Medical Practice Act and so cannot legally practice. However, by one of those curious contradictions that legislatures sometimes enact, she is required to register the births she attends. The fact that she complies with the law in this particular has been occasionally used to convict her of illegal practice; but the midwife is, in general, tacitly allowed to practise in Massachusetts, and she is encouraged to register births in many cities.

Those who have been most interested in improving obstetrical practice in Massachusetts have steadily opposed all plans to license, train, or supervise midwives on the ground that all efforts in this direction are worse than futile. An investigation made in 1909 showed 104 midwives to be practising in that city and the most important mill towns of the State. This number seemed so small in view of the very large number of recent immigrants in Massachusetts, that it is always cited in support of the theory that the Massachusetts policy of prohibiting the midwife by law and ignoring her in the administration of the law has made the problem much less serious than in New York and other States where something more has been attempted. The *Report of the Massachusetts Commission on Immigration* (1914) showed, however, that the earlier report greatly underestimated the number practising in the cities and towns

The Immigrant and the Community

covered in the investigation, and says that "although contrary to law, an increasingly large number of immigrant women are attended during childbirth by midwives, many of whom are untrained and irresponsible" and urges "the medical profession and the State to face this problem at once and to decide on some method of protecting immigrant women from the absolutely untrained and irresponsible practitioners." [15]

European practice would have proved a valuable source of information as to what might be done in the way of standardizing midwifery, but the opponents of supervision have insisted that rules and regulations which could be enforced in Germany, Austria, Italy, or Denmark could never be successfully administered in the United States. This reasoning will not, however, allow us to disregard the successful beginning that has recently been made in England, where conditions were in many ways analogous to those in this country In England as in the United States, many midwives who were ignorant and untrained were already practising. Their practice there was more general among the poor than in this country. After an extended investigation of the whole subject and in the face of considerable opposition, an act was passed in England in 1902 to become completely operative only in 1910. After that time any woman desiring to be registered or licensed as a midwife was required by law to be a graduate of a training school, to pass a written and oral examination given by the Central Midwives' Board, and to conform to the rules and regulations regarding the practice of mid-

[15] See pp. 193-196

The Immigrant and the Public Health

wifery established by the Central Midwives' Board.

The actual supervision of the midwives is done by the inspectors who are employed by the local supervising authorities. The success of the supervision must of necessity vary under this system of local administration of the law. But Miss Carolyn Van Blarcom, at present Secretary of the Illinois Society for the Prevention of Blindness, reported, after a study of the system in the rural districts as well as the manufacturing towns, that the inspectors have apparently introduced a new kind of inspection. The midwife is visited at home, she is accompanied on calls, and her patients are occasionally visited by the inspector; but no attempt is made to frighten or intimidate her The object of this inspection is not so much to discover the woman who is untrained as to teach the old, *bona fide* midwife, who is usually untrained, and to counsel and advise those who have attended good schools but are still inexperienced practitioners. The English regulation of midwifery seems, therefore, to be an attempt not only to raise the standard for future licensing, but by patient visiting and advice to improve the methods of the old midwife, who because of her following could not be successfully abolished by law.

This seems to be a system applicable to the situation in the United States. The greatest obstacle to regulation is the fact that in this country the midwife is used principally by the immigrant women, while in England the fact that her patients were English may have influenced public opinion.

To bring about immediate improvement in the

The Immigrant and the Community

standard of care given immigrant mothers and their babies, the States should require by statute for all midwives: (1) training in a school of midwifery approved by the state Board of Health; (2) licensing after examination; (3) annual renewal of license without cost provided the midwife has observed the rules and regulations of the Board of Health; (4) supervision of the practice of the midwives by the state or city boards of health.

Until there are reputable schools of midwifery, however, the passage of laws making such requirements would be of little use. It is, therefore, important that efforts should be first directed toward the establishment of such schools. In the investigation made by the Immigrants' Protective League the midwives were asked whether they would take such a course were it offered. Some replied that they were too old, some that they were too busy, and a few thought that their training was entirely adequate. Seventy one said that they would be glad to attend school if it offered practical work. In Chicago, such a school would logically be connected with the Cook County Hospital, in which there is a great maternity ward. As medical students are not admitted to this ward, this would not mean the sacrifice of medical students to the training of midwives. It would mean an immediate improvement in the standard of care given many women and new-born children and the gradual elimination of the entirely untrained and therefore dangerous practitioner at present so disastrous to a large group of peculiarly helpless members of the community.

Although the raising of medical standards and the

The Immigrant and the Public Health

improvement of the public health may seem to be a scientific rather than a social problem, little progress can be made unless the scientist makes some study of the human reaction to the program he seeks to carry out. In a cosmopolitan population that reaction cannot be easily and simply determined, for not only social and economic but racial differences must be carefully considered.

CHAPTER VII

THE IMMIGRANT AND THE POVERTY PROBLEM

THE fear that immigration increases poverty and pauperism found more general expression seventy years ago than it has at the present time. The declaration that the United States is being used as "the dumping ground for the known criminals and paupers of Europe" was not only more frequently made from colonial times down to 1882, but the charge had in it more of truth then than since that time. In the period from 1830 to 1850, when the rack-rent system and the loss of the potato crop brought famine and death to Ireland, and in 1845, when floods ruined the crops in the valleys of the Danube, the Elbe, the Main, the Moselle and the Rhine, the Irish and the Germans [1] came to the United States in large numbers to escape the poverty at home.

The great majority of those who came paid their own way or were assisted by their relatives or friends, especially by those who were here in the United States. But some English, Irish,[2] German, and Swiss[3] were deported to the United States because they were receiving or must soon receive relief, and the local government wanted to be relieved of their support. In Ireland, landed proprie-

[1] J. B McMaster, *A History of the People of the United States*, Vol VII, p 221.
[2] S C Johnson, *A History of Emigration from the United Kingdom to North America*, Chap IV.
[3] H. P. Fairchild, *Immigration*, pp. 67-68.

The Immigrant and the Poverty Problem

tors sometimes paid for the transportation to America of their own dispossessed tenants and of others whose poverty would make them a charge upon the parish and so increase the rates for the landlord class. In Great Britain and Ireland emigration funds were collected by philanthropic societies, and trade unions tried the experiment of providing their unemployed members with money for emigration, in the hope that this would equalize employment and raise wages.

Under the Poor Law Amendment Act of 1834, the parishes of England were first given statutory power to deport their paupers — a practice which had been followed to some extent before this specific authority to use the poor law funds in this way had been given. Most of those who were sent by the English Poor Law guardians or immigration societies at that time, as at the present, were transported not to the United States but to Canada in response to Canada's desire for English immigrants. In 1847 the English Poor Law System was extended to Ireland, and here, too, poorhouses and deportation were looked to as the cures for the poverty that the landlord system had produced in Ireland [4] From May 1, 1850, to April 1, 1851, 1721 Irish were deported to America; but of these only 263 came to the United States.[5] Squatters on government land were sometimes given passage money to the United States by the English Commission on Public Lands because "it was too late in the season to send them to Canada and therefore they sent them to New York." In one

[4] S. C Johnson, *A History of Emigration from the United Kingdom to North America*, pp 80, 86, 91.
[5] Edward Everett Hale, *Letters on Irish Emigration* (1852), p. 9.

The Immigrant and the Community

instance, each of the deported "squatters" was given one pound by the Government when he landed in the United States.

In 1851, there was a total immigration to the United States of 379,466. Of this number, 221,253 came from Ireland.[6] The number of those who were sent by relief organizations — public and private — was therefore very small compared to the total number who came; but many of those whose friends in the United States sent them steamship tickets and those who were able themselves to get together enough money for the passage had been so starved in Ireland and were so ill provided for what was in those days a truly perilous journey across the Atlantic, that they had to be taken care of immediately upon their arrival in the United States.

In a series of letters written to the Boston *Daily Advertiser* in December of 1851 and January, 1852, Edward Everett Hale reviews these facts.[7] This was a time when support for the Native American party was growing in Boston and throughout New England, and when the religious and racial hostility which accompanied it demanded drastic action against the foreigner. It was also a time when the people of New England were united in the common purpose of preventing the return to slavery of any Negro fugitive who escaped from the South.

The recommendations of Dr. Hale with regard to the poor Irish were quite different in spirit from those made by the "Native American party." He was amazed that the English authorities, without the "slightest

[6] *Report of the United States Immigration Commission*, Vol, 3, p 24.
[7] Edward Everett Hale, *Letters on Irish Emigration* (1852).

The Immigrant and the Poverty Problem

shame" at the course they were following, should have resorted to the deportation of paupers as a means of meeting the Irish problem. But he was not the less eager to have the Government and the people of the United States realize the opportunity and the obligation that the coming of these poor Irish immigrants had created.

He reminded the people of Boston that the Irish were "fugitives from defeat, or without a metaphor, fugitives from slavery." "Every Irishman who leaves Ireland for America," he said, "seems to be as really driven thence by the intentional or unintentional arrangements of stronger nations, as if he had made a stand in a fight on the beach of Galway, and been driven by charged bayonets into the sea. We are," he said, "or ought to be, welcoming these last wrecks of so many centuries of retreat."

The same figure of speech that Dr. Hale used to describe the Irish was used by another writer to describe the departure for America of the German flood victims of the forties. The long lines of carts piled with the little furniture they were taking with them, it was said, might be mistaken for a "convoy of wounded, the relics of some battlefield, but for the rows of little white heads peeping from beneath the ragged hoods."[8] Dr. Hale reminded the people of Massachusetts that the method then used in dealing with the Irish was to "tax them first and neglect them afterwards . . . to send them back to Ireland at the public expense, poor creatures who are

[8] Littell's *Living Age*, No. 129, October, 1846, p. 201, quoted in McMaster, *A History of the People of the United States*, Vol. VII, p. 222.

The Immigrant and the Community

as entirely fugitives from a grinding slavery as if their flight had been north instead of west "[9] To-day, the country as a whole "suffers with one heart" over the Belgian, Polish, Jewish, Servian, and Irish victims of twentieth-century barbarism But were these same people, to whom our sympathy and generous gifts have gone, to reach us as refugees, we would deport many of them, even though all their surviving relatives were in the United States; and those whom we admitted we would as a Government "tax first and neglect them afterwards," as Dr. Hale said of the Irish in the nineteenth century.

Dr. Hale's plea in 1851 was that "the state should stop at once its efforts to sweep them back. It cannot do it. It ought not to do it. It should welcome them; register them; send them at once to the labor-needing regions, care for them if sick, and end, by a system, all that mass of unsystematic statute which handles them as outcasts and Pariahs. The Federal Government, having all the power, should use it; not growling in its manger, as it does, and only hindering those, upon whom, in its negligence, the duty falls." Dr. Hale's recommendation it is probably needless to say was not carried out.

Until 1882 there was no general federal regulation of immigration. The individual States, especially New York and Massachusetts, attempted to prevent the landing of dependents by requiring the shipmaster to give bonds covering a five-year period for those whom he brought to the United States and who were judged by the exam-

[9] *Letters on Irish Emigration*, p. 53.

The Immigrant and the Poverty Problem

ining officers likely to become public charges. These state laws, which attempted to meet the expense of the inspection necessary for the enforcement of the law by means of a head tax, were declared unconstitutional. For this reason, state attempts at regulation were abandoned; and this work was undertaken by the Federal Government

The first general regulation of immigration by the United States was made in 1882. The excluded classes under the law passed in that year were lunatics, idiots, and those who in the opinion of the inspectors were likely to become public charges. The Act of 1891 tried to prevent "assisted immigration" by providing that persons who were assisted or whose passage was paid by another, unless it was affirmatively shown that they met the requirements of the law in other respects, should be denied admission. This act took the enforcement of the law out of the hands of the state boards of immigration, which had been allowed to enforce the Act of 1882, and created a federal Bureau of Immigration under an officer called at that time Superintendent of Immigration and now known as the Commissioner-General of Immigration. The Act of 1903 added "beggars" to the list of persons excluded on the general ground of dependency; that of 1907 denied admission to those certified by the examining surgeon as having physical defects affecting their ability to earn a livelihood.

The numbers excluded for these and other causes since the adoption of the law of 1907 are shown in the following table: [10]

[10] See Table XVIIA, *Annual Report of Commissioner-General of Immigration*, 1915.

The Immigrant and the Community

Causes of Rejection	1908	1909	1910	1911	1912	1913	1914	1915
Unable to be self-supporting*	4,611	4,828	16,239	15,103	10,470	12,164	22,321	16,551
Afflicted with contagious diseases	2,847	2,308	3,033	2,735	1,674	2,457	3,143	1,613
Afflicted with tuberculosis	59	82	95	111	74	107	114	89
Idiots and imbeciles	65	60	56	38	54	72	82	33
Feeble-minded persons	121	121	125	126	110	483	995	302
Insane persons (including epileptics)	184	167	198	144	133	198	197	128
Criminals	136	273	580	644	592	808	755	276
Prostitutes and other immoral women	124	323	316	253	263	367	380	291
Procurers of prostitutes	43	181	179	141	192	253	254	192
Contract laborers	1,932	1,172	1,786	1,336	1,333	1,624	2,793	2,722
All others	780	896	1,663	1,718	1,162	1,405	2,007	1,914
Total number rejected	10,902	10,411	24,270	22,349	16,057	19,938	33,041	24,111
Total number admitted	782,870	751,786	1,041,570	878,587	838,172	1,197,892	1,218,480	326,700
Total immigrant arrivals	793,772	762,197	1,065,840	900,936	854,229	1,217,830	1,251,521	350,811
Per cent. rejected for all causes	1.4	1.4	2.3	2.5	1.9	1.6	2.6	6.9

*Included in this group are all immigrants certified by the examining surgeon as having "physical or mental defects affecting ability to earn a livelihood," as well as "paupers and beggars," and those certified as "likely to become a public charge."

The Immigrant and the Poverty Problem

It will be seen from this table that the most frequent cause for rejecting immigrants is the decision of the inspector or the Board of Special Inquiry that they will not be able to be self-supporting. In 1914 out of a total number of 33,041 excluded, 22,321 and in 1915 out of a total of 24,111 excluded, 16,551 were sent back for this reason. There has been a greatly increased interest in better care for the feeble-minded in recent years, as well as much discussion of the added burden of poverty and crime that results from their presence in a community. This is quite clearly registered in the increased numbers excluded for this reason.[11] For example, 121, or approximately 2 out of every 10,000 applicants for admission were excluded as feeble-minded in 1908 as compared with 995, or 8 out of every 10,000 applicants in 1914, and 302, or 9 out of every 10,000 applicants who were in 1915 excluded for this reason. Generally speaking, the exclusion laws are more rigidly enforced from year to year. The inspection has been especially rigid in the past year (1915), when 6.9 per cent. of all those who sought admission were excluded. Prior to that time the exclusions had been less than 3 per cent.

It is not difficult to agree with the fundamental principle on which these restrictions of immigration are based. People who are already dependent upon public or private charity or those who it may be reasonably assumed will shortly become so, should be cared for by the community in which they were born or in which they have, in the language of the so-called Law of Settlement, acquired a legal residence.

[11] The Law of 1917 (sec. 3) adds to the excluded classes "persons of psychopathic inferiority."

The Immigrant and the Community

This doctrine that each community should care for its own poor is not only considered "fair," as the saying goes, but it is recommended sometimes on the ground that by keeping the poor at home they must, by their very presence, remind the community that a thorough-going change in social and economic conditions is necessary if the causes which make for poverty in that community are to be eradicated. And charity organization societies would doubtless testify that in general it is easier to care satisfactorily for a person and to make him self-supporting in his native environment than in a new one.

But, however correct in theory, this legislation is extremely difficult to enforce with even a reasonable approximation to justice and efficiency. Injustices were discovered in connection with the attempts to make each county and State in this country and each parish in England support its own poor. Serious restrictions were sometimes placed on the movement of persons from place to place inside a country, because one community feared that it might have to bear the burden which "belonged" to another community.

Students of social history know how seriously the poor suffered from the narrow localism that found expression in the old settlement laws of England. During the latter part of the seventeenth and practically the whole of the eighteenth centuries free migration from parish to parish was not permitted. Until 1795 a laborer could not move from one village to another unless the parish authorities of the village that he wished to leave were willing to grant him a certificate guaranteeing support by the original parish in case he should ever become a public charge. The parish authorities of the

The Immigrant and the Poverty Problem

village that he wished to enter would not admit him without such a certificate, lest they might at some time be obliged to support an additional pauper, for every laborer was at that time under suspicion of becoming at some time a public charge. These "Laws of Settlement were in practice, as they were on paper, a violation of natural liberty"; and "probability of expulsion, 'exile by administrative order,' as it has been called, threw a shadow over the lives of the poor." [12]

The parish officers believed that by thus treating with suspicion and distrust every stranger in the community they would keep under control the disease of pauperism, and enormous sums of money were wasted in determin-

---

[12] J. L. and B. Hammond, *The Village Labourer*, pp. 115 and 120. It is interesting to note that Adam Smith, writing in 1776 of the oppressive character of the old settlement laws, found in them a serious obstruction to the free circulation of labor. When a laborer, he said, "carried his industry to a new parish, he was liable to be removed, how healthy and industrious soever, at the caprice of any church warden or overseer, unless he .. could give such security (that he would not become public charge) . . . a security — which scarce any man who lives by his labour can give. . . ." The result in England of this system, said Adam Smith, was that it was "often more difficult for a poor man to pass the artificial boundary of a parish, than an arm of the sea or a ridge of high mountains," and he finally said, "To remove a man who has committed no misdemeanor from the parish where he chooses to reside, is an evident violation of natural liberty and justice The common people of England, however, so jealous of their liberty, but like the common people of most other countries never rightly understanding wherein it consists, have now for more than a century together suffered themselves to be exposed to this oppression without a remedy. . . . There is scarce a poor man in England of forty years of age, I venture to say, who has not in some part of his life felt himself most cruelly oppressed by this ill-contrived law of settlements" (See *Wealth of Nations*, Bk. I, chap. 10, part II) During the nineteenth century the English poor law and the poor laws of our American States have made deportations illegal until a man has actually become a public charge. It is interesting, therefore, to note that the old and oppressive method of deporting men and women when it is suspected that they might become public charges has, in America, been transferred to the immigration law in quite recent years.

The Immigrant and the Community

ing the disputed questions of legal residence under the Settlement Act. But, unfortunately, the poor became poorer when this was the remedy upon which reliance was placed.

While, under our Federal Constitution, citizens of one State cannot be denied admission to another State, nevertheless, if citizens of one State after change of residence and before acquiring "settlement" become charges upon the public, they can be and are returned by the local poor masters or supervisors to the State and county where they have a legal residence. Until very recent years, this was done without any preliminary investigation and without regard to peculiar hardships which would and often did result from this insistence that legal residence should be the sole basis for determining what should be done for those who were sick or poor. Men and women were sometimes taken to the border of a State and left to make their way as best they could to the community which was obliged by law to care for them. County and state officials in this country, like the parish officials in England, "made a record" on the vigilance they showed in driving out of their jurisdiction these unfortunates. Little by little, this practice has been improved. Investigation, notice to the authorities in the former jurisdiction, and deportation only when the best interests of the person to be helped will thus be served, are now the rule not only with the best private relief agencies but with many public ones.[13]

[13] See E. T Devine, *Principles of Relief,* Appendix II, "Charitable Transportation"; and *Seventh Biennial Report of the National Conference of Jewish Charities* (1912), p. 236 on "Transportation Decisions."

The Immigrant and the Poverty Problem

In our relation to other countries, however, the Law of Settlement is still in the early eighteenth century. Internationally, we are enforcing it much as the parishes of England did in the seventeenth and eighteenth centuries. Under the United States Immigration Law, those who are judged likely to become public charges, or are found to be insane or feeble-minded, or are in some way not legally qualified to enter the United States, or those who within three years after their admission to the United States are found to have entered in violation of the law or to have "become a public charge because of a cause existing prior to their coming," are returned to Europe by the steamship line without expense to the United States Government or to the deported immigrants.

Attention has been called to the fact that the most frequent cause for which the immigrant is excluded at the ports is that it is believed he will become a public charge. Very often the only evidence that is before the inspector and the Board of Special Inquiry, which passes on the question of his admission or rejection, is the immigrant himself. He is often taken out of the long line because he is old or undersized or frail looking, and sent to a doctor for further examination. The doctor may recommend his exclusion because he is "afflicted with poor physical development" or "deformity of chest," because he is "undersized" or has a hernia or some "constitutional inferiority." Sometimes the inspector is of the opinion that the man or woman will not be able to get work and is therefore in the language of the law "likely to become a public charge." The ability of the

The Immigrant and the Community

immigrant's relatives or friends to assist him should, however, be a factor in such decisions, and it is therefore important that a statement of their resources should reach the port.

But the Pole or the Italian who has been here only a few years does not at all understand what he must do to prove his ability and willingness to help support the brother or sister who is detained. If he consults the notary public of the neighborhood, he is often charged a very high price and then poorly advised as to what he should or should not do. Over and over again, it happens that a girl is deported before word of her arrival has reached the relative who sent for her; and she is sent back to Russia, for example, with no word from them expressing their regret that they were denied the opportunity of doing for her the things they had affectionately anticipated doing.

The present law is so indefinite that it leaves the question of who may or may not be admitted almost completely to the discretion of the Secretary of Labor, who has the final decision in cases that are appealed. The official decisions have not been regarded as constituting precedents that must be followed in similar cases as they arise, and so the outcome is always uncertain. The result is that again and again one has to agree with the stricken relatives, who have received word of a deportation order, that no explanation of why the decision was made can be given. When asked regarding the admission of the brother or sister or mother for whom some eager immigrant youth in this country is hoarding his savings for a prepaid ticket, there is no

The Immigrant and the Poverty Problem

possible means of advising him how the decision will probably go.

This means cruel and needless self-denial on the part of those in the United States who send money or tickets to Europe, and failure and even disgrace for those who sell or mortgage their little holdings when they start to America and so have nothing to which they may return when excluded.

Since the outbreak of the present war, because of the danger of their being captured on the return voyage, the Government has not been deporting all those whom it has excluded. The difficulty of indefinite detention at the ports of all these was at once apparent; therefore those whose relatives or friends could furnish bonds guaranteeing their return without expense to the Government whenever in the opinion of the Department of Labor deportation should become safe, have been allowed to land temporarily. Unfortunately this ruling released the steamship company from meeting the expense of deportation as required by the Immigration Law. Moreover, the obligations of these bonds were frequently not understood by those who signed them. The friends of the immigrant are familiar with only one type of bond. This is one frequently required, which guarantees that the immigrant will not become a public charge. Relatives failed, therefore, to grasp the full significance of this temporary admission. It raised the false hope that if the brother or the sister "made good" he or she would be allowed to remain. For example, a Greek who arrived at Ellis Island in August, 1914, was certified as having "a physical defect" (in his case a very slight

The Immigrant and the Community

one) "affecting his ability to earn a livelihood," and was ordered excluded. Ocean travel was not then considered safe, and the man was allowed to land temporarily under bond. In November, when demand was made for his return, his relatives were amazed. He had been working for a fruit dealer ever since his arrival in Chicago and had been entirely self-supporting. The Chicago doctors pronounced his defect a very slight one that could be cured by an operation that the man was willing to undergo. An appeal was made to allow him to remain, but the Department considered the ruling of the examining doctor at the port to the effect that it was doubtful whether the man could support himself better evidence than the fact that he had actually been self-supporting since arrival, and insisted upon the fulfilment of the bond.

The deportation of those who are discovered within three years [14] after their admission to have entered the country unlawfully or to have become public charges on account of causes existing prior to their coming, presents difficult problems, also.

Having discovered that a man or woman has some mental, physical, or moral affliction and is for this reason in need of skilled social treatment, it is customary to ask about the length of his residence in the United States before rendering the service needed If he has not been here three years, he is reported for deportation quite regardless of whether by so doing the United States has violated the standards now established for intelligent social treatment.

[14] The Law of 1917 (sec. 3) extends this to five years

The Immigrant and the Poverty Problem

One of the first difficulties involved in the carrying out of this law is the separation of families which it often necessitates. For example, an immigrant German girl who did fine embroidery in the dressmaking section of one of the largest department stores in Chicago was sent to an Illinois hospital for the insane because of melancholia and in the course of time was reported to the immigration authorities for deportation. She and her mother had been the last members of the family to come to the United States; her brothers and sisters were citizens with many social and business connections in Chicago, and the girl had no near relatives in Europe. She had been in the United States less than three years, and she had had one such attack before coming. The doctors thought her recovery from this second attack was a matter of a few weeks but could not undertake to say that she would not be subject to another. She was, therefore, clearly deportable under the law. But if she was sent back alone, how could her recovery be expected? If her mother accompanied her, it meant in the event that the girl did not recover a hard and lonely old age for the mother. Fortunately in this case the girl's relatives were able to secure a bond guaranteeing that her hospital expenses would be paid by her relatives in the event that she suffered another attack, and she was allowed to remain.

A Polish widow who came to the United States in 1907 told the immigration inspector that she was coming to join her husband, because she had been warned that unless she made this false statement she and her two sons would not be permitted to land and would be compelled to return to the village in Galicia, where there

The Immigrant and the Community

were no schools for the children and no prospects for the future except the black poverty which was the common lot of the landless peasant. She had no one in Chicago except some acquaintances — *landsleute* — to help her solve the problem of supporting herself and her two sons. The first year after she came was one of serious and widespread unemployment; and she suffered as did many others. A kindly neighbor explained to her that poor widows could get food and coal from the county authorities in America and then went with her to the county agent. She was given a basket of groceries, but the investigation that followed showed that she had been in this country less than three years. By receiving this one dole of food, she has become technically a public charge; so she was arrested by the United States inspectors and ordered deported. This order was subsequently reversed and she was allowed to remain. Since that time, although in off-seasons she has found it very hard to keep the boys well clothed and well fed on the small wages she earns in a pickle factory, she has never again been an applicant for public relief, and the boys are now self-supporting.

Sometimes, because of the conditions at home, the return may mean a quite terrible experience for those deported. This is illustrated in the case of a Russian-Jewish woman and her two children who applied for admission to the United States during the summer of 1916, and the settlement of whose fate has been postponed until the end of the war. They had come from a town near the Russian border which had been taken by the Germans and retaken by the Russians several times. The

The Immigrant and the Poverty Problem

husband and father was a baker and had sold bread to the Germans when they first entered the town. For this he was shot by the Russians when the Germans were driven out. The widow decided to come to America, where she had two married children, a sister, a brother, and many cousins. She got to Ellis Island, but the medical examination showed that one daughter was feeble-minded. The child could not return alone. When the soldiers were in the town the mother had kept the child hidden for weeks at a time in constant fear that she would be discovered and mistreated. Her terror and despair when told the United States laws denied her a refuge for her children can be imagined. We do not, of course, want organized importation of the insane, the feeble-minded, or the subnormal to the United States. But we should admit the occasional ones who come and who for obvious reasons can be better cared for in the United States than at home. Their care would create no new problem in the community, nor are such instances sufficiently numerous to constitute a real burden.

Another hardship connected with the exclusion and deportation of immigrants is due to the fact that in legislating we have had in mind only what must be done to protect the United States against the undesirable immigrant. In consequence, proper care for those who are deported is not provided for by law. Nationally, we still follow the policy of irresponsible "dumping" of those whom we exclude. Having decided to refuse admission to an immigrant or to deport one who has been admitted, we do not take adequate measures to assure ourselves that these people whom we compel to return

The Immigrant and the Community

ever reach their own village or even their own country. An immigrant who came from Russia but sailed from Bremen or Hamburg or Rotterdam is returned to the port from which he set sail; and what becomes of him afterward we make no concern of ours. That we should feel responsible for the safe return home of the insane, the feeble-minded, and the poor whom we turn back would seem to be, while not a legal, certainly a moral obligation.

Some years ago, a Hungarian girl was taken to the County Hospital in Chicago. She was the cause of much trouble and concern because, although obviously very ill, she was refusing treatment. The doctors and the nurses were unable to speak her language and so unable to overcome what seemed a childish wilfulness on her part in refusing to permit examination and treatment. The Immigrants' Protective League was able to arrange for proper care and to arouse her interest in her own recovery. But she was equally difficult to deal with when she was well; for she was unable to keep any job, gave away her clothes, did not know or care what wages were paid her, and was generally quite irresponsible. She was eventually adjudged feeble-minded and deported. Through correspondence, the Immigrants' Protective League had learned from the Hungarian village authorities that she was an illegitimate child who had run away and that the girl's mother had had much difficulty in supporting herself and the girl. We saw the girl off on her long journey with many misgivings. She had sailed on a French steamer from Havre and was to be returned to that port. We had arranged for her to be met and cared for by a private agency in France, and

The Immigrant and the Poverty Problem

another organization in Hungary had notified the French society that it would meet and care for her on her arrival in Austria. But as she was sick when she landed in Havre, she was sent to a hospital; and when dismissed from the hospital several months later, she had to make her way alone and unaided to her home village, which she reached only after many mishaps.

Deportation is a popular remedy because it seems a short and easy way out of any difficulty that presents itself in connection with an alien. For example, a Russian-Jewish boy of eleven was reported to the Immigrants' Protective League as "subnormal and incorrigible," and it was believed by those making the report that he ought to be deported. His father had died in Russia, and the mother had started with her six children for the United States. Four of them were turned back at the port of embarkation by the steamship company because medical examination made by the company's physician showed they had trachoma — a contagious disease of the eyes — and would therefore be denied admission to the United States. Arrangements were made for the care and treatment of these children, while the mother, a daughter who was over fourteen years of age, and this small son continued their journey. On their arrival in Chicago, the mother and daughter took up the burden of supporting the three of them, sending some money back to Russia, and saving enough to bring over the rest of the children when their eyes should be finally pronounced cured.

This program admitted of very little care for the boy. He was soon assigned to the subnormal room at the

The Immigrant and the Community

public school and was making life a burden to his teacher and the principal. The first visit to the boy convinced the officer of the Immigrants' Protective League that he needed a physical examination. A visit to the doctor showed that the boy was very seriously in need of glasses, that he had adenoids which needed removing, that his teeth had been much neglected, and that his hearing was deficient. With the remedying of these defects and arrangement for more satisfactory home supervision and care, the boy has changed greatly. Instead of being subnormal, he is now considered one of those mentally restless children who must be constantly employed to keep him out of mischief. Deportation to Russia would not have helped him in any way. The intelligent application of existing resources for the help of such children is giving him the chance every child should have.

American cities are sometimes obliged to meet the problems that result from the fact that Canada is also guilty of the same kind of irresponsible "dumping" that the United States practises in the rejection of immigrants. For example, many who want to go to Eastern Canada from the Western part of the United States come to Chicago and from there take a train into Canada. The immigration regulations of Canada deny admission to any one " who has come to Canada otherwise than by continuous journey from the country of which he is a native or naturalized citizen " This rule, adopted to exclude the Hindu, excludes also the foreign-born men and women who have resided for a period of

The Immigrant and the Poverty Problem

years in the United States but have not become American citizens. As this and other provisions of the Canadian law are not well understood by residents of the United States, many who seek admission are turned back at the boundary. Deporting under the Canadian law does not mean returning the excluded person to the place from which he set out; he is refused admission to Canada, and the railroad which brings him to the Canadian border is required to take him back to the place from which it brought him. And so in a railroad center like Chicago, people who came from Washington, Texas, or Arkansas are carried back free of charge, only as far as Chicago. Their friends and connections may be a thousand miles away and their funds quite inadequate to support them even while they look for work in Chicago. Canada assumes no responsibility for them, just as we take the position that what becomes of the person we exclude is a matter of no concern to the deporting Government.

Some effort has recently been made by the United States Bureau of Immigration to arrange to connect the deported immigrants with private organizations in Europe, in the hope that these organizations will undertake to see that the insane man, the girl deported because of immorality, the woman who is feeble-minded, and those who are poor or sick, reach their relatives and friends and are connected with the European agencies which will see that they are given the special care and assistance their condition renders necessary In coöperation with official control much can be done by the

The Immigrant and the Community

private agencies, but no private agency can, and indeed should, undertake to do what can be effectively done only by official, international agreement.

To what extent these restrictions, by which the United States in recent years has denied admission to all those who because of mental or physical defect were deemed "likely to become public charges," have resulted in a reduction of poverty in the United States cannot be determined scientifically. Untrustworthy generalizations as to the extent of dependency among the foreign born, especially those from southern and eastern Europe, are frequently made

The United States Census enumeration of the insane and feeble-minded in institutions in 1910 showed that the ratio of the foreign-born whites in the insane hospitals of the country to every 100,000 of the total foreign-born white population was 405.3; while the ratio for the native-white population [15] was only 168.7. But these figures should be corrected on the basis of age, since there are relatively fewer children in the foreign-born population, and insanity is less frequent among the children than among the adults. The census points out that "for all ages combined, the ratio for the foreign-born is twice as large as it is for the native; but there is no such disproportion between the ratios in any one of the age groups." [16]

The census of the feeble-minded in institutions showed the ratio of the feeble-minded among the foreign-born whites to be 9 3 per cent. to every 100,000 of the foreign-born whites, while the ratio for the native-born

[15] *Insane and Feeble-Minded in Institutions, 1910,* p. 25
[16] *Ibid.,* p. 26.

The Immigrant and the Poverty Problem

whites was 26.5 to every 100,000 of population, so that the foreign-born are contributing only about one third as many of these mentally deficient to our institutions as are the native-born.[17]

The report of the United States Bureau of the Census on *Paupers in Almshouses, 1910,* furnishes information as to the relative extent of public institutional relief among the native-born and foreign-born and the relative amount of pauperism among the various races in this country.

It will be recognized at once that the number of paupers who are cared for in the almshouses of the country does not measure the extent of dependency. Many, both native- and foreign-born, who are not self-supporting remain in their homes and are cared for in whole or in part by public or private charity. Many others are in private institutions. Statistics showing the nationality of those cared for in all these ways are not available. Moreover, if we were able to classify by nationality those receiving all the kinds of relief given in a year, we still would not have measured the extent of the kind of poverty that is a serious matter from the standpoint of community welfare. For there are also families which live close to the margin of existence and in which as a result the children cannot be properly fed and clothed; cannot be given the education, the care when sick, the good times when well, which they ought to have if, when men and women, they are going to contribute in proportion to their ability, to our community life. None of these families so long as they do not

[17] *Insane and Feeble-Minded in Institutions, 1910,* p. 188.

The Immigrant and the Community

receive public or private charity are ever counted in any poverty statistics.

The figures as to the number of paupers in almshouses are, therefore, enlightening only in so far as they indicate whether poverty and pauperism is a matter of nationality or race, as some people have believed it to be. The enumeration made in 1910 showed that the ratio of paupers for every 100,000 persons of foreign birth in the country was 248 2, while for every 100,000 native-born whites of native parentage the ratio was 64.7, so that the foreign-born are contributing to almshouses about four times as many paupers as the native-born.[18]

In the three out of the four northern geographical divisions of the country, where most of the foreign-born whites and their children live, the ratio of almshouse pauperism is, however, higher for the natives of native parentage than for the natives of foreign or mixed parentage.[19]

During the period which has seen the great increase in immigration from southern and eastern Europe, there has been an increase in the total number of paupers, but the relative amount of pauperism has decreased. Thus the ratio per 100,000 population was 132 in 1880, 116 6 in 1890, 100 in 1904, and 91 5 in 1910. The decrease among the native-born whites has been greater than among the foreign-born, but the latter has decreased from 348 8 per 100,000 foreign-born persons in 1880 to 248.2 in 1910.

The following table shows by country of birth the number of foreign born in the almshouses and the

[18] *Paupers in Almshouses, 1910*, p. 25.
[19] *Ibid.* p. 29.

The Immigrant and the Poverty Problem

hospitals for the insane per 100,000 of the representatives of each country in the population as a whole.[20]

Country of Birth	Paupers per 100,000 Population	Insane per 100,000 Population
Ireland	1,048.5	974.3
Switzerland	410.9	602.4
France	390.7	523.7
Scotland	313.0	325.2
England and Wales	304.7	386.5
Germany	300.3	551.2
Canada, English	160.3	342.3
Scandinavian countries	151.2	515.1
Canada, French	137.1	252.1
Austria-Hungary	75.4	235.6
Russia	43.7	231.2
Italy	31.8	136.2
All others	64.4	160.7

This table shows that among the immigrants the Irish have a much higher ratio of almshouse pauperism (1,048.5 paupers to every 100,000 Irish born in the population) than those of any other nationality, while the recent immigrants have by far the lowest ratio of almshouse pauperism — a ratio of 75.4 for Austria-Hungary, 43.7 for Russia, and 31.8 for Italy.

These figures as to the relative amount of pauperism among the native and the foreign-born need to be considered in connection with a number of other facts that enter into the problem. In the first place, the greater number of paupers among the foreign-born as compared to the native-born is, as the census report points out,

[20] *Paupers in Almshouses, 1910*, p. 28, and *Insane and Feeble-Minded in Institutions, 1910*, p. 31.

The Immigrant and the Community

"due in part to the age distribution of the foreign-born, among whom there are fewer children than among the natives." Generally speaking, dependent children are not found in almshouses, and such dependents would not be included therefore in this enumeration. In the next place, the proportion of men among the foreign-born is greater than among the native-born; and almshouse pauperism is more common among men than among women, who are more frequently cared for by private charity.

The proportion of foreign-born white men under forty-five years of age who are paupers is about the same as for the native-white men of the same age. "But in the age groups over forty-five, and especially in those over sixty, the ratios for the foreign-born are far in excess of those for the natives."[21] This means that the foreign-born man has less frequently been able to lay by enough to support himself in his old age and that he has fewer friends or relatives in this country or that such as he has are either unable or unwilling to care for him and so he is sent to the "poorhouse" to wait for death. The large number of old people who are found in almshouses would, in a measure, account for the greater ratio of those belonging to the old immigration who are compelled to go there, since the percentage of old persons among the Italians and Russians, for example, is relatively very much smaller than among the Irish and Germans.

But back of age and sex and nationality are the causes that make men and women the pitiful charges upon

[21] *Paupers in Almshouses, 1910*, p. 25.

The Immigrant and the Poverty Problem

public charity, which the census reports calls by the ugly name of "almshouse paupers." Certain causes of pauperism, such as industrial accidents and industrial disease, are much more common among the immigrant than among the native American group, and there is also the fact that, generally speaking, the immigrant, because of his ignorance of the language, his lack of training, and the prejudice against him, is at the bottom of the scale industrially. For these reasons his wages are more frequently inadequate, and he is, therefore, unable to provide for sickness and old age. As a larger per cent. of the newly arrived immigrants live on the margin, so a larger per cent. are pushed over for one reason or another into that unhappy group of public dependents which we are considering.

This evidence can, it would seem, be accepted as showing that such dependency as exists among the foreign-born is not due to race or nationality. What relation the increase in the population through immigration bears to the causes of poverty and to dependency is discussed elsewhere. It is to these causes, and not to the birthplace of the victims, that the public must give its attention before real improvement can be expected.

Pending the long, slow, uphill work that is involved in our progress toward social and industrial democracy, there is the question of the care and treatment of those who are now, because of one reason and another, charges upon either public or private charity. Attention has been called to the fact that in excluding immigrants and deporting them from the United States we do not follow the recognized standards of humane and intelligent social

The Immigrant and the Community

treatment. But there are many dependent foreign-born who are not deportable, because they have been here longer than the three-year period [22] during which the Immigration Law authorizes deportation or because their dependency is in no way traceable to a cause existing prior to their coming, and who must be temporarily or permanently supported in this country. The charity organization worker asks in what ways the "treatment given the dependent family" should be modified when those families are recently arrived immigrants. Is the problem of "family rehabilitation" different when the father and mother have come from Russia, let us say, or Italy, or Hungary?

In the first attempt which is made to gather the facts from which some working plan for the family may be made, the charity worker discovers that she cannot proceed as she does when the family is native-born or has resided for many years in the United States. There is, first of all, the language barrier, which so frequently exists because the parents cannot speak English; their racial characteristics and the social traditions that govern the family and community relationships must be understood before any suggestions may be made that will help in the family's adjustment to the new American environment. (The relatives and friends to whom inquiries and appeals for help should first go are in Europe.) The immigrant understands us no better than we understand him. His immediate misfortune which has rendered assistance necessary only adds suffering to the confusion of standards emigration often produces.

[22] Under Law of 1917 (sec. 19) this has been made a five-year period.

The Immigrant and the Poverty Problem

If, as too often is the case, reliance is placed on a child, a neighbor, or an interpreter who is without education or training for social work, how can we hope to help the family through the difficulty that has sent them to some social agency for advice or assistance? Is it to be expected that the American who is sent by a public or private relief society to help this family will be able to secure the coöperation of the family in such plans as she works out on the basis of the inadequate information which she gathers in this way?

We shall never be able to give to the non-English speaking, the same standards of care or help that we give to those who know the language, until we have trained social workers who belong to the immigrant nationalities. American social workers must also be familiar with the history and social life of the Pole, the Slovak, the Italian, the Greek, and other nationalities, and must appreciate the fact that, while nationalities are much more alike than they are unlike, those differences that we might call superficial become of the greatest importance in dealing with men and women who are sick and discouraged, whose children are becoming delinquent, and who are finding the greatest difficulty in understanding American life.

CHAPTER VIII

THE IMMIGRANT AND INDUSTRIAL DEMOCRACY

THE possibility of taking advantage of the immigrant because he is ignorant of our language and unfamiliar with the agencies, both public and private, to which he might appeal for help is the opportunity which the unscrupulous agent, the irresponsible private banker, the land shark, or the shyster lawyer does not neglect. So, too, his employer is often able to take advantage of the immigrant solely because his ignorance of the language makes him unaware of the terms to which he is agreeing. For example, in the late spring of 1914, eight Bohemians came to the office of the Immigrants' Protective League. They were cold, hungry, and exhausted from a long walk back to Chicago. They had been sent out in February by a Chicago employment agency to work in excavating for railroad construction in a part of Wisconsin which the engineer described as "an uninhabited country with no roads to speak of except such trails as the contractors made to haul in their supplies" Five days after they began work, as a condition of their being supplied with the overshoes which they so greatly needed, the men were required to sign a contract which made them not employees but subcontractors. According to the agreement which they were thus forced to sign and the terms of which no one of them understood, they were not to be paid until the work of all of them had

The Immigrant and Industrial Democracy

been approved by the engineers of the railroad. The contract also specified that the laborers were to pay rent for the cars, the trucks, and tools supplied them and that they were to bear the cost of constructing the camp and opening the roads which had been built in part before they arrived.

One of the men who acted as "straw boss" and who spoke some English had had several years' experience in railroad construction work. He was, however, unable to read and write English and would have been absolutely unable to comprehend the language of the formal contract even if it had been read to him. Three of the other men spoke a little English but could not read and write it. The others had been in the country only a very short time and could speak no English at all. Several of the men had a good common school education and were of more than average intelligence. The rates of payment for earth, loose rock, or solid rock excavations which the contract specified and which the men regarded as a "piecework" basis of payment, had been made clear to them. At the end of eleven weeks they were dismissed, according to the men's story; according to the contractor's, they left their work voluntarily.

When they asked the company for their wages at the end of that time, the eight men who had worked for eleven weeks were told that no wages were coming to them, but that, on the contrary, they were in debt to the company $110.06. For this eleven weeks of work they had received, according to the contractor's statement, $11.69 worth of clothes and their board. The "board" was of very poor quality; for example, only $3 worth of

The Immigrant and the Community

meat of any sort was furnished the eight men during the month of April. How much in debt they would have been had they remained until they finished the job, the engineer did not estimate for them. The assistant engineer suggested that the men undoubtedly thought they would make at least day wages on this subcontract and that this was the reason for their dissatisfaction with the company. These facts were submitted to the Wisconsin Industrial Commission, but the Commission was unable to do anything for the men, and the suggestion was made that they give their case to a lawyer in a town near the camp. The lawyer, however, felt that it was useless to bring suit because, he said, "there had been a number of suits growing out of the contract in question and the workingmen had fared ill in every case." No lawyer could be found in the town who was willing to take the men's case.

Suit was therefore instituted in Chicago. This remedy involved the delays and the expensive appeals by which a company can usually, if it so desires, wear out the men. While in this case the men were able because of the interest of the Immigrants' Protective League to see the suit through and to collect their wages, their utter helplessness without such assistance was clearly apparent. They were convinced that this construction company deliberately took advantage of them. Such an experience could not fail to make them bitterly distrustful in their future relations with their employers. Moreover, the knowledge they gained of the expense and delay which is involved in an appeal to the law could not make them feel that a reasonably satisfactory way of de-

The Immigrant and Industrial Democracy

termining the merits of such a dispute has, as yet, been worked out by society.

While instances of this sort are all too frequent, they cannot be said to be general or widespread. A degree of isolation, resulting from the place of work or the fact that the men affected have no compatriots in the community, is necessary for the success of this kind of gross exploitation

Discussion of such injustice as this and the means of prevention would, therefore, come more appropriately under the general subject of the exploitation of the immigrant rather than the economic effects of immigration In connection with the latter, the questions usually raised are: (1) whether or not the immigrant supplants the native-born workingmen to the disadvantage of the latter; (2) whether the immigrant is responsible for the evils of our present industrial system: the overemployment of those who work excessively long hours, the underemployment of those who are unwillingly idle many weeks or months during a year, the low wages, the insanitary workshops, and the lack of adequate protection for life and limb; (3) whether the immigrant has delayed the organization of the workingmen and women into trade or industrial unions; or (4), to put it in a much broader way, whether the immigrant has prevented or greatly delayed the coming of industrial democracy in the United States.

The importance of the immigrant in industry is indicated by the following table, which gives the total number of persons and the number and per cent. of the foreign-born white persons who were engaged in manufac-

The Immigrant and the Community

turing and mechanical industries each decade from 1870 to 1910.[1]

Census Year	Total Number of Persons Employed	Number of Foreign-born White Persons	Per cent. of Total Persons Employed who are Foreign-born
1870	2,541,149	827,101 *	32.5
1880	3,587,715	1,092,609 *	30.5
1890	5,091,293	1,597,118	31.4
1900	7,112,304	2,175,686	30.6
1910	10,875,223	3,394,891	31.2

* The census figures for 1870 and 1880 include colored as well as white persons. The number of foreign-born colored, however, is so small that they could not affect the conclusions.

These United States census occupation statistics show that while the number of the foreign-born wage-earners employed in manufacturing and mechanical pursuits has increased more than fourfold since 1870, the total number of those employed in these industries has increased at a slightly higher rate. The increase in the number of foreign-born employed in industry has, therefore, barely kept pace with the expansion of industry, but has not grown relatively in importance in spite of the greatly increased immigration from southern and eastern Europe. Professor Page in his study of " Some Economic Aspects of Immigration before 1870 " found that there was up to that time no serious competition between the immigrants and the native Americans. " The native held possession

[1] Ninth Census of United States (1870), Vol. I, pp. 708–714; Compendium of Tenth Census of United States (1880), Part 2, pp. 1372–1377; Eleventh Census of United States (1890), Part 17, Occupations, p. 20; Twelfth Census of United States (1900), Special Reports Occupations, Table 2; Thirteenth Census of United States (1910), Vol. IV, Table VI.

The Immigrant and Industrial Democracy

of the field . . .; they owned and controlled the resources of the country, and they created and administered the plans for further development; they were economically as well as politically the ruling class, and while free to choose their own vocation and location, they were in a position to assign the immigrants to such work as they themselves were unwilling or unable to do. In the main, they set the immigrants to the performance of the heavier, coarser work; and to the extent that this new force sufficed to do such work, they were able themselves to withdraw from it and use their energies in higher and more remunerative fields." [2]

That the native-born have continued to do this down to the present time is indicated by the industries in which the native-born now predominate. For example, in the building trades the last census showed 2,257,506 native-born wage-earners, while the number of the foreign-born was only 850,875; in the automobile factories, an industry which has seen its origin since the period of the so-called new immigration, the native-born workers number 76,313 and the foreign-born 28,864; while in the "ready-made clothing" industry, which has grown into one of importance in recent years, the number of the native-born is 182,917, of the foreign-born 335,309; in the blast furnaces and rolling mills there were 180,089 native-born to 202,512 foreign-born; in the construction and maintenance of streets, roads, sewers, and bridges the native-born employees numbered 91,176 and the foreign-born 109,183 Likewise, although the employees of the steam railroads number 1,010,493 native-born to 400,992 of

[2] *Journal of Political Economy*, Vol. 21, p 53.

The Immigrant and the Community

foreign birth, the laborers employed on the railroads were 146,435 native-born to 228,849 foreign-born. In other words, the "displacement," in so far as it has occurred, has been in the unskilled and less desirable work. The census statistics of occupations, therefore, seem to indicate that the conclusions of Professor Page with regard to the utilization of immigrant labor still hold true, and immigrants are still being set to perform "the heavier, coarser work," leaving the native-born free to "use their energies in higher and more remunerative fields"

Many people are, however, of the opinion that if the native-born had remained in a majority in those industries in which the foreign-born workers now predominate, the low standard of wages and working conditions which are so frequently met with would have been supplemented instead by what they call an "American standard of wages and working conditions." But native ancestry is not a safeguard against exploitation, nor a guarantee of successful organization against all efforts toward that end.

During the summer of 1916, the attention of the people of Illinois was called to the unsatisfactory conditions which are sometimes found in localities where the immigrant has never penetrated. A strike of the fluorspar and lead miners of Rosiclare — a small mining town in southern Illinois — occurred at that time. An inspector from the state factory inspector's office was sent there to look into alleged violations of the state factory act. He submitted a report which gave in addition to a statement of the number and kinds of violations which he discovered, some facts about the town and its people He re-

The Immigrant and Industrial Democracy

ported that the company-owned houses, from which the strikers were then being ejected, were built on posts or piles of rocks about four feet from the ground. "Rough boards with battens over the cracks to keep out the rain" were used in building the two- and three-room houses. The furnishings of these "homes" were equally poor — "no carpets, no pictures, nothing but beds, a few chairs, a table, and a stove." The inspector reported he found poor cistern water, outhouses near the houses, and no screens during the summer. Altogether the picture that he gave was one not only of poverty but of squalor as well.[3] The representative of the Illinois Federation of Labor reported that women as well as children went barefooted because they had no money for shoes; that village officers who did not comply with the demands of the company were driven from the town; and that the rights of the people were generally defied by the "gunmen" who were brought in as strike-breakers.[4] These miners who were living in this way were not recent immigrants from southern or eastern Europe, but Americans of British stock whose fathers and grandfathers were born in this country. They had come to Illinois from Kentucky and Indiana and had not been "driven out" of Pennsylvania when the so-called Slav invasion of that State began. Although most of the immigrant miners of Illinois had been unionized for many years, these Americans were taking the first difficult steps toward that end,

[3] Report of C. M. Brown, Deputy Inspector to Oscar P. Nelson, Chief of the Department of Factory Inspection. Published in the *Illinois State Federation of Labor Weekly News Letter*, Vol. II, No 16, p 1.
[4] Victor A. Olander, "Labor Day, 1916," *Life and Labor*, Vol. VI, No. 9, p. 131.

The Immigrant and the Community

and the unions composed largely of the foreign-born from southern and eastern Europe were taxing themselves to help the Americans of Rosiclare to secure not only a higher wage but their legal rights.

Responsibility for the accidents which occur in mines and foundries is often laid to the ignorance of the immigrant employees rather than to the neglect on the part of the State to require adequate safeguards. Moreover, when there is undisputed evidence of public neglect, the immigrant is often held responsible for that neglect. This conclusion is reached on the theory that Americans, while indifferent to what the Pole or Italian suffers, would not permit the native-born American to suffer in the same way. They hold that the same number of accidents occurring to American workmen " would incite a storm of indignant protest which would not be stilled until remedies were provided, if those who are subjected to such conditions were our own kin brothers." [5] Undoubtedly, because the language barrier isolates the immigrant, we are unacquainted with the injuries and losses which come to the foreign-born and so less roused to action by them. But that Americans could be relied upon to come to the support of workmen who are their " kin brothers " has not yet been proven.

The state regulations designed to protect the health and safety of the miners in Illinois applied for the most part only to coal mines; so these American lead-miners in Rosiclare had not secured the benefits of regular inspection When the story of these men was told, although attention was called to their American ancestry, it did

[5] H P Fairchild, *Immigration*, pp. 346-347.

The Immigrant and Industrial Democracy

not "incite a storm of indignant protest" in Illinois. The people who listened and sympathized and wanted to help were the ones who want better working conditions for all workingmen and women. The Rosiclare miners told the same sordid story of patient suffering that the immigrant often tells. But in the course of the strike the old difficult questions of the superiority of property rights over human rights were raised, and men divided on those issues rather than on the nationality of the people concerned.

In the strikes of the immigrant miners of West Virginia, of Colorado, of Michigan, and of Minnesota, the American public learned of what were called un-American standards of living and of what many believed to be an un-American subversion of courts and militia to the interest of the mine owners. Can the responsibility for all this be shifted to those newcomers among us, or must we recognize that the American public is still divided on the fundamental issues which lie back of this struggle?

One critic of the immigrant finds that it is the presence of the immigrant that has forced "the American workingman in self-protection to resort to the labor or industrial unions — to the closed shop, boycotting, strikes, and the like — thus bringing to our people a long train of evils."[6] While the American trade unionist has sometimes condemned the immigrant, he would condemn much more strongly this conception of the trade or industrial union as one of "the evils" of our present industrial life and would be quick to reply that high wages, short hours, and good conditions of work were no substitute

[6] Frank J. Warne, *The Immigrant Invasion*, p. 315.

The Immigrant and the Community

for the principle that workingmen through their representatives shall have some voice in determining the conditions under which they work. If it is the immigrant who has forced collective action on the working people, he has been an important factor in forwarding industrial democracy in the United States.

To some people, low wages seem to be entirely due to an oversupply of labor, and they regard the labor struggle as primarily one in which the laborers are themselves arrayed against each other in the struggle for better conditions.

The policies of the older trade and craft organizations were no doubt in some measure affected by the crude popular statements of two economic theories that so powerfully influenced thought a generation ago. The first of these was the doctrine of the "wages-fund" and the second the Malthusian theory of population. By the narrow logic of these theories, members of the most intelligent section of the working class were led to believe that the only way to make real progress was through an organization whose membership was restricted. A limited membership and very much higher fees for the foreign-born were therefore regarded as necessary to protect them against competition.[7]

The time when the trade unionist fears the competition of those outside his ranks is when he has been compelled

---

[7] It is scarcely necessary to point out that the belief that immigration should be restricted because immigration has produced or will produce an "oversupply" of labor is a popular theory often supported by vague references to these economic doctrines stated in their crudest form. Dr Isaac A. Hourwich's well-known study of *Immigration and Labor* (Putnam's, New York, 1912) is an invaluable contribution to the discussion of this subject.

The Immigrant and Industrial Democracy

to resort to an endurance test in the settlement of a dispute with his employers. The success of every strike depends on whether the strikers can win the support of their own group and so prevent the employer from filling their places. If the strike is a strike of the relatively unskilled, the strike-breakers may be recruited from the newly arrived immigrants. If it be a strike of telegraphers, the immigrant would not be the offending strike-breaker. That men will be found to take their places if the price offered is high enough, is one of the facts that the unionists understand when they begin the struggle. The strike-breaker is never loved by the trade unionist, who calls him by the ugly name of "scab," but when to the feeling that he has betrayed his own class and gone over to the "enemy" is added race prejudice, the resentment lingers longer and often includes all the unoffending members of the race.

It is frequently said that the immigrant has been preferred by employers because he is "more docile" and will, therefore, submit to a kind of discipline and to conditions of work and payment which American workmen would never tolerate. Preference for the non-English speaking immigrant over the man or woman who has the same strength or the same skill is not found by those who try to secure employment for immigrants. On the contrary, a knowledge of English usually commands an increase in wages. For example, the wages of the immigrant servant girl, high as wages go, are higher as soon as she learns English. So the "all-around machinist" who is so rare a product in America that the foreign-born has practically no American competitor in

The Immigrant and the Community

this field, can earn more when he knows English because, for obvious reasons, a knowledge of English has a real commercial value In fields where the immigrant might be a competitor of the American, the immigrant is often denied the opportunity to work until he has learned English. Thus, before the war, no non-English speaking person was accepted at the employment office of a firm employing many thousands of relatively unskilled men and women. In this instance the employees were not unionized; so the policy cannot be said to have emanated from the employees

There is much conflicting testimony about the immigrant workman. After the excitement had subsided and people tried to talk dispassionately of the causes of the great strike in Lawrence and the related ones which followed in other Massachusetts towns, many employers said that it was because their "workmen were foreign-born and without respect for law or authority of any kind" that they had suffered in this way, and they believed that teaching their employees English would insure them against similar uprisings in the future; while others felt that, except for the fact that the mill operatives were foreigners, this struggle would have come twenty years earlier.

Sometimes in the effort to prove that the southern or eastern European is responsible for the bad industrial conditions in America, comparisons favorable to the past are made which are without foundation in fact. For example, one writer quotes Harriet Martineau to show that there was "a state of bliss in the Lowell cotton

The Immigrant and Industrial Democracy

mills "[8] when she visited the United States in 1830 and was so much impressed with the intelligent girls she found in the mills. And he asks us to contrast this "state of bliss" which she found with the conditions now existing in Lowell and the other New England mill towns. He does not call attention to the fact that from 1810 to 1860, when the American girls worked in the mills, there was no "field of employment for the educated woman who wanted to or was compelled to earn her livelihood outside of her own home." And so, although these early mill operatives were Yankees and often well educated, the conditions under which they worked would not be tolerated to-day, in any State in which we would say that a beginning in factory legislation had been made. Hannah Borden's day in a Fall River mill is probably fairly typical. "She rose at four, took her breakfast with her to the mill, and at five had her two looms under way. From seven-thirty to eight-thirty she had an hour for breakfast, at noon half an hour, and the looms did not stop until half-past seven at night."[9]

The long hours, insanitary mills, crowded boarding houses, compulsorily supported corporation churches which the American girl in the mills endured are forgotten, and we are asked to believe that there was something approaching industrial democracy in the mills of New England before the standards were dragged down by the immigrant. Whether conditions in the mills would have improved more rapidly had the American girl preferred weaving to school teaching or clerking, is a

[8] Frank J Warne, *The Immigrant Invasion*, p. 190.
[9] Edith Abbott, *Women in Industry*, p. 127.

The Immigrant and the Community

matter of conjecture. At any rate, the Yankee girls left the mills to the incoming Irish immigrants with working conditions wholly unstandardized, and their descendants should be all the more eager to help the Polish and Lithuanian girls who are in the mills to-day in their struggle for better conditions.

It has been urged that the failure to make real headway in the trade union movement is due to the fact that certain races do not make good trade unionists. Writing in 1901 Professor Commons said of the Jew[10] that "his individualism unsuits him for the life of a wage-earner, and especially for the discipline of a labor organization." The Jew's conception of a trade union, Professor Commons found to be that of a tradesman rather than that of a workman. "The Jew joins the union when it offers a bargain and drops it when he gets, or fails to get, the bargain." This judgment took account only of a part of the Jew's history. It recognized that his long residence in, but not of, Russia and indeed other nations, might have delayed the development of his sense of responsibility for governmental action, which is what is generally meant by the "individualism of the Jew." But it failed to take account of the fact that the sacrifices he has been compelled to make for his religion have produced in him a fierce devotion to his ideals. With religious persecution ended, many of the Russian Jews have given to the labor movement the same patient and self-sacrificing devotion which his adherence to his religion taught him in Russia. That this devotion, which has in it a spiritual element, gives to the move-

[10] *Report of the United States Industrial Commission,* Vol. XV, pp. 325, 327.

The Immigrant and Industrial Democracy

ment a driving force, trade unionists who are not Jews now realize.

If the Jewish wage-earners were for a time more interested in "the discussion of socialism and the philosophy of the labor movement"[11] than in organization, that period of discussion has brought them into the movement with a wider appreciation of what they wanted to accomplish. In view of the important part the Jews have played in the labor movement in recent years, Professor Commons would probably not say to-day that the Jew is a failure as a trade unionist. If he did, his judgment would be at variance with that of many employers who believe their Jewish employees are the "instigators" or the "initiators" of the "demands" which they "persuade" their "satisfied" fellow-workers to make.

The Jews more than other trade unionists are showing themselves to be unwilling to be hampered by the trade union traditions of a past generation. And it has been unions composed largely of Jewish workers and led by Jews that have worked out the first machinery for the kind of continuous collective bargaining which the complete division of labor and piecework payment now necessitates.

While in the ranks of organized labor as well as among scholars, statesmen, and the clergy, the narrowest race prejudice is sometimes found, it is on the whole very much less common. The doctrine that some people are inferior because they are of a different nation or a different race and do not, in consequence, need or care for good homes and an opportunity to give to their chil-

[11] *Report of the United States Industrial Commission*, Vol. XV, p. 327.

The Immigrant and the Community

dren an education which will develop all their possibilities both for leadership and for service, is contrary to the fundamental principle for which workingmen and women have organized. And the trade unionist who lives in the present does not indulge in that kind of statement

Out of the very fact that here in the United States all the races of the world are working together in a single city, in a single industry, or are united in a single union local, is coming a new kind of power and of spiritual outlook which those of one race who work together can never know. The American workmen should be the first, therefore, to recognize the international aspects of his problem and to ask international coöperation in solving it.

But an appreciation of what the immigrant has done and might do in the labor movement does not mean that the presence of the immigrant has not created new problems in the organization of the workers. Perhaps it would be more correct to say that the multitude of tongues and the barriers of nationality and religion have complicated the work of organization. Unfortunately this complication has been too frequently disregarded in the efforts made by organized labor to enlist the immigrant workers. The English-speaking organizer has too often concluded that the southern or eastern Europeans were not " good union material " only because they could not understand English

For example, in a recent strike in an industrial town near Chicago the majority of the men were recently arrived Russians, most of whom could speak no English.

The Immigrant and Industrial Democracy

There were some Lithuanians and a considerable number of Greeks. The girls were Polish and Lithuanians. Their demand for higher wages and shorter hours had been provoked by an increase given to only one small group of workers. The industry was not organized. The men realized that because of their ignorance of English and of American procedure they were at a special disadvantage in dealing with their very powerful employer. They appealed to the Federation of Labor, and organizers who knew only English were sent to help them. Some speakers who knew Polish were later secured from another union, but they were not experienced organizers. The strike failed. It might seem to some to have been because these nationalities lacked the persistency necessary for success. It may have been due to many reasons. Certainly the strikers could get none of the encouragement which comes with consultation with those who have had experience in disputes between laborers and their employers, for the leaders of the strikers could not talk with the Federation organizers.

The unions have sometimes made the same mistakes in dealing with the immigrant that they have in their attitude toward the workingwoman. The American-born workingwomen and the women of the old "immigration" as well as the foreign-born workingmen have sometimes been excluded from the unions and at the same time denounced as underbidders. If admitted, it has been thought unnecessary to recognize or consult the leaders in the ranks of the women or of the immigrants, and then both have been condemned because they did not have more group consciousness or more capacity for

The Immigrant and the Community

leadership. That both the American women and the immigrant from eastern Europe are incapable of collective action and abstract devotion to principle is a conclusion often reached on insufficient evidence. To-day both the workingwomen and the immigrant are playing their part in the labor movement, and there is a growing feeling that all laboring people must go forward together regardless of sex, or race, or place of birth. And it is this feeling of a common purpose that gives real power to the labor movement. The possibility of securing higher wages and shorter hours for themselves is not the only one that attracts the workers to collective action The results measured in these terms are all too often not worth the sacrifice involved. But measured by the gains which will come to their children and the children of others outside of their own ranks if the organized workers of to-day bear their part of the struggle, the sacrifices for the cause seem small.

In recent years much emphasis has been laid on the economic effects of immigration, and it has been repeatedly said that the social and political effects have been greatly exaggerated in past discussions of the subject. Thus Professor Jenks and Mr. Lauck on the basis of their experience in connection with the United States Immigration Commission say that the immigration problem " at present is really fundamentally an industrial one, and should be principally considered in its economic aspects " [12]

Before undertaking to formulate an immigration

[12] Jenks and Lauck, *The Immigration Problem*, p. 197.

The Immigrant and Industrial Democracy

policy on the basis of its economic effects, we should remember that there is in the United States and in European countries, also, an increasingly large group of people who are convinced that political and social reconstruction will never be accomplished until the economic life of the country is placed on a sounder basis. They are, also, equally convinced that we cannot expect to get very far toward the goal of democracy in our economic relationships without a revamping of our social standards and a widening of the sphere of political action. There are, on the other hand, many who are not converted to political action as a method of settling our economic or social ills. In this day of industrial expansion and reorganization, economic and industrial questions are the most difficult to harmonize with our old political ideas and institutions.

Many trade unionists as well as many capitalists are unwilling to accept the idea that fundamental political changes are needed before we can give a larger measure of happiness and equality to all men and women. Most of these people believe we should be able to find some road to reform which will involve no break with the old traditions.

The trade unionist frequently objects to political action because he thinks the same ends can be best accomplished by organization. In accordance with this theory, the American Federation of Labor has repeatedly gone on record as opposed to securing an eight-hour day through legislation, thus repudiating any appeal to organized public action to protect the workers against the long hours which the employer might impose on them.

The Immigrant and the Community

There has not, however, been this feeling about political action with reference to the immigrant. The contract labor provisions of the Immigration Law were enacted through the efforts of organized labor and are intended to protect the American workman against the importation of the foreigner because it was believed that without such restriction the employer could defeat the workman in the event of a strike, or when a strike was about to occur, by dismissing the dissatisfied native worker and substituting the foreign-born whom he would bring to this country under contract to work. The first prohibition passed in 1885 made it unlawful for any person to assist or encourage in any way the importation or migration of any foreigner into the United States under any kind of contract to perform labor or service, and declared all such contracts null and void. The penalty the law carried was a fine of $1000 for its violation. The administrative provisions of the law were strengthened by amendments in 1887 and 1888. In 1891 the encouragement of immigration by promise of employment through advertisement abroad was forbidden, and the steamship companies were prohibited from encouraging immigration "either by writing, printing, or oral representation," except by means of ordinary commercial letters or advertisements. Under the laws of 1903 and 1907, assisting or encouraging immigration by " offers or promises of employment or in consequence of agreements, oral, written or printed, expressed or implied, to perform labor in this country " is forbidden. Special provision is made by the law for bringing in skilled laborers, domestic servants, and the

The Immigrant and Industrial Democracy

members of certain professional classes. In the case of the first mentioned, this can be done only after submitting evidence that such labor cannot be obtained in this country and with the consent of the Secretary of Labor.

The Contract Labor Law is, in some sense, a measure of the changed public attitude with regard to the rights of the workman. During the colonial period and for some time after the adoption of the Constitution, criminals whose sentence was "transportation" to the colonies and many others whose only offense was their poverty, were sold to service for a period of years by the master of the sailing vessel that brought them over. As late as 1818 and 1819 the indentured servants or "redemptioners," most of them German at that date, were sold at public auction exactly as the Negroes were sold in the slave markets except that the redemptioner's term of service was limited and once free his color did not proclaim his former slavery.

During the Civil War, President Lincoln and the North generally thought that immigration should be encouraged. Advancing the passage money was the method of "encouragement" which it was believed would be effective, and so in a law passed in 1864 and not repealed until 1868 provision was made that all contracts which were entered into in foreign countries by immigrants to the United States and which pledged their wages to repay the expenses of emigration, were valid and enforceable in the courts of the United States and territories. To-day, we would say that the enforcement of any labor contract by requiring specific performance

The Immigrant and the Community

of the contract would be "involuntary servitude," but this was exactly the method of assuring repayment of passage money advanced to the immigrant that was provided for by statute in 1864. From legalizing the bringing in of redemptioners or prohibiting the entrance of any one who has had even a verbal offer of work, has involved a wide change of policy.

During the same years when Congress was strengthening the Contract Labor Law, it was also making more effective the exclusion of all those who seemed "likely to become public charges." In doing this we were involved in certain inconsistencies. The peasant who is planning to come to the United States is told that he will be excluded if the inspector decides he will not be self-supporting, but he will also be excluded if he comes with a promise of employment, or, in other words, submits evidence of his ability to be self-supporting.

The full measure of the prohibition which the Contract Labor Law lays down has been and always will be impossible to enforce. Still it has served some useful purposes It has probably prevented employers from bringing in immigrants during times of industrial disputes, and it has also to some extent protected the immigrant against his own ignorance of American wages and of the purchasing power of American money. For although in the absence of such a law, he could not be compelled to carry out any contract which he might make either abroad or in this country, the immigrant's ignorance of this fact and his fear of a possible penalty for "breaking his word" would in many instances hold him to the work after he had learned that under the

The Immigrant and Industrial Democracy

terms of his contract he was being underpaid by his employer.

The Contract Labor Law is, perhaps, not the best means of accomplishing the ends for which it was enacted. It has been suggested that prohibiting the importation of immigrants as strike-breakers and requiring that all contracts under which they are brought in at other times should provide for not less than the current rate of wages, would more nearly accomplish the kind of protection desired.

But no modification of the immigration law will enable us to avoid meeting the issues involved in the settlement of certain fundamental questions regarding social policies. The vote in Congress on the restriction of immigration indicates that both parties to this controversy are willing to strike at the immigrant. Because of his ignorance of English and the fact that he is so frequently unskilled, the immigrant is at the bottom of the scale industrially. More than other workers, he suffers from the evils of our present industrial system. But to advocate a literacy test, designed to exclude those immigrants whose early opportunities were so few that they were not taught how to read and write, on the ground that the adoption of such a test is a step toward the regularization or the democratization of American industry is merely to delude one's self with the belief that a short cut can be discovered.

For example, the unemployment which comes with the present organization of certain industries into two seasons — one of overwork and the other of idleness — cannot be solved by restriction. Neither can restriction

The Immigrant and the Community

solve the question of who should bear the cost, the employer or the worker, of the months or weeks of idleness which come with these seasonal trades.

For the trade unionist to vote against political action as a means to the permanent settlement of certain difficulties with their employers and at the same time to advocate political action to curtail the opportunities of those who are weaker industrially than themselves cannot be defended in principle. It is, of course, within our legal rights; and the discrimination, because it accords with a religious and race prejudice which is all too general in the United States, becomes a " labor " measure which the opponents of labor eagerly unite in supporting. Professor Ross's theory that we are justified in denying to those of other countries the privileges we are ourselves enjoying on the ground that we can best serve the world by giving the world an example of standards which are worth copying, is the argument which aristocracy always offers in defense of its privileges. That the American boy or the American girl is entitled to a freer life or better economic opportunities than the Polish girl or the Italian boy is no more susceptible of proof than is the doctrine that the sons and daughters of certain ones in our midst should have privileges and opportunities which the State denies to all the others.

CHAPTER IX

THE EDUCATION OF THE IMMIGRANT

THE past year has seen the development of great interest in the question of whether or not the immigrant has responded in full measure to what the public has imagined were the opportunities offered him to make himself a real part of the American community to which he has come. There has, however, been no corresponding effort to find out to what extent these opportunities have really been extended to him.

The great body of immigrants who have been coming to the United States for the past twenty years are between the ages of sixteen and twenty-five — past the age of compulsory school attendance. They have come in the largest numbers from southern and eastern Europe, and often from those districts where the peasantry is denied the opportunity of coming in contact with the culture of its own country. They have been largely representative of people like the Poles, the Bohemians, the Jews, and the Slovaks, who have been made subjects to another people and have felt themselves to be the victims of social, political, or religious discriminations. According to the Thirteenth Census, the number of the foreign-born in the United States was over thirteen and a half million in 1910 and the number of those who were native-

The Immigrant and the Community

born of foreign parentage was about a half million less. At that time only 19 3 per cent. of the white population of New York City was native-born of native-parentage, of Chicago it was 20 4 per cent., of Boston 23.5 per cent., of Cleveland 23.6 per cent., of Detroit 24.7 per cent., and of San Francisco 27.7 per cent. In Chicago, thirty-six nationalities are represented, and Chicago's immigrant population is not more complex than that of most American cities.

The duty and the opportunity of the National Government and of the local community with regard to the immigrants who have been coming to the United States is clear. It is twofold: (1) to protect the immigrants against fraud and exploitation so that such traditions as they cherish with regard to America will not be lost in their first contact with us; (2) to give them an opportunity to learn the English language and to secure such a working knowledge of our laws and institutions as will enable them to join with us in the work of making the United States a really effective democracy. To do this does not mean that a new kind of service unknown to American traditions should be undertaken in behalf of the immigrant. It does mean, however, that community organizations and institutions shall be established and maintained, not for an imaginary homogeneous Anglo-Saxon population, but for the population as it is.

Our failure to protect the immigrant against organized exploitation and to give him the opportunity of acquiring the information that would enable him to protect himself has been shown to be the cause of much needless suffering and unnecessary loss both to the immigrant and

The Education of the Immigrant

to the community. Our educational policy also has sometimes completely ignored the problems of the immigrant.

Some years ago at a meeting of the National Conference of Charities and Corrections, the subject under discussion was what could be done in both day and evening schools to prepare more successfully the immigrant children and their parents for American life. An " educator " who was present rose and, with a display of a very popular kind of Americanism, said that we had an " American system of education " in this country and that if it did not suit the immigrant, he ought not to come, or, having come, if he is dissatisfied, he should go back. It was, of course, quite evident to those who listened that this educator would resent any interference with his " system " on behalf of the American boy or girl just as he did on behalf of the Italian or Lithuanian man or woman. The problem of adapting successfully our school system to meet the needs of the community has not been created by the presence of the immigrant; but each national group is a new element to be considered if the adaptation is to be scientifically made. A real service is, therefore, rendered the native American, as well as the immigrant, in every demand that the schools be made flexible and be constantly adapted to changing conditions.

It has been generally assumed that the training which the immigrant child needs is the same training which has been worked out for the American-born child. In an investigation made by the Massachusetts Commission on Immigration, some of the superintendents reported that " no distinction is made between the foreign and the

The Immigrant and the Community

native children" in their schools, as though this showed a commendable freedom from prejudice. As a matter of fact, the most careful adaptation of educational methods is needed.

In most cities the only special provisions made for immigrant children are the so-called "steamer" classes, in which the child is supposed to learn English rapidly in order that he may be placed in the grade in which, so far as his general education goes, he belongs. Except in a few places, however, no special methods of teaching have been worked out and utilized in teaching English in these classes. It is said that the methods employed in Porto Rico and the Philippines are far more effective than any in use in our schools; probably because more professional interest has been given the teaching of English in these Island possessions than in New York, Pittsburgh, Chicago, or Cleveland. We might, at least, use in behalf of our immigrant population the methods developed in the schools we have established for the Filipino and the Porto Rican children.

Occasionally, newly arrived immigrant children are put in classes organized for backward or subnormal children, or subnormal or backward children are put in the "steamer" classes; and grave injustice is thus done to both groups.

If the immigrant problem is to be met, no narrow conception of education can be followed The children of recent immigrants come from homes where the economic handicap is the greatest; from neighborhoods near which vice districts, disreputable saloons, and gambling-houses are tolerated by a political administration of our cities;

The Education of the Immigrant

and from vicinities where congestion, bad housing, and dirty streets send the children to school to learn more than reading, writing, and arithmetic. Under the present system, American habits of dress, speech, and manners are very rapidly acquired; and in the narrow field of teaching reading, writing, and arithmetic to the children of the immigrant the schools have probably met the expectations of the public. But this equipment is not an adequate protection for them against the temptations they have to meet. Although the percentage of crime is smaller among our foreign-born citizens than among the native-born Americans, the records of the Juvenile Court of Cook County show that more than three fourths of the children brought into that court are of foreign parentage.[1] These children have not, except in a very few cases, committed " crimes." Any man whose boyhood included the larks usual to that age would be likely to conclude, after reading over the Illinois or Colorado definition of delinquency, that it was just as well there were no juvenile courts when he was a boy, as he would have been the despair of judges and probation officers. The American father or mother whose child commits these small misdemeanors is able, by the substitution of a new and wholesome interest for the dangerous one, to prevent the commission of more serious offenses. But the immigrant parent finds this extremely difficult to do. His children, because of the rapid strides they have made in the public schools, have become the interpreters of America to him. Many things on which the old-world father and mother frown, they are told " all the kids do

[1] See Breckinridge and Abbott, *The Delinquent Child and the Home* (Russell Sage Foundation), Chapter III.

The Immigrant and the Community

here "— a statement sometimes correct and at other times dangerously incorrect. The American mother who has found herself quite helpless before similar arguments, which clearly indicate that the boy or girl thinks her standard old-fashioned, can appreciate in some measure the difficulty of the Italian or Polish parents. For them it is much intensified by their peculiar dependence upon their children. These foreign-born parents speak to the boss, the landlord, the policeman — all the great in their world — through their children. In such a family the oldest child usually refers to the children as "mine." "Mine fader's got to get work because mine Charlie hain't got no shoes," he explains as the reason for making an appeal to you for advice as to where his father's services may find a market. When such a child becomes tired of the burden of responsibility he has so early assumed and makes a few gay excursion with his gang, his father's word of warning is little heeded; and so the assistance of the judge of the juvenile court and the probation officer are necessary to convince him that the sport he is having at the expense of the man who keeps the neighboring fruit stand is a dangerous kind of sport for him. What is really needed is a reëstablishment of the parents in the eyes of the immigrant child. Our juvenile court judges and probation officers are trying to do this; but with the best intentions in the world we are usually widening the gap between the parent and the child by the policy we are following in our public schools. In our zeal to teach patriotism, we are often teaching disrespect for the history and the traditions that the ancestors of the immigrant parent had

The Education of the Immigrant

their part in making. This often means disrespect for the parent himself. Some teachers, with a quick appreciation of the difficulty the family is meeting in the sudden change of national heroes and standards, are able to avoid mistakes of this sort by making it clear that, for example, the story of the achievement of Italian nationalism is a thrilling one to us and that we are all indebted to the Bohemians because of their long struggle for religious liberty. A little Greek boy who is a friend of mine explained, " My teacher likes me because I tell her stories of the Athens." Whether Miss O'Grady really cared for the stories he told of the city from which so few of our Greek immigrants come and whose history and traditions are yet so intimately loved by them all, I cannot say; but I do know that both the school and Athens occupied a different place in the eyes of the boy because of the seeming interest of the teacher.

To meet her opportunities, the teacher must know the parents of her pupils and the organized social life of the national groups to which they belong. She must know the history of the country from which they come and must keep constantly in mind the problems created by the old home and the racial background. She has, also, to remember that although immigrant parents will always look to their children to help in understanding America, a too conscious attempt to educate the parents through the children may end in a dangerous reversal of family relationships.

The recent Cleveland Foundation Survey of Education showed that approximately one half the children in the elementary schools of Cleveland are from homes in which

The Immigrant and the Community

a foreign language is spoken. The United States Immigration Commission's investigations of the public schools indicated that the percentage of children whose fathers were immigrants was 71.5 in New York, 67.3 in Chicago, and 63.5 in Boston.

The numbers involved, therefore, warrant the expenditure of such time and thought as are necessary for the most careful working out of methods that will "educate" the immigrant children along American lines and at the same time will not destroy the traditions round which the family life has been built.

While the children of foreign-born parents show a lower percentage of illiteracy than do those of the native-born, securing the prompt enrollment in school of every immigrant child is a matter of great importance. His period of attendance will be short, in any event, because family needs will probably send him to work at the earliest possible moment. If the United States Immigration Bureau, which knows the name and the destination of every immigrant child admitted, would notify the school officers of the local community to which the children go, and by a follow-up system impress local officers with the nation's interest in the matter, the immediate enrollment of all these children could be easily secured. For a number of years, the Immigrants' Protective League received the names, addresses, and nationality of all children between six and sixteen years of age who came to Illinois by way of Ellis Island. These names were sent by the League to the truant officers or superintendents of schools in the various cities of the State. The reports received from them indicated some

The Education of the Immigrant

of the inadequacies of the enforcement of the Illinois compulsory education law.[2] But in most cases those who responded to the request for coöperation were intelligently interested in the enforcement of the law. One school superintendent, writing of a thirteen-year-old South Italian boy, said, "The boy had given his age as sixteen and was at work in the mills" when located, but "will report at school on Monday." Another, speaking of a twelve-year-old German boy, said his "parents had intended to put him to work but the law was explained to them." Another said of a seven-year-old Slovak boy that his attendance was secured after three visits, this number having been necessary because the child was found to be "really afraid to go to school." Other reports showed similar situations. All these school officers recognized that they would probably not have known of these children had they not received notices of their arrival from the League.

This experiment demonstrated that a simple form of cooperation can and should be worked out between the Federal Government and the States, so that the names of these immigrant children will be sent, without the intervention of a private agency, directly to the school authorities all over the country. There is a greater value in such visits as those described than results from securing the attendance of the individual children at school. These visits not only impress the entire foreign neighborhood with the thoroughness of our educational system, but an intelligent visitor will discover bad conditions that

[2] See Abbott and Breckinridge, *Truancy and Non-Attendance in the Chicago Schools* (The University of Chicago Press), Chap XVIII.

can be corrected and will refer them for correction to the proper agency.

A discussion of the education of immigrant children would be incomplete if some reference were not made to the private or parochial schools that these children attend in such large numbers. They are sent to these schools by their parents for two reasons: (1) because of the religious instruction given and the general religious influence of the school; and (2) because Polish, Lithuanian, Greek, Bohemian, German, or some other foreign language is taught in these schools and not in the elementary public schools. While with many parents the first is the reason for preferring these schools, with many others it is the second, and if the language of the neighborhood were taught a few hours a week in the public schools, these parents would not prefer the parochial schools.

This eagerness on the part of the foreign parents to have their children learn to read and write in their native language is difficult for many Americans to understand, but the explanation is simple. In addition to the cultural value of knowing two languages, it should be remembered that the peculiar isolation of the mother keeps her from learning English and often leaves her in almost complete dependence on her native language; and so for the sake of the family life, a knowledge of that language by the children is necessary. The devotion to their own language is strongest among the Bohemians, Poles, Slovaks, Lithuanians, and others who come from countries in which, because they have struggled for years to resist the efforts of the government to stamp out their language

The Education of the Immigrant

and to substitute German, Russian, or Magyar, freedom of language has come to be regarded by them as an evidence of liberty. Not to teach their children the language for which they and so many of their friends have made great sacrifices would be a supreme act of disloyalty.

Some parents, however, prefer the public schools, and think that Saturday and Sunday classes such as are usually maintained by the Bohemian Freethinkers, or classes held after the regular public school session like the "Heder" schools of the Jews in which the boys are taught Hebrew, or summer schools such as have been maintained by the Women's Auxiliary of the Polish National Alliance, are sufficient for acquiring the foreign language. And many, of course, of every nationality think it unnecessary for their children to know more of their native language than they can pick up at home, and are quite contented therefore with the public school education.

Some private or parochial schools are maintained by the Protestant churches. Of these the largest number are German and Scandinavian Lutheran, but there are a few Slovak and Magyar Lutheran or Presbyterian schools also. Wherever a "Greek Community," as they call the organization that maintains the Orthodox Church of the Greeks, can muster thirty or forty children, a school is usually established in the basement of the church, in a flat building, or in any room that can be secured. But the great majority of these bilingual schools are Roman Catholic; and criticism of them has therefore usually raised the religious issue, and the demand for state regulation of these schools has seemed to be legislation specially

The Immigrant and the Community

aimed at that church and not to accord, therefore, with our ideas of religious freedom.

Insistence on educational standards is, however, necessary if compulsory education rather than compulsory attendance at school is the aim of our compulsory laws. Some of these bilingual schools are so poor as to furnish no real educational opportunities to the children who attend.

The poorest of them are probably the Greek. From some of these the child goes to work, knowing neither Greek nor English, foreign in speech and manner, and fearfully handicapped when he comes to compete with the child who has been to the public school or to a good private school. Some of the Roman Catholic schools are almost as bad.

This is due to the fact that these parochial schools are organized and maintained by the individual parishes; and when the parish is composed entirely of poorly paid working people, the money that can be raised is quite inadequate for maintaining a good school. For example, one sometimes finds in such schools more than one hundred children in a first grade taught by a single teacher, who fortunately for her own peace of mind knows nothing of the educational progress that has been made in recent years. Usually in such classes the children recite in concert; and the childish voices, droning in Polish or Lithuanian, can be heard out on the street before the school is reached In the best of these parochial schools, and good ones are not hard to find, only the religious instruction and the history of the

The Education of the Immigrant

mother country are taught in the foreign language, and the rest of the instruction is in English. But in some, English is taught as a foreign language by teachers who speak it with an accent and far from fluently. As a result, one occasionally meets American-born children who because they attended such a school are unable to make themselves understood in English.

It has already been said that because of the short periods of attendance, because of their language, and other handicaps, it is especially important, if they are to be educated in the most elementary sense, that the teaching given these immigrant children shall be especially efficient.

Obviously, for the sake of the child as well as the community, these private schools should be subject, then, to some regulation. It can, perhaps, best come by state enforcement of a statute providing that children shall be regarded as truants if they are attending a private school in which English is not the language of instruction and which does not "equal in thoroughness and efficiency and in progress made," to use the language of the Massachusetts statute, the public schools in the same city or town. Those to whom working certificates are given should in every case be required to pass the prescribed educational tests in English. These were the recommendations of the Massachusetts Commission on Immigration based on an investigation which showed that "many of these parochial school teachers have but a limited knowledge of the English language; comparatively few speak it fluently; some do not speak it at all.

The Immigrant and the Community

Such lay teachers as are employed are, generally speaking, wholly unqualified." [3]

The recommendations of the Massachusetts Commission encountered much Catholic opposition. However, they also received Catholic support. Certainly, the Church does not stand for the educational inefficiency found in some of these Catholic and non-Catholic schools; and an honest and not unfriendly effort on the part of the State to raise the standard of teaching and to reduce the size of the classes in these schools should have the same support that an effort to improve professional standards in medicine receives, whether the medical school is public or private

The general American attitude has in the past been that the immigrant is only a one-generation difficulty and that all we had to do was to see that the children got a good *American* education and then we need have no anxiety about the future of the country. But gradually we have come to see that the education of the child, except on the formal side, will not be successful if his parents are thus neglected. And some of us, too, are disturbed at the wastefulness of ignoring the possibilities in the immigrant himself and are realizing that the contributions which he might make to American life ought to be quite different from any that his children or the American of native parentage can make.

In planning any new program for the education of the adult immigrant, the main difficulty is a complete lack of

[3] See the *Report of the Massachusetts Commission on Immigration*, Mass House No 2300, p 147, for a detailed discussion of this subject See also Abbott and Breckinridge, *Truancy and Non-Attendance in Chicago*, Chapter XVIII, "The Special Problem of the Immigrant Child."

The Education of the Immigrant

definite ideas as to what can be accomplished. Anything, however little, which the evening schools have managed to do has been counted as so much pure gain. There is, however, a growing demand that the education of the adult be put on an entirely new basis. To meet this demand, it would be necessary to decide at the outset what we ought to expect to accomplish in any program adopted.

People who have been stirred by the nationalism which the present war has developed have said that "we ought to get the immigrants into our evening schools and teach them American ideals." These enthusiastic patriots seem quite unconscious of the fact that, because the immigrant is so inadequately protected against fraud and exploitation and because he so frequently suffers from racial discrimination, it is perhaps necessary to get him into a room and to tell him how different our beliefs with regard to social and political equality are from our practices. But until we live these beliefs we cannot honestly represent them to the immigrants as American.

There are others who think that it is necessary to teach the strangers among us the "fundamental Americanisms," for they fear that the traditions of the country will be destroyed by the "invading hordes." We should probably rather seriously disagree among ourselves about what these fundamental Americanisms are; but I suppose most of us would like to class religious toleration as one of them. When we remember how long, judged by this standard, it took to Americanize our Puritan ancestors, it is a surprise to find that people believe that such principles can be taught by ten lessons in Americanism

The Immigrant and the Community

Many Americans have in mind as of first importance a change in the superficial habits of the immigrants — their dress, housekeeping, and family celebrations. And yet no one of us really sees any danger to American life in the use of black bread instead of white, or in the wearing of a shawl instead of a hat.

There are others who find that one of the greatest lessons of the war has been to demonstrate the need of "molding" the immigrants into true Americans as fast as possible. But this cannot be accepted as an educational end either for children or for adults. The "molding" process is contrary to sound educational standards It means ironing out individual, as well as group, differences. It means that the native Americans set themselves up as the "true American type" to which the immigrants must conform This would, of course, be reckless in its disregard of the talents and capacity of other peoples. It would also be so stultifying to the native Americans that it probably would seriously endanger any future development of those who are descendants of the "old stock."

Fortunately, the educational needs of the adult immigrants are of the definite sort that can be met. Those who see them as they arrive and after they have encountered many of the ugliest aspects of American life know that they come with some knowledge of industrial conditions in America — that is a reason for their coming. But of labor laws designed for their protection, of the employment agent and his practices, of possible markets for their skill, of what is a fair wage in America, they know nothing at all. They know that we have a

The Education of the Immigrant

republican form of government — that, too, is a reason why they come. Most of them know something of the history of the country and of the principles it has championed. But they do not have any concrete knowledge of the machinery through which democracy expresses itself or is prevented from expressing itself in the United States. They do not understand the history that is being made in the United States to-day.

We are relying on our public evening schools to teach the immigrant English and to give him the information he needs to enable him to take his part in our community life. Chicago is not especially behind other cities in the educational provision which it is making for the adult immigrant; but that Chicago is not doing what, in the interest of the community as well as of the immigrant, should be done, is obvious.

According to the United States Census in 1900 there were in Chicago 69,771 foreign-born white persons ten years of age and over unable to speak English; in 1910 the number was 184,884. By 1916, it is estimated the number was more than 200,000. In 1900 there were 46,624 foreign-born white persons over fourteen years of age who were unable to read or write in any language; in 1910 the number was 75,580. How much effort is being made to offer these people the opportunity of learning the things they need to know, very few people in Chicago have stopped to inquire.

In the spring of 1915, with the coöperation of the superintendent of schools and the superintendent of evening classes, an investigation of the evening schools in Chicago was made by the Chicago School of Civics and

The Immigrant and the Community

Philanthropy and the Immigrants' Protective League. Only a few of the facts learned in that investigation can be given here. During that year, of the 17,613 who were enrolled, only 7 per cent. attended as many as 70 out of 80 evenings of the session and 23 per cent. attended less than 20 evenings. The record of illiteracy was not kept by the schools; but the principals of the evening classes so far as they had information on the subject thought that practically no illiterates were in the schools.

The inference drawn from such figures by those who do not know all the facts is that the immigrant is to blame for this showing. Two of Chicago's leading newspapers recently called attention editorially to the large number of non-English speaking residents in the South Chicago district and the small number that had taken out their citizenship papers. The superintendent of evening schools reported that his South Chicago classes have not been well attended. The papers quite rightly reasoned that something was wrong. But even superficial investigation would have indicated the real source of the difficulties The men who are employed in the steel mills of South Chicago work twelve hours a day for one week on a day shift and the next week on a night shift. The classes the city offers these men meet four evenings of every week throughout a term of twenty weeks, just as they do in the other parts of the city That so many of them should have attended evening school under these circumstances is a proof of their great eagerness to learn English.

The Education of the Immigrant

In order to gain some first-hand information as to the reason why those who had evidenced their desire to learn English by enrolling in the evening school dropped out in such large numbers, the Immigrants' Protective League visited in the spring of 1916 all those who had left three of the evening schools and whose names and addresses could be secured. These schools were situated in typical foreign neighborhoods in the northwest, west and southwest parts of the city.

Of the 554 whom we tried to interview, we were unable to locate 115, 112 had moved from the neighborhood of the school, and 33 had left the city to do farm or railroad construction work. The reasons given by the others were as follows:

```
Industrial causes .......................169
   Overtime work ..... ......... ...69
   Changed from day to night work..37
   Changed jobs, unable to get to
      school by 7 P. M. ...... ......36
   Fatigue after the day's work......27

Dissatisfaction with school ................. 51
   No classification of students  .... 6
   Discouraged over progress ........17
   Teacher unable to speak their
      language ....................22
   Indifference of teacher ........... 4
   Change of teacher ... ..  ....... 2
Illness or some family difficulty .......... 49
All other reasons ......................... 71
                                          ___
                                          340
Counted twice ..........  ................46
                                          ___
Total ................ .  .. .. ... ..294
```

The Immigrant and the Community

Ways by which a large number of these people might be kept in attendance at evening school immediately suggest themselves. Those who leave on account of overtime work said that they were planning to return in the fall when the term began. But they will hardly have enrolled before the Holiday rush will demand exhausting overtime work. To meet this difficulty, classes should be offered throughout the year. During periods of normal immigration the largest numbers arrive during the spring and summer; so a summer term is much needed on this account. The plan of beginning the evening classes in October and closing them in March was never adopted with a view to securing a large attendance of those for whose benefit the classes are offered, but because tradition has kept the school houses locked for several months a year. The evening schools receive students at any time during the session; but new classes are not organized nor is the work widely advertised except in the fall. The frequent formation of new classes and a follow-up system would secure the re-attendance of most of those who leave on account of illness or with the beginning of the busy season in their trade.

Chicago conducts one very interesting and successful day school for adults near the center of the business district. Students are allowed to attend the whole day or such part of the day as they are free. A large number of waiters, dishwashers, and other hotel and restaurant employees in the Loop District, and others who come from various parts of the city attend this school. But it is too far away from many of the largest immigrant districts to enable those who work at night to attend.

The Education of the Immigrant

Classes meeting in the late afternoon are very much needed in other parts of the city, if those who do night work are to be given any opportunity to learn English.

Men and women whose work ends at six o'clock in the down-town district find it impossible to reach home and to get ready for school by seven o'clock. These men and women all said that they would be glad to attend a class beginning at eight o'clock It should, of course, be possible to have classes beginning at both seven and eight o'clock. But for the Polish girls who worked ten hours in a laundry, for the Ruthenian girl who did dish-washing ten hours in a restaurant, for the seventeen-year-old Polish boy who worked in a foundry, for the seventeen-year-old Russian Jewish girl who was eager to learn but who said it was a choice of work or school and she must choose work — for these and others who found themselves too tired to attend after the day's work — some radical change in our educational program is needed.

The Massachusetts Commission recommended the establishment of a compulsory part-time system for all those under seventeen years of age in the hope that they would not only be taught English but be given such additional general and vocational training as would meet their needs. It is to be hoped that employers eventually will be compelled to allow all their employees who are unable to speak English a short period for instruction during their working hours. Some employers would be willing to do this now; and the schools should hold themselves ready to conduct these classes, provided reasonably satisfactory teaching conditions are guaranteed.

The Immigrant and the Community

The practice of employing as night school teachers only those who are also employed in the day school is general. In cities where this is not done the teaching force is recruited from students and young lawyers and doctors who find this work a convenient way of supplementing their incomes. In neither case are really professional standards possible. No great improvement in the teaching can be hoped for until specially trained teachers are employed to do the evening school work. In some of the large classes which are composed of old and young, illiterate and educated, and taught by a weary teacher, the class work is necessarily so poor that only the most ambitious and the hopelessly stupid remain.

Books intended for adults are now generally used; but the Cleveland Survey [4] reports that men employed in one of Cleveland's steel mills were found copying "I am a yellow bird. I can sing. I can fly. I can sing to you," and in another they were reading "Little drops of water, little grains of sand." Books in which the words and pictures are based on the work and life of the immigrant men and women are now available and in such general use as to make Cleveland seem conspicuously behind other cities.

Miss Addams tells the story of one eager teacher at Hull-House who felt the need of making some connection between the life of the class and the teaching of English. As no text-book of this sort could be secured at that time, the teacher prepared a series of lessons herself. The class was to begin with the sentence "I get

---

[4] Herbert Adolphus Miller, *The School and the Immigrant*, p 92 (Cleveland Foundation Survey Education, Vol. 20).

The Education of the Immigrant

up early every morning." That in theory was to be followed by "I wash my face," and so on until they had been through the regular morning routine as she conceived it. The plan was outlined to the class, a group of Italian girls, who could speak some English but could not read or write. They were all home finishers of men's ready-made clothes — at that time one of the sweated industries in Chicago. The girls entered enthusiastically into the plan. They began according to the scheme with "I get up early every morning," but followed in concert with "I sew pants all day." With these girls, as with the rest of us, the work they are doing seemed the important thing, and eating and washing were after all mere details, relegated to the background when it came to a discussion of the day's program. It is needless to say that after this experience the lessons given the girls were based on the tailoring trade.

Immigrants of all nationalities usually think that the employment of their own people as teachers would greatly increase the effectiveness of the evening school work. While this might be open to question, there is no doubt that it would increase the attendance — an important consideration. Certainly, if teachers speaking the foreign languages are not employed, some one who can talk to those who cannot speak English is needed to enroll and classify them, to help the teachers in the first few lessons, and to hold conferences with the pupils from time to time so that difficulties encountered may be explained. The Lithuanian visitor of the Immigrants' Protective League found that one of the men who had dropped out of evening school on account of overtime

The Immigrant and the Community

work had learned a great many English words which he did not understand and was touchingly grateful when she stayed to go over them with him.

We should long ago have recognized that much of the opportunity for education which is offered the adult immigrants should be in their native language. Many of the older men and women will never learn English, and with others it will be many years before they will understand it easily. Most of them have lived in the country, and are having their first contact with the problem of city life in the United States. They need at once a knowledge of the city's water and milk supply; of its sanitary regulations; of the labor laws designed for their protection; of the naturalization requirements; something of the history of the United States; and more of the problems of municipal government with whose right solution they, as much as any one else, are concerned. The public libraries are beginning to meet the cultural needs of the immigrant, but books with concrete information along these lines are not available for the educated and would not be used by those of little education or by the illiterate. These people must be reached by moving pictures explained by lecturers who speak their language.

Very few attempts have been made to reach the immigrant mothers. Moving pictures, talks in their own language, and lessons in English, if offered at convenient hours and places, would secure the attendance of these women in large numbers

A few ambitious mothers enroll each year in the regular evening school classes, but they usually find it im-

The Education of the Immigrant

possible to continue in regular attendance for long. Among those who dropped out of the three evening schools in Chicago that the Immigrants' Protective League covered in its investigation was a Russian-Jewish woman of thirty-six who has five children. She attended forty-one evenings that winter but finally had to give up because she found it interfered too seriously with her family duties to go four evenings a week. She still wants to return but does not think she ought to do so until the children are older. The extension of the visiting teacher idea to the educational work for the older immigrant women which Los Angeles has inaugurated will undoubtedly show the great value of this personal work among the women and lead to organized group work which will meet their needs.

There are other special problems. For example, local communities cannot be asked to make provision for teaching English to those who are employed in the temporary construction camps, and yet as these workers move from camp to camp and are out of touch with all Americanizing influences it is especially important that some plan be made for giving them some elementary preparation for citizenship.

Following the precedents in vocational education, the national and state governments should assist the local communities in providing the special classes which the presence of the immigrant necessitates. This could be done by means of a percentage reimbursement of the local community for expenditure for the education of the adult immigrant, provided the character of the work done were approved by a supervising officer. The expense of

The Immigrant and the Community

providing schools for construction camps should be entirely divided between the nation and the State. The smaller industrial towns, in which large numbers of recently arrived immigrants live, are at a special disadvantage in their efforts to meet the educational needs of the population. Because the amount of taxable property is relatively small, with the same sacrifice that is made in richer communities, these industrial towns are unable to give adequate educational opportunities both for the children — American and foreign-born — and for the adult immigrant. The difference in the ability of local communities to do this work could be equalized if the per cent. of the reimbursement were in a measure dependent on the local tax rate for school purposes.[5]

The education of the immigrant is a national as well as a state and local problem. The present public interest in the hyphenated American bids fair to result in increased racial friction and distrust. If the United States realized the opportunity that the education of the immigrant offers and if school men would undertake by professional research to supply the standards at present lacking in this neglected field, this feeling of alarm and suspicion might be utilized to promote the permanent good of the country and of the immigrants.

[5] See *Report of the Massachusetts Commission on Immigration,* House No. 2300, p 142, for a concrete suggestion of how this plan might be worked out.

CHAPTER X

THE IMMIGRANT IN POLITICS

Our policy in the treatment of our foreign population has generally been to ignore the fact that it is foreign. We act as if, by pretending that the foreigner knows our social, industrial, and political problems, we can bring it about that by some miracle he will come unaided into a knowledge of these problems. Now and then we suddenly conclude that we cannot rely on this national faith-cure treatment, and we become much alarmed about the "menace of our foreign-born population." This has been especially true of our attitude toward the immigrant in politics.

During the period of the Know-Nothing agitation, from 1840–50, it was feared that too many immigrants would be naturalized; and under the slogan of "America for Americans" many people demanded that a twenty-one year period of residence should be required of the alien before the vote be conferred on him and that public offices should go only to the native-born.

There are people to-day who, as Governor Altgeld said, find in the circumstances of their birth the only reason they have for thanking God that they are not as other men. This group is eager to take advantage of the present nationalism to secure a favorable hearing for their argument that, inasmuch as they displayed such

The Immigrant and the Community

wisdom in the choice of a birth-place, they are to be regarded as the possessors of qualifications which peculiarly fit them for public office.

But there is another group of people who think, not that the immigrant is too eager to become a citizen and that in consequence the domination of American politics may pass from the native-born, but that he is not eager enough to avail himself of the opportunities offered him to become naturalized and that, in consequence, the danger of having a large and permanently alien population in our midst confronts us. Thus we find the United States Immigration Commission considering it as evidence of the superiority of a race when a large per cent. of those eligible had availed themselves of their privilege to become American citizens.

In connection with its industrial investigation, the commission secured from 68,942 men information as to their citizenship. It was found that among the so-called "older" immigrants more than 70 per cent. were naturalized or held their first papers, except in the case of the French-Canadians and Mexicans; while of the "newer" immigrants the percentage was less than 50 per cent., except in the case of the Bohemians and Moravians, the Hebrews, the Finns, and the Austrians. The numbers in the different races from whom information was secured by the Commission varied so greatly, however, as to make it impossible to accept these conclusions as indicating the assimilability of the various national groups. For example, according to the percentages the Armenians appear to be more eager to become citizens than the North Italians or the Poles; but the comparison

The Immigrant in Politics

was made on the basis of information secured from 171 Armenians, 4069 North Italians, and 10,923 Poles.

It is certainly true that with all races the numbers who become citizens vary with the length of time the race or nationality has been coming to the United States in considerable numbers, as well as with the time the individuals under consideration have been here.

Some anxiety has been expressed during the past year because many of the men employed in our so-called "basic industries" owe their allegiance to a foreign power, and a few employers are making it necessary for aliens to become citizens in order to secure the promotion to which they are entitled on the basis of skill or length of service. These employers see a danger that is not social or political but military; and they are resorting to economic pressure to make men devoted and valuable citizens.

These employers, however, who regard it as a patriotic duty to do what the Government itself would not do — compel naturalization — are increasing the fears of those who believe the economic necessities of the immigrant make it impossible for him to vote independently.

A new naturalization law was passed in 1906, which provides for greater uniformity of procedure in the different States and so makes corrupt local political control much more difficult than formerly. At present, the immigrant may declare his intention of becoming a citizen at any time after he is eighteen years old. He is required to give facts concerning his age, birth-place, residence, etc, and also the details of his arrival. His petition for naturalization may be made two years after

The Immigrant and the Community

making his declaration of intention and after five years' continuous residence in this country; it must be signed in his own handwriting, and with it a verification of landing must be filed.

His petition is examined and verified by the federal examiners during the ninety-day period which must elapse between the filing of the petition and the naturalization. In order to prove his residence, he must produce two witnesses who have known him for a period of at least five years. The fees amount to five dollars, one dollar for filing the declaration of intention and four dollars for filing the petition and securing the final papers. No alien who is unable to speak English can be naturalized. And as naturalization is confined to free white persons or aliens of African nativity or descent, all the yellow races are denied the privilege of becoming American citizens.

The candidate for naturalization, at the time of filing his petition, is given a simple test of his knowledge of our political history by the naturalization examiners who are attached to the Federal Naturalization Bureau. If he does not meet these tests satisfactorily, he is advised to attend evening school and is re-examined when he appears before the Naturalization Court. The declaration of intention, therefore, serves no useful purpose and should no longer be required. Moreover, amendment of the petition should be possible so that slight technical errors which are discovered may be corrected and new witnesses may, when necessary, be substituted for those named on the original petition.

Another desirable change relates to the naturalization

The Immigrant in Politics

of women. At present the citizenship of a married woman is that of her husband — a foreign-born woman who is married cannot acquire citizenship independently and an American-born woman who marries an alien becomes a citizen of Italy or Russia or some other foreign country.

A further objection to the present naturalization law is the cost of naturalization. The amendment of the old law increased the expense of naturalization, and this operates as a deterrent to many men whose family necessities make naturalization too great a family sacrifice. To the $5 which he pays in fees must be added his loss of work during the two days when he must file his petition and appear in court, and the payment he must make to his witnesses for the time they lose. If the court is crowded and his petition has to be postponed, the expense is increased by that amount so that men often pay more than $25 for their citizenship papers. This expense does not impress the immigrant with anything except his own poverty. Citizenship should not and cannot be made valuable either by making it costly or technically difficult to secure. The simple expedient of holding night sessions of the courts should long ago have been adopted, so that loss of working time would be unnecessary.

If we desire to make the old-world people, who are accustomed to dignified official procedure, feel that they should not undertake lightly the new responsibilities and duties of American citizenship, some sort of impressive ceremony is needed. Many young people who feel very solemn over the renunciation of their allegiance to the land of their fathers and the assuming of citizenship in

The Immigrant and the Community

this country, are ashamed that their emotions should be so stirred by anything which they find Americans apparently regard as so casual and unimportant. Something of a ceremony has been tried in a number of localities and the effect has always been wholesome.

But it is not with the process of naturalization but with the way the rights of citizenship are used that we are concerned in determining what is or might be the influence of the immigrant in politics. Many people believe that political assimilation of all the diverse groups that are coming to us cannot be accomplished and that because of the immigrant vote, instead of advancing politically, we are having great difficulty in holding on to the gains which we have made at great sacrifice in the past.

It is difficult to determine the part played by the foreign-born in national politics. A clear issue between the foreign and native-born voters has never been presented. Like most native-born, the immigrants have usually been members of either the Republican or the Democratic party — the Irish in largest numbers are Democratic, as the Germans, the Scandinavians, and the Poles are Republican. But in the great struggle over slavery, the foreign-born voters did render the cause of freedom a great service. The immigrants then as now preferred the North; and the South tried to believe that it did not want the Germans, the Irish, and the Scandinavians who were pouring into the North at that time, saying that if the South was left in the peaceable possession of its slaves the North was welcome to the " paupers and convicts " who were coming from Europe [1]

[1] James F. Rhodes, *History of the United States*, Vol. I, p 355.

The Immigrant in Politics

The foreign-born voters and their sons were a new element to be won by one side or the other in the controversy of that day. The early German immigrants were originally Democrats, but as the question of slavery became the only issue between the parties, they became Republicans. As Von Holst[2] has pointed out, "they felt themselves Americans, not citizens of this or that individual State" and the state-sovereignty argument did not appeal to them. This foreign-born element in the electorate decided the controversy over which the native Americans were so hopelessly divided. Their support elected Lincoln in 1860 and turned the balance in Kentucky and Missouri for the Union.

The Irish, the Swedes, the Norwegians and, until the present time, the Germans, and others who come from northern and western Europe have been looked upon as presenting very few political difficulties. They have been coming to this country for the last sixty years or more and have had time to make good Those who come now find prosperous friends and leaders in their own group whose ability has given them a place in American esteem, and the recent immigrants of these nationalities do not therefore meet the prejudice which the southern or eastern European still has to overcome. This has, of course, not always been the case. In the forties, the Native American, or Know-Nothing, party regarded the immigrants from northern Europe as a menace to the republic and was able to build up something of a national following on the anti-alien issue. Now this feeling has been trans-

[2] H Von Holst, *Constitutional and Political History of the United States*, Vol. IV, p. 427.

The Immigrant and the Community

ferred to the recent arrivals. We have learned that there are, for example, good Swedes as well as bad Swedes; Swedes who are good business men and Swedes who fail in everything they undertake; Swedes who are unselfishly interested in the cause of good government and Swedes who have time for nothing except personal gain. In other words, we have learned to accept or condemn the Swede as we accept and condemn the Anglo-Saxon American, as individuals and not *en masse*.

With the immigrants who come from Russia, Austria-Hungary, Greece, and Italy the situation is quite different. They are unlike the people we have known in certain superficial characteristics — in their dress, their food, and their amusements. We are shocked when we find that the polite and good-natured Greek who keeps a shoe-shine parlor or a fruit-stand has neither the beauty of an Apollo nor the statesmanship of a Pericles, and we lament the degeneration of the Greek race. And on such weak evidence as this, the present immigrants are sometimes condemned as " undesirable "— without moral, industrial, or political possibilities.

There are other reasons offered, however, for the belief that the new immigration has been the cause of serious confusion and even corruption in municipal politics. Large colonies of these people from eastern Europe, they tell us, are found in those parts of our cities where vice and graft flourish and the corrupt politician gets his majorities. It is true that, because of their economic necessities and their ignorance of English, the immigrants must live together in the poorest, most congested, and gen-

The Immigrant in Politics

erally least desirable parts of the city. The bad conditions of such a district cannot, however, be laid at the door of the foreigner.

The segregated vice districts, disreputable saloons, and gambling houses are supported by those who live in our so-called "better" neighborhoods. In these "tough" districts the foreigners constitute the only hopeful element.

They are, after all, a rather selected group when they reach our cities; for only the more ambitious of the peasantry of Europe will undertake the journey to America, and the qualifications for entrance debar many of the undesirable among them. Their simple honesty and their thrift are not always an adequate preparation for the temptations of city life and the pressure of economic necessity. Forced by an indignant public opinion, the police keep the demoralized and vicious out of other parts of the city; but if an immigrant demanded the same protection for himself and his family he would probably be silenced by the reply that he did not appreciate the great blessings of liberty and industrial opportunity which the republic offers him. To expose these foreigners to conditions dangerous in their effects both on themselves and on the community may be unavoidable at present, but to ignore them as possible instruments in the improvement of these districts is quite unintelligent.

In the past, this hopeful element has been left to the tender mercies of the ward politicians, and has been allowed to learn from the bad housing, the poor streets, and the open vice which are their daily experiences how

The Immigrant and the Community

law may profitably be defied in America. The hold of the boss upon the people of such neighborhood was first clearly explained by Miss Addams in her book on *Democracy and Social Ethics*. It is soon known that he has favors to bestow or to withhold; and that the police of the district have much respect for what he says. But it is not by corrupt manipulation or police oppression, so much as by friendly service, that the politician gets his first hold upon these people. With all of them a job is an immediate and frequent necessity during the first few years in America. Although the number of men an alderman can put on a city's payroll has been greatly reduced by the extension of civil service, certain aldermen still make it their political business to get men jobs Owing to a quite unbusinesslike management of the hiring of men by large employers of casual labor and the desire of public-service corporations to hold the support of aldermen, the political bosses are able to get men hired or dismissed by these companies. One Italian showed me a letter that he said had secured him several jobs. It was from an alderman in the Nineteenth Ward of Chicago whose reign has been long and notorious. It read: "This is a neighbor and a friend of mine Please give him work." And long after the man has passed from the group of laborers who are dependent upon casual and irregular work and has become the prosperous owner of a grocery store, he will remember his "neighbor and friend" and be glad to do for him any small favor that he can. The only favors asked of him will be at election time, and in his gratitude the Italian

The Immigrant in Politics

will in all probability vote against his own and the city's interest.

This is not because this man and others like him are not interested in the city and the country. Most of them are people in whom emotional patriotism is very strong. Fourth of July is more generally celebrated on Halsted Street than in other parts of Chicago. And every Sunday, American and Italian flags precede the band that plays the funeral march of some Italian, and for great religious festivals the Greek church is decorated on the one side with Greek and on the other with American flags. There have been several election scandals in Chicago's Ghetto in recent years, and yet the Russian-Jews of that district are giving their evenings to academic discussions of the fundamental concepts of liberty and lament American indifference to governmental questions. Undoubtedly, here as in the so-called better neighborhoods a great deal of moral steam is going to waste because the confusion of local with state and national issues makes it impossible for the recently naturalized voter to cast an intelligent ballot. For example, a Bohemian who has been here six or seven years, whose time has been well occupied in learning English under great difficulties and in holding his job, finds a quite different political situation from the one he has known in Prague To expect him to inform himself about the various federal, state, and local issues and, what is much more difficult, to discover how the hundred or more candidates really stand on these issues, is manifestly absurd The absurdity is the greater because we have not planned to give him the

The Immigrant and the Community

kind of disinterested guidance or help which we have found it necessary to give to native-born Americans.

Because of the bewilderment in which the newly made voter sometimes finds himself some Americans conclude that our political institutions are menaced by the immigrant vote and think these " foreigners " ought to be excluded or the privilege of voting withheld from them for a very much longer period of years. But knowing as we do the bewilderment of many Americans, it is much more reasonable to argue that our complex population is an added reason for consolidating the various local governing bodies and simplifying elections.

An increased use of the referendum is also much needed. It is extremely difficult to explain to an Italian voter why he should vote for John Smith and not for Sam Jones, when both are claiming to be the possessors of all political virtue and intelligence, and the latter is on the same ticket with the Italian notary public who, to the glory of Italy, is a candidate for the legislature this year. But if a question of policy is submitted the case is different; personal valuations are not necessary, and men vote for something they can understand.

In 1907, a Democratic alderman, one of the so-called " gray wolves " whom the Municipal Voters' League has been unable to defeat, was reëlected from the Nineteenth Ward in Chicago. He received 4478 votes out of a total of 6225 votes cast, which shows how complete the hold of a boss may be on a neighborhood in spite of repeated efforts to dislodge him. The same year, in that ward, 3393 votes out of a total of 5975 were cast against the adoption of a street car ordinance dealing with com-

The Immigrant in Politics

plicated issues of street car service. The long struggle over the transportation problem, which was temporarily settled by this ordinance, was one on which difference of opinion among intelligent voters was inevitable; and it is interesting to find that this difference of opinion was registered in about the same vote in wards composed largely of foreign-born voters and dominated by one of the "gray wolves" of the city council as in the university neighborhod or on the well-to-do "North Side" of the city. In the spring election of 1915, a number of bond issues were submitted to the voters of Chicago. These were $500,000 for a new contagious diseases hospital, $60,000 for a dormitory for the farm reformatory for boys, $250,000 for a penal farm colony for men and a House of Shelter for Women, $700,000 for a municipal garbage reduction plant, $600,000 for more playgrounds and bathing beaches, $663,000 for fire stations, and $1,199,000 for new police stations. All these bond issues carried — the last by the narrowest margin, the contagious diseases hospital by the largest, and the playground and bathing beach bonds by the second largest majority. In the Nineteenth Ward, all the propositions also carried. The one providing for more playgrounds and bathing beaches, however, received the largest vote, and the contagious diseases hospital and the municipal garbage reduction plant seemed to the Italian and Russian-Jewish voters of that ward next in the order of importance.

While not the way in which the city as a whole voted, this was exactly the conclusion reached by the voters of the Seventh Ward, which is said to contain a larger per

The Immigrant and the Community

cent. of intelligent and independent voters than any other in the city. At the same election the Seventh Ward reelected to the city council Professor Merriam, a great leader in municipal reform, while the Nineteenth Ward returned an alderman whose record has been repeatedly condemned by the Municipal Voters' League.

The police station bonds did not carry in eighteen out of thirty-five wards of the city. In two of these eighteen wards the Americans of native stock predominated over the foreign-born voters; in six the foreign-born voters belonged very largely to the "old immigration"; while in ten of the eighteen wards opposing this bond issue the "new immigration" was largely represented. Bonds for new police stations had failed in previous elections — a vote of disapproval of Chicago's corrupt and inefficient police system rather than of unwillingness to replace our insanitary and immoral underground cells by new and modern ones. The need of new stations had been emphasized by a number of Chicago's civic and reform organizations preceding the election of 1915; so there had been more propaganda in behalf of this particular measure in the native than in the foreign-born districts. But, because of the petty tyranny they suffer at the hands of the police, it would undoubtedly require much more persuasion to get the foreign voters to favor new stations, which would mean better quarters for the officers as well as for those who are arrested

That our police system needs reforming, that we need better and cheaper transportation, more schools, and better enforcement of the health ordinances, the Polish and Italian workman knows better than the native-born

The Immigrant in Politics

voters; but under the present system of boss control he often votes in effect against every reform measure which comes before the city council. What we need to cure these evils of democracy is more democracy; and, if the presence of the foreign-born makes this more obvious, the immigrant will have served us well.

To utilize, in the interests of the community, the honest desire of many of the foreign-born for better municipal conditions, not only should we have simplified governmental machinery and wider use of the referendum, but the leaders of these newer immigrants should be drawn into the general reform movements of our cities. In the belief that it is necessary to separate municipal questions from neighborhood and party interests through permanent organizations that would unite all those interested in the cause of good government, city clubs, municipal voters' leagues, and national, municipal, and civic leagues have been formed. Because they are known to be disinterested and nonpartisan, these organizations have been trusted to give correct statements on the records of candidates and issues; and, as a result, the path to an honest and intelligent vote has been made much easier for American voters. They have felt the conscious security which comes with numbers and able leadership.

The naturalized citizens from northern and western Europe, having been here long enough to establish their political usefulness and to speak English as fluently as any of us, have also had a part in the movement; but the intelligence and eagerness of those who come from southern and eastern Europe is little utilized by political reformers. Although the recently naturalized voter may

The Immigrant and the Community

be able to speak English, he is often quite dependent on his mother tongue, and special time and special consideration should therefore be given to the question of how he can be enabled to understand what the real issues are.

Health departments, in cooperation with the child-saving and other philanthropic agencies of the city, have used this method of direct appeal in their efforts to reduce the death-rate among babies. The situation of the mother is exactly analogous to the political difficulties of the foreign-born. The mother, more anxious than any one that her child should live, has to have it carefully explained to her why she must not buy milk in pails from her next-door neighbor who has always been a good friend to her, and she has to be told why although she fed her baby what she herself ate in Poland — mainly milk and black bread — it would not do to give the baby what she and many of her neighbors around the Stockyards regard as the American diet — beer and sausage.

The foreigner must adapt his old political creed to American conditions just as the mother must modify her rules for rearing her children, and, because the organized community makes no effort to explain the American issues to him, he often acts blindly. Until the public schools give the minimum preparation required for citizenship and also offer illustrated lectures and careful, unbiased instruction on current political questions, in the language of the immigrant as well as in English, we cannot hope for much improvement.

In addition to this, an opportunity should be given these people to unite directly through their own organizations in the work of civic reform associations. To

The Immigrant in Politics

preach to them through their own press the gospel of good government, to urge them to vote against some particular boodler, or to vote for the man we are convinced will give them improved street car service, is not enough. Men cannot be held by the promises of immediate utilitarian results to work for political reform at considerable personal sacrifice; for the results rarely come when expected and the sacrifice seems to have been entirely useless. If, however, they are part of a large movement, they can count some victories as well as some, perhaps many, discouraging defeats; they can feel that in their next endeavor they will be stronger because they know the cause is stronger, and the Italian who gets discouraged in the boss-ridden ward in which he lives can be told what they are planning to do in Pittsburgh and what is still left to do in Cleveland. It is the more important because the Bohemians, Greeks, Poles, and other foreign-born groups are the only hopeful, healthful elements in certain diseased parts of our cities; and if those parts of the city are ever to be really improved, these groups must be drawn into the larger reform movements.

But the attitude of reform organizations is after all very much like that of the political party. "If the German vote is necessary to swing this election, there is no use spending money on anybody but Germans," they say. Consequently, all the information that is regarded as necessary to enable the American voter to cast an intelligent ballot is given to the German but not to the Italian, the Greek, the Bohemian, and the Pole.

When he does attempt to do anything for the foreigner,

The Immigrant and the Community

the "good citizen" is often too easily discouraged. He is much disappointed and even grieved to find that the foreign press cannot always be relied upon to further the principles for which he stands. He forgets that his experience with American newspapers should not have led him to conclude that American newspaper men have been uninfluenced by our prevailing commercialism and are ready to stand for political idealism quite regardless of the effect such a policy may have on the advertising or the circulation departments of their papers.

When the suggestion is made that if the newspapers cannot be relied upon, pamphlets explaining the situation should be mailed the foreign-born as well as the native-born American, he wonders about the expense, and so these new voters are left to the same old influences

But if the "good citizen" is doubtful about the importance of the foreign-born, the ward boss knows it pays to keep track of these new voters. Party leaders are generally concerned only with the partisan outcome of an election, and so, although they denounce the "boss" in party platforms and in their public utterances, they measure out to him the rewards which keep him loyal and active and they prevent the passage of laws which would undermine his power and create a more wholesome political life. And it is the indifference of the reformer and the support which the disreputable politician is given by his party leaders that enables him to keep his hold upon these people.

If we are going to continue to follow this policy in the future, the community will continue to suffer. And because the community pays the real costs of our political

The Immigrant in Politics

shortcomings, the careful training which is necessary to change the situation should be undertaken by the community in its schools. It may not matter whether the Italian or the Slovak vote is for or against a particular measure at this time; but it is important in the long run that these thousands of Slovaks, Ruthenians, Italians, and others should be given a chance to ally themselves with the best element in the community and to assist us in making the United States a real democracy.

The Socialist party carries its educational campaign to all these groups. Every large foreign neighborhood has its Socialist paper printed in the language of the colony, has its branch organizations which are informed of the efforts of other branches in other parts of this country and of Europe. They, therefore, feel the inspiration which comes from being a recognized part of an international as well as a national movement. Trade unions are also slowly recognizing the necessity of working in the same way, and local unions whose meetings are, for the time being, conducted in Italian, Polish, or Yiddish, are coming to be not uncommon.

Organizations among these people, permanent in character, and which should be prepared to take up the next issue when, or before, the last one has been settled, are very much needed. Intelligent and able leaders can be found among the foreign-born who would be able to mobilize the honest, undirected enthusiasm which many of these people have for civic progress. National prejudice is at present preventing those of us who are agreed upon what should be done from working together for the accomplishment of a common end. If we were able to

The Immigrant and the Community

come together it might be that in this affiliation between the American and the naturalized American, respect for the political experiences of both groups would develop and much other good might then result. Little by little we might come to believe that our Anglo-Saxon ancestors did not possess a monopoly of all political wisdom, and our community life might become richer by an appreciation of the contributions which others among us might make.

CHAPTER XI

THE IMMIGRANT AND AMERICAN INTERNATIONALISM

DURING the last two years Americans have grown increasingly conscious of the interdependence of the United States and Europe. The closing of markets and trade routes with the consequent poverty and ruin that came during the first year of the war and our present almost embarrassing prosperity have compelled attention to our oversea interests. But the war has also taught us that commerce is not the most important bond which unites us with Europe.

Chicago has almost from the beginning been involved in the war in a very real sense. During those first bewildering days in August of 1914, the representatives of all the Slavic groups in Chicago met on the West Side in the belief that Servia's cause was their own; and from that day to this in our great foreign communities news from Europe has taken precedence over our domestic occurrences. The long lists of the killed and wounded are published in the foreign language press here and are scanned with the same anxious fear as in Vienna or Warsaw.

Those who have friends or acquaintances among our local immigrant groups have heard from month to month new stories of suffering, of death, and of a silence imposed by the censors that is almost as hard to endure as death itself. A young Polish girl, who scrubs marble

The Immigrant and the Community

for ten hours a day came to the office of the Immigrants' Protective League for sympathy in October of the first year of the disaster. She knew that we understood how many sacrifices she had made to send her mother the money to buy a cow and how much joy she had had in knowing what a help it would be to the family. A letter had just brought the news that the cow had been taken by the soldiers the first time that the army swept over Russian Poland. She was able to bear this almost cheerfully because, as she explained, her passage money had been repaid; and she knew that she was still able to scrub and could save the money for a second cow, and was glad to feel she was able to help them. But since then no word has come; and the girl has asked again and again and again whether we think her mother and her young sister have escaped and are, by some miracle, alive and undishonored, and what has become of her two older brothers. A Russian man who has been in this country three years tells how he left his wife and two children in a village in Western Russia. At the approach of the Germans in the winter of 1915, they were ordered to go to Moscow. On the journey, which they made in company with so many others, the two children died. What his wife has suffered, he can only imagine. She has not yet secured a permit to leave Russia. He has, however, sent her a steamship ticket and hopes she will soon be allowed to join him. But as the children were the center of the plans they had made when he emigrated, he can hardly bear to think of her coming alone.

There are thousands of immigrants working patiently in our mills and factories who have had no word from

The Immigrant and Internationalism

their old fathers and mothers or younger sisters and brothers since Poland, Lithuania, and the territory about Lemberg, where the Ruthenians live, as well as Servia and Belgium, were desolated by the war. We have taken little notice of these foreign-born among us except as we have looked askance at them and suspected them of a possible disloyalty to the United States. Such relief as America has sent has in general not been thought of as going to the sisters and the brothers and the children of these men and women who are here in the United States. American gifts have gone to a Poland and a Servia that are known to us only through history and the printed stories of disaster and not in the intimate personal way in which we might have known them, from the Poles and the Servians who are in our midst. We Americans have lacked the imagination to achieve an internationalism which should be ours because of our immigrant population.

Foreign-born citizens of the United States we know have played an important part in the politics of Europe in the past. Every movement looking toward more democratic organization in the "old country" has counted upon the emigrants in the United States for moral and financial support. And more than one European government has been convinced during the past fifty years that, except for American support, it could have suppressed discontent at home.

We have known of Irish oppression and the Irish desire for national expression, and we have realized that American sympathy has helped to keep Irish hopes alive. The average American knows something of the

The Immigrant and the Community

partition of Poland and has been able to appreciate the feelings of the Poles who are fighting in German, Austrian, and Russian armies, not for Poland but for the three conquerors of Poland. What would be a possible and just solution of the Polish question has received little attention. Of Bohemian discontent we have known something; but of Lithuanian, Ukrainian, and Croatian desire for local autonomy or independence, Americans have in general known nothing. And yet, here in our midst are men and women who have played an important part in the struggles of these people toward a national life.

The Jews who emigrated from Russia and Roumania before the war have heard that suspicion has increased the racial prejudice since the war and has resulted in new discriminations against their people. And so the Jews are asking Americans to exert their influence in behalf of equal political rights for the people of their faith. The Hungarians are asking us to consider how their very existence is threatened by the encircling Slavs; the Austrians, that we inform ourselves as to the measure of self-expression which Austria has accorded its various groups. Those of German stock have wanted us to understand what Germany considers are the real barriers to world friendship. And we have failed during the past year to see the great suffering that is back of these appeals that are disturbing our peaceful existence. We have even forgotten that it may be difficult for these people who live in daily fear of the news of family disaster to maintain their self-control and to view the situation in its larger aspects

The Immigrant and Internationalism

And so, suddenly irritated at the over-zealousness of a few, we have turned upon all the foreign-born in our midst and are challenging their patriotism, their interest in the country in which their children have been born, in which they have invested their little capital and their very life itself.

As a matter of convenience, we have ourselves labeled the man who was born in Poland, or Ireland, or Germany the Polish-, the Irish-, and the German-American. Many Americans, indeed, have insisted on these classifications in order that their prejudices might find expression in preferring one over the other in employment and in political and social recognition. Now, we are attacking them for a practice for which we even more than they are responsible. The Democrats expressed their fear in a demand for "America First"; the Republicans asked for "Undiluted Americanism." The tyranny of this kind of "Americanism" must react upon us all. William Graham Sumner in his *Folkways,* written in 1907, illustrates the control that watchwords or slogans exercise over public opinion and calls special attention to the fact that this tyranny is greatest in the use of the words "Americanism" and "American." "If," he says, "a thing is to be recommended which cannot be justified, it is put under 'Americanism.' Then we see what 'Americanism' and patriotism are. They are the duty laid upon us all to applaud, follow, and obey whatever a ruling clique of newspapers and politicians chooses to say or wants to do."[1]

Any criticism by the foreign-born of our international

[1] See p. 177.

The Immigrant and the Community

policy subjects the man making the criticism to the charge of preferring a foreign power to the United States. A discussion of his propositions on their merits is not granted.

We have among us millions who know by experience what universal military service means. The catchword of "democratic" has been applied to this service, and a discussion of the plan on its merits has thus been made more difficult. The testimony of the Russian, the Austrian, and the German in our midst would show how far from "democratic" the burdens of conscription are. These men are only too eager to tell from their own experience that two years of military training for those boys who through poverty have known from childhood the heavy responsibilities of life, always means a loss of two years of school or trade training which would have enabled them to rise a step and to put their sons several steps ahead. To the rich, whose fathers have been concerned only lest their sons shall grow up undisciplined and irresponsible because they have had every desire gratified from childhood, two years of military service means no corresponding sacrifice of career and opportunity Many immigrants have come to the United States solely for the purpose of escaping military conscription; and they are, of course, bewildered by the present demands made by the so-called advocates of national defense. One old Jewish woman who moved from Russia to Canada with her sons that they might not have to endure military service in the Russian army, arrived in Canada at the time of the outbreak of the war. Fearful lest conscription should be adopted in Canada, she came to the United

The Immigrant and Internationalism

States as soon as she was able to do so, arriving just as the militia was being mobilized to move to the Mexican frontier. She thinks any mother can understand the aching fear with which she thinks of her young sons being taught the gospel of international hatred, and her willingness to move again if it is necessary to keep her boys from being trained to kill. But the foreign-born fear to speak because their opposition would be challenged as a display of loyalty to the " old country " or a lack of affection for their chosen country, when the newspapers are demanding that they be " all-American."

This unwillingness to allow the foreign-born among us to express their feelings and opinions is, as Sumner pointed out, a denial of the doctrine that " governments derive their just powers from the consent of the governed," and it might perhaps be in point for one of these many " hyphenated citizens " to ask whether we consider the Declaration of Independence un-American. How much suffering this fostering of our national egotism will cause our immigrant population, few people realize. It is increasing our racial prejudice, our fear of those whom we sometimes call the " inferior peoples " who are coming to " dilute the old American stock " and to " destroy the old American ideals." The group in the United States who are yielding to this popular outcry against the foreign-born seem to assume that, because the civilization of the United States is higher than in some of the more backward communities from which the peasant comes to us, the American aptitude for civilization is also higher.

Professor Franz Boas has pointed out that the

The Immigrant and the Community

" tendency to value one's own civilization as higher than that of the whole rest of mankind, is the same as that which prompts the actions of primitive man, who considers every stranger as an enemy, and who is not satisfied until the enemy is killed " [2] During the past year we have had this primitive tendency lauded as the highest expression of Americanism.

This magnifying of the possible disadvantages of our cosmopolitan population has resulted in the neglecting of its advantages. How many of what are called American traits are due to geographic influence, to frontier life, or to a distinctly racial contribution cannot be determined by conjecture. To what extent, for example, the Scandinavians have made the history of Minnesota different from the history of Tennessee, Colorado, or Massachusetts, cannot exactly be determined. It is even more difficult to say what influence the Scandinavians might have exerted were they not controlled or limited by the common insistence on the American standard. But that into the development of Minnesota has gone Scandinavian intelligence, hard work, and devotion to the larger public welfare, cannot be questioned.

Professor Page of the University of Virginia has called attention to our failure in the past to learn from the immigrant the methods of intensive farming that he practised when he arrived. The American farmer of a generation or two ago was usually satisfied with very meager returns from farming because he counted as his real profits the rapid increase in the value

[2] *The Mind of Primitive Man,* p 208

The Immigrant and Internationalism

of his land. Careful, painstaking farming which the European knew interested him very little "Any methods of the foreigners different from those already in vogue, being 'outlandish,' were held in suspicion and contempt." So the foreign farmer "strove to learn and to adopt the methods of the American farmer rather than to apply the more intensive methods that had developed in Europe."[3] Frederick Law Olmsted was especially struck by the contempt that the American farmers in Texas showed for the methods of farming practised by the German immigrants. Undoubtedly, this insistence that the immigrants adopt our ways has lost us much, not only in Texas but in every part of the country to which immigrants have come in large numbers.

During the colonial period as well as during the past decade, the immigrants have been numerically an important factor in the life of the country. The Irish, the German, the Scandinavian, the Italian, the Bohemian, the Pole, the Russian Jew, and all the others who have come have contributed as well as received benefits from the opportunities afforded them in the United States for contact with each other and with the Anglo-Saxon American. Together they have builded this country, and the shirkers and the slackers in that building have been individuals and not a race.

The coming of the so-called "new immigrants" to a city like Chicago and many others of the Middle West has been coincident with their development. Chicago

[3] T. W. Page, "Some Economic Aspects of Immigration Before 1870, II," *Journal of Political Economy*, Vol. 21, p 39

The Immigrant and the Community

has teachers, lawyers, doctors, bankers, and manufacturers; skilled and unskilled laborers; aldermen, congressmen and judges; men and women who are progressive, reactionary, and revolutionary in their political and social theories; men and women who belong to the dependent and defective classes — who are Bohemians, Germans, Poles, Italians, Russian-Jews, Irishmen, Greeks, and Americans of Anglo-Saxon descent. Any enumeration of the foreign-born citizens who are distinguished leaders in the nation or in their own localities, of property owned, of movements forwarded or initiated by those who belong to the "new" immigration would be no measure of the contributions that they are making to our common life

Flattered by a too ready acceptance of American habits, we have generally concluded that this proved the desirability of the immigrant, forgetting that a sudden and complete surrender of social habits and standards means the kind of wholesale imitation which is always a sign of weakness. As a result, we have neglected a precious opportunity to enrich our American life. For we have not been able to see that, if encouraged to express his own characteristics, the Slav and the Italian would give to American life the color, the gaiety, and the self-expression which Puritanism denied to it and which no reading of Russian literature or attendance on Italian opera can give to the Anglo-American

This negative policy that has failed to utilize our immigrant possibilities is in danger of being changed to a positive one that is intended by means of social and political pressure to impress our foreign-born citizens with

The Immigrant and Internationalism

our superiority. This method of assimilation is not a new one in Europe; and the Poles from German or Russian Poland, the Finns, the Lithuanians, or Little Russians from Russia, the Bohemians from Austria, or the Slovaks from Hungary know it too well. The evidence which they offer proves overwhelmingly that this method of assimilation is not only cruel but unsuccessful.

It has always been embarrassing to Americans to have distinguished visitors from abroad call attention to the fact that the United States is not a "nation" in the European sense of the word; but it is none the less true that unity of religion, unity of race, unity of ideals, do not exist in the United States. We are many nationalities scattered across a continent, with all the difference in interest and occupation that diversity of climate brings. But instead of being ashamed of this diversity we should recognize that it offers us a peculiar opportunity for world service.

The demand for "nationalism" in Europe has been a democratic demand that a people shall be free to speak the language which they prefer and to develop their own national culture and character so that all the peoples of Europe may associate together as equals. Here in the United States, we have the opportunity of working out a democracy founded on internationalism If English, Irish, Polish, German, Scandinavian, Russian, Magyar, Lithuanian, and all the other races of the earth can live together, each making his own distinctive contribution to our common life; if we can respect those differences that result from a different social and political environment and see the common interests that unite all people, we

The Immigrant and the Community

shall meet the American opportunity. If instead we blindly follow Europe and cultivate a national egotism, we shall need to develop a contempt for others and to foster those national hatreds and jealousies that are necessary for aggressive nationalism.

The day of American isolation is past, and in the future we must have our part in the settlement of world questions. If, in entering world politics, American commercial interest determines our international policy, we shall have added only a new brand of national selfishness to the world problem. Even if we were able to make a policy founded on commercialism feared abroad, we could not make it respected where respect counts most — among the American people. For at a time when we are trying to throw off the control of commercialism in our national and city life, we would not, consciously, strengthen its power internationally. Some Americans have felt the necessity of imitating Europe slavishly and have tried to develop among us national hatreds that could be used to persuade us to action. This groping for an approach to internationalism neglects the internationalism that is so peculiarly American.

Is it too much for us to hope that the United States may develop a foreign policy which will grow out of the understanding resulting from the fact that those who have come to us, with all the racial and religious hatreds which are the result of oppression and which have been carefully nurtured in support of a selfish nationalism at home, have lived together in the United States on the same street, in the same tenement, finding the appeal of a

The Immigrant and Internationalism

common interest greater than the appeal of a century of bitterness?

Because of its foreign-born citizens, the United States is in a peculiarly advantageous position to urge that the terms of peace which will end this war shall make for a lasting settlement. For a genuine American public opinion will be presented not only through diplomats to the courts and parliaments of Europe but through the intimately personal connections that our people have with the people of Europe it will be presented to the people of Europe — humble and distinguished alike. The demand that we understand where right lies in the present controversy has been made because each side has realized this peculiar potency of American public opinion. Sir Roger Casement's declaration that his statement was addressed, not so much to the court before which his fate was being decided, as to the United States, where he believed that public opinion would decide the fate of Ireland, had behind it the same conviction.

If we are to respond to this appeal, if we are to give up our provincialism, the American people must understand the questions that are to be determined when the terms of peace are made.

The United States is committed to a change in its traditional policy of avoiding all entangling alliances. During the campaign of 1916, both President Wilson and Mr. Hughes declared themselves eager to assist in the formation of a League of Nations with a view to preventing future wars. If the United States is to enter a League of Nations to preserve a peace that shall be agreed upon at the close of this war, we should have something

The Immigrant and the Community

to say about the terms that we are to assist in making permanent. We do not want to enter an unholy Holy Alliance committed to the suppression of all forms of liberalism that may appear in the future. American interest in a just recognition of the rights of the oppressed or dependent nationalities of Europe is a peculiar one. Their cause should be our cause, because of the democratic principle on which it is founded and because here among us are millions of "Americans" driven to this country by the very oppression these nationalities are asking the United States to assist in ending. If we are to raise our voice in behalf of those who are not themselves admitted to international councils, we should have an American public opinion that will enable our representative to speak in no uncertain terms.

It is not necessary for us to go to Europe to acquire a first-hand knowledge of the questions that the oppressed of Europe are asking to have settled rightly. For here among us are the humble men and women who have themselves suffered from a denial of the freedom they are asking the world to give to their people; here are also "intellectuals" who have had their part in leading the movements at home. Here are all shades of opinion — the reactionary Russian who finds himself in agreement with the reactionary American who fears the development of democracy; here is, too, the Russian who is ready again to suffer Siberian imprisonment if it would promote the cause of liberalism in Russia. This is the Russian who realizes that recognition of the rights of the Pole, the Jew, the Finn, the Lithuanian, and the Ukrainian is necessary if the Russian himself is to be really

The Immigrant and Internationalism

free. Here are Bohemians, liberal and reactionary, Catholic and Freethinker, agreeing in their desire for an independent Bohemia; here are Poles of all parties united in the support of "Free Poland." And finally, here too are the Americans of many generations whose neighbors, friends, and business associates come from all these groups and who have been a part of that American internationalism which is founded not on diplomacy or force but is the result of the understanding which has come with the necessity of living and working together.

If we can learn to listen to those who have suffered from a denial of self-government in Europe, we may be able to avoid American imperialism and to give to the Filipino, the Porto Rican, the Negro of Santo Domingo and of the United States, the rights to self-government that we have thus far denied them.

"Americanism" is much more a matter of the future than of the past. It is to be hoped that we shall have the courage to be unlike Europe in both our nationalism and our internationalism and that we shall have the imagination to use the possibilities which are ours because we are of many races and are related by the closest of human ties to all the world.

CHAPTER XII

THE IMMIGRANT'S PLACE IN A SOCIAL PROGRAM

In the preceding chapters, evidence has been given of the discouraging sacrifice of ideals and the needless suffering and loss which result from our failure to protect the immigrant against exploitation; to advise him with regard to the employment which offers him the largest future; to give him adequate opportunities to prepare himself for intelligent participation in the community life; and, in general, to take him and his needs into account in our plans for social and civic betterment. The needs and possibilities of the immigrant have had little place in more than a century's discussion of immigration. The question before the public has always been, Who among those desiring to enter the United States should be denied admission?

This question is prompted by the general distrust of any stranger, by an exaggeration of our own virtues and a minimizing of the virtues of others. To the old Greeks, every non-Greek was a "barbarian," and there are many Americans to-day to whom every immigrant is likewise a barbarian. This may be a modern survival of that primitive loyalty and suspicion which was regarded as necessary for the preservation of the tribe. Every one not a member of the tribe must, of necessity, be looked upon as an enemy. It is only as intercourse increases and the oppor-

The Immigrant's Place in a Social Program

tunities for mutual helpfulness are understood that the members of a tribe or nation are convinced of the value of the friendship of other peoples. Unfortunately many Americans do not meet the recent immigrant either in business or in social life, and because they do not know him they are ready, like the primitive man, to regard him as the enemy of our social order. Without information, these Americans are led by their prejudices to accept sweeping condemnations to the effect that our political corruption is due to the immigrant's ignorance and inexperience; that crime and poverty can be traced to him; that the declining birth-rate among the native Americans is the result of his coming; that he is responsible for our backwardness in giving political recognition to women; and other evil results are predicted for the future. Professor Ross, for example, maintains that American women must eventually lose their reputation for beauty because of the mingling of what he calls "mongrel types," which the new immigrant represents! Indeed, there is scarcely a national defect that has not been charged by some one at some time as due to the influence of the immigrant.

Thus to attribute all our social and political difficulties to the immigrant is a popular explanation of our shortcomings, for it releases us from any responsibility for existing evils and lays upon us only one obligation — to get rid of the immigrant. If national deterioration can be prevented only by restricting immigration, then the only question to be settled is the method of restriction. Certain measures designed to protect the public health and public morals were easy to agree upon, but the controversy over further "measures of protec-

The Immigrant and the Community

tion" has continued. Public interest in this controversy is the explanation of our failure to give thoughtful consideration to the question of how those who are admitted can be best adjusted to our complicated social, political, and economic life.

The school teacher, the probation officer, the playground supervisor, the social worker, all those who are asking what can be done by public and private agencies to break down the barriers of language, of prejudice, and of misunderstanding which now isolate the immigrant, find the discussion of the restriction of immigration of no practical help. On the contrary, much of what is written from this standpoint is so colored by race or religious prejudice that it has tended to create new barriers or strengthen old ones. Professor Cross of the University of California thinks it is time "that we were learning that, after all, our opposition to immigration is for the most part a matter of racial prejudice." Many who might be said to be unprejudiced have known neither the immigrant nor the problems of poverty at first hand, and inasmuch as the immigrant group is the poorest in our midst, they have often made the mistake of concluding that the wretched conditions of living that they find among these groups are racial characteristics, when they are in fact the results of poverty and common to the poor of all nationalities, immigrant and native-born alike.

At the present time, there is rather general insistence that the evidence against the immigrant has been strengthened since the new immigration from southern and eastern Europe has so greatly increased. It is urged,

The Immigrant's Place in a Social Program

first, that the greatly increased numbers that have been coming during the past twenty years have made assimilation impossible, and, second, that the immigrants from southern and eastern Europe are racially less desirable than those from northern and western Europe.

The United States has always had a complex population. Prior to 1850, the Census did not determine the nativity of the population, so just how complex it was in the earliest history of the country we cannot determine with exactness. Professor Ripley says that "for the entire colonies at the time of the Revolution, we have it on good authority that one fifth of the population could not speak English and that one half at least was not Anglo-Saxon by descent." [1]

This indicates that a larger proportion of the people of the country were unable to speak English in colonial times than the proportion shown by the Census of 1910, which is especially remarkable in view of the fact that the immigration of the last two decades has come largely from the non-English speaking countries. Thus the problem of Americanization is older than the "new immigration"; older, indeed, than the nation itself.

In the federal census of population for 1910, two interesting tables [2] are published which show the proportionate number of foreign-born in our population since 1850, when census enumerators first recorded the nativity of the population One, which is given below, shows that although our immigrant population has increased

---

[1] Ripley "Races in the United States," the *Atlantic Monthly*, Vol 102 (1908), p 745.
[2] *Thirteenth Census of the United States* (1910), Vol. I, Population, p. 129.

The Immigrant and the Community

very greatly during this period of sixty years, the proportion of the foreign-born to the total population has remained almost stationary for half a century.

Census Year	Total Population	Foreign-born	Per Cent. Foreign-born
1910	91,972,266	13,515,886	14.7
1900	75,994,575	10,341,276	13.6
1890	62,947,714	9,249,560	14.7
1880	50,155,783	6,679,943	13.3
1870	38,558,371	5,567,229	14.4
1860	31,443,321	4,138,697	13.2
1850	23,191,876	2,244,602	9.7

In the words of the census commentator, this table shows clearly that "the proportions of the native and foreign-born population have not changed greatly since 1860." In that year the foreign-born constituted 13.2 per cent. of the whole population, and at the close of the century, in spite of the vast immigration during the succeeding four decades, the foreign-born constituted 13.6 per cent. of the population, and during the next decade this had increased only to 14.7 per cent.

The second table shows the per cent. of increase from decade to decade during this period.

Census Year	Foreign-born Population	Increase Since the Preceding Census	
		Number	Per Cent.
1910	13,515,886	3,174,610	30.7
1900	10,341,276	1,091,716	11.8
1890	9,249,560	2,569,617	38.5
1880	6,679,943	1,112,714	20.0
1870	5,567,229	1,428,532	34.5
1860	4,138,697	1,894,095	84.4

The Immigrant's Place in a Social Program

According to these census returns, the percentages of increase in the number of the foreign-born have not been so large in the last two decades as in some earlier periods, and the number of native-born has been relatively greater since the source of immigration shifted from northern and western to southern and eastern Europe. This fact, together with the greatly increased number of socializing agencies, should mean that the problem of "Americanization" is much simpler now than a century ago. Moreover, it is the total numbers of those who come rather than the percentage of increase which is a measure of the practicability of carrying out a comprehensive program for service among them.

The percentage of increase in the foreign-born population was greatest from 1850 to 1860 (84.4). Those who came during that decade were principally the Irish and the German fugitives from famine and war. Their entrance into the country was not without widespread and often bitter comment. The Native American, or Know Nothing party was the organized expression of the opposition to the German and the Irish immigrant. Then, as now, people were much concerned because the country was being populated by the "lowest dregs of Europe"; then, too, people were discouraged because the immigrants tended to "congregate in centers which were already overpopulated" instead of going to regions which the native-born American had avoided in selecting his own home.

Since the beginning of the twentieth century the number of immigrants who have entered the United States is 13,554,043 — about four times as many as made

The Immigrant and the Community

up the entire population of the United States in 1790. Between the year 1908, when emigration statistics were first recorded, and the year 1916, there were 2,397,606 immigrants who left the United States presumably to return to their homes in Europe. On the assumption that the movement back to Europe was as great during the preceding years of the century, the net increase to the population since 1900 by immigration is nearly nine million. For numbers such as these, it is possible and even necessary to ask national consideration in formulating some policy that will properly relate to our American institutions these millions who have come from such widely different environments.

The change in the source of our immigration is a matter of common knowledge. Thus, of the 8385 who came in 1820, 92.4 per cent, came from northern and western Europe. In 1840, out of a total immigration of 84,066, 95.2 per cent. also came from northern and western Europe. Although the percentage from this section grew smaller each decade after 1840, it was not until 1896 that the majority of those who came were from Russia, Austria-Hungary, Italy, and neighboring states. By 1900, 72.4 per cent of the total immigration came from that part of southern and eastern Europe. This change has also been registered in the census statistics of the foreign-born population, although less rapidly than in the immigration statistics. For example, in 1880, 29.4 per cent of the foreign population of the United States were German by birth and in 1910 only 18.5 per cent.; in 1880, 27.8 per cent., and in 1910, 10 per cent. were from Ireland; in 1880 only 9.9 per cent of the foreign-born came from

The Immigrant's Place in a Social Program

England and this per cent. had decreased to 6.5 by 1910; in 1880 only .5 per cent. came from Russia and Finland but by 1910, 12.8 per cent. of all the foreign-born in the United States gave Russia as their place of birth; the per cent. from Austria-Hungary also increased from 2 per cent. in 1880 to 12.4 per cent. in 1910, and those who came from Italy from .7 per cent. to 9.9 per cent. of the foreign-born population during the same period of time.

This has seemed to many people to present the really threatening aspect of the present immigration. There has been much concern lest the virility of our racial stock be destroyed by the absorption of constantly increasing numbers of those who belong to quite different ethnographical groups. It is, however, important to ask ourselves whether such fears are based on prejudices rather than on such facts as are available.

According to Professor Boas, there is no scientific basis for the assumption that there is a "mongrelization" taking place in America different in kind from what has been taking place for "thousands of years in Europe." Nor is there a "more rapid intermixture going on" here than those which occurred in earlier times. "The difference," Boas finds, "is based essentially in the masses of individuals concerned in the process." What effects the intermixture which is now going on may have upon "the ultimate type and variability of the American people cannot be determined at the present time," he continued, "but no evidence is available that would allow us to expect a lower status of the developing new types in America."[3]

[3] Boas, *The Mind of Primitive Man*, pp. 260 and 261.

The Immigrant and the Community

Most of those who are very much concerned about the future American type have already decided upon the "superior type" that they desire to see dominant here. Thus, more than a decade ago, Professor Munsterberg discovered that the Americans derived their "spirit of independence and self-determination" from the Germanic races. For this reason, he found "the German, Swedish, and Norwegian newcomers have adapted themselves at once to the Anglo-Saxon body politic, while the French have remained intrinsically strangers" But he feared there might be worse than the French in store for us, for he asks, "But what is to happen if the non-Germanic millions of Italians, Russians, and Turks are to pour in unhindered?" His prejudices led him to conclude "that they will drag down the high and independent spirit of the nation to their low and unworthy ideals."[4] This has been said in substance many times with other nationalities named as the ones that will prove "a menace" or "a reinforcement of our national traditions." No one has ever thought of his own racial stock as undesirable. To each, his own people seem to be freedom loving and capable of self-government. It would be in accordance with our belief in democracy as well as with the findings of anthropologists to accept as true that there are no races whose superior merit entitles them to special consideration and others who should be denied self-expression and equal opportunities for progress.

Those who know the immigrant peoples find that whether they belong to the "old" or the "new" immigration they are all much more alike than they are unlike,

[4] Munsterberg, *The Americans*, p. 163.

The Immigrant's Place in a Social Program

and that the really important differences, those that separate the desirable from the undesirable citizen or neighbor, are individual rather than racial. In other words, there are more important differences between individual Englishmen, Germans, or Russians than there are between Russians and Germans, or Germans and Englishmen. It is, however, easy to magnify superficial differences into irreconcilable ones. Those people whose habits and social customs he has never understood, whose language is quite unrelated to English, the American finds "strange" and even "suspicious." When he is told that millions of men and women, largely from those districts of Europe, of which before the war he had not even heard, have become residents of the United States in the last sixteen years, he is alarmed as well as amazed. He is likely to insist that they cannot possibly be assimilated and that we must in self-protection keep out "these hordes of Europeans." Sometimes he takes the optimistic view that although he knows nothing of the process he is sure that the immigrants are being absorbed into our social and political life because he himself knows this or that naturalized American who came to this country fifteen or twenty years ago with no assets except his own courage and thrift and who is now a great power for good in the community. As a matter of fact, neither of these conclusions is altogether correct. There is no doubt that we are absorbing the immigrant into our national life, but we are doing it with a reckless disregard of the suffering and the loss of idealism which our *laissez-faire* policy inevitably entails. And, on the other hand, we cannot measure the success of our immigration policy

The Immigrant and the Community

or lack of policy by the achievements of those possessed of the unusual kind of ability which enables them to overcome all obstacles.

In order to formulate a program which will prevent unnecessary failures and will enable us to utilize more fully the potential contribution of each race, we need to understand the intellectual, the social, and the economic life of the peasants in their European homes, and we need to know the special difficulties that they encounter here in the United States.

That the immigrant usually changes from a simple to a highly specialized and complex industrial life is a matter of common knowledge. During his first years in America he must, in consequence, abandon many old customs and adopt new standards of social relationships. He is usually young and suddenly released from the restraints which village life always imposes. And yet, as a rule, he meets this crisis simply and successfully. Sometimes, however, a tragic moral downfall or a general demoralization of family standards can be traced to this cause. Before any progress can be made toward eliminating the hardships of adjustment to our American life, these difficulties must be recognized and understood. The school teacher, the judge of the juvenile or of the municipal court, or the social worker, is in no position to help the immigrant out of his bewilderment and confusion unless he understands, not in a general way but concretely, the conflict with traditional standards of judgment which his life in the new world has brought

An understanding of the peasant's life in his European home is not easily acquired. To many Americans, the

The Immigrant's Place in a Social Program

so-called foreign colonies in New York, Chicago, Pittsburgh, or Cleveland seem to be reproductions of sections of Italy, Greece, Poland, or Russia The visitor to the Greek colony near Hull-House is at once struck by its un-American character. He tries to recall his long-forgotten college Greek and is gratified to find that he is able to make out that one coffee house is called the Café Appolyon and another the Athena; he is amazed to find that the barber shop in the same block is called " The Parthenon Barber Shop " On the night of the Greek Good Friday, which usually comes about two weeks after Good Friday is observed by the Western World, the stores in the Greek colony are draped with purple and black and there are rows of lighted candles in the windows of the tenements and the shops. At midnight a solemn procession of Greek men and the few women who make up the "colony" follow the priest and the sepulcher, which is borne from the church. The American who watches them for the first time as they march down the street carrying their flickering yellow candles and chanting their Greek hymns, asks himself if he is really in the United States. But after a moment's reflection he must realize that this particular panorama could be enacted only in an American city. For the procession is led by six burly Irish-American policemen, and along the walks are Americans of Polish, Italian, Russian-Jewish, Lithuanian, and Puritan ancestry watching with mingled reverence and curiosity this celebration of a holy day. And the young Greek, as he looks out on the crowd that hems in the procession and hears the impatient clang of the Halsted Street cars, tries to control his aching home-

The Immigrant and the Community

sickness as he remembers the Good Friday procession in the village in Tripolis from which he came.

To the immigrant, the street on which he lives here is so unlike the one on which he lived at home that he believes it to be thoroughly American. Those who know the village or the city life of Europe know that these "foreign neighborhoods" are neither Italian, nor Polish, nor Russian, nor Greek. Nor are they American. A sympathetic knowledge of the life and hopes of the people of such a neighborhood is rare among Americans. An understanding of their racial history and the course of their social and economic development in Europe is still more unusual. In our attempts to help those who have been unable to make the necessary adjustments to the new conditions they encounter here, we usually act, therefore, quite without the information which is necessary for a proper diagnosis of the source of their difficulties. As long as the individual cases are not properly diagnosed, successful treatment is only a happy accident and cannot form the basis for a program of prevention. Most Americans are quite unconscious of the need of understanding the immigrant before they undertake to make plans for the carrying out of which his cooperation is necessary. There are some who resent the immigrant as an outsider whose troubles they should not be asked to consider, and they are, in consequence, impatient of any demands which his presence in the community makes upon their attention. As a rule our social policies are based on the assumption that it is the part of wisdom to ignore the complex character of our population and to build all our social and political institutions with

The Immigrant's Place in a Social Program

a view to meeting the needs of an imaginary homogeneous people. This is in part because we have felt these racial or national differences an evidence of the inferiority of the immigrant, and so this assumption of identity seems to be a generous willingness on our part to overlook the inferiorities of other races. To take account deliberately in our social planning of these differences in customs, Americans have felt would be a dangerous recognition of "un-American" habits and traditions. By assuming an identity which does not exist, we have expected by a sort of faith-cure process to hasten the coming of that happy time when all those who come to the United States shall have become exactly like the native American.

This policy is as wrong in principle as it will always be unsuccessful in practice. We cannot expect our foreign-born citizens to make a genuine and valuable contribution to American life if they are asked or encouraged to become only the imitators of others. Many of the habits and customs which the immigrants bring would form a valuable contribution to our community life. None of them should be foredoomed to extinction simply because they are different from those that have existed here.

The immigrant does not create new problems that can be solved apart from the general problems of our community life. Because he belongs to the group in the community that is weakest, economically and politically, what the immigrant suffers is a measure of the extent, but not an evidence of the cause, of our failures. If, for example, our city governments are corrupt, the most flagrant evidence of that corruption will usually be found

The Immigrant and the Community

in an immigrant community, because here administrative officers can defy decency without fear of the condemnation of American public opinion. But the corruption is in no sense confined to such neighborhoods; those who organize it and profit by it are not there. Eliminating the immigrant would not end it. To delude ourselves with the belief that except for his presence among us we would have been able to avoid these fundamental difficulties in our social and economic relationships, is only to delay the solution of those difficulties. Prejudice against the immigrant only confuses the issue.

All of this is not saying that the immigrant does not complicate American life. We shall never have settled, for example, what recreation is needed to reduce delinquency among girls until we have considered what special forms of recreation are necessary in order to appeal to the young people of each nationality and at the same time not run counter to the social traditions of their parents. We cannot hope that our social and political institutions will meet the needs of all the people unless we recognize and plan for all the people instead of limiting our consideration to the relatively small Anglo-Saxon element in the population. We cannot make a social program to meet "American" needs if we make it for a homogeneous population

The immigration problem, is, therefore, not so much a problem in assimilation as in adjustment. To assist in such adjustments, we must take account, first, of those traditions and characteristics which belong to the immigrants by reason of their race and early environment, and,

The Immigrant's Place in a Social Program

second, of the peculiar difficulties which they encounter here. These two elements in the problem must be known before we can attempt to reach reliable conclusions. It need not be pointed out that it is impossible to work out a permanent scheme of adjustment. Changes in the sources of immigration must be constantly kept in mind. Advancing social and educational standards will make what is recommended for both the immigrant and the native American to-day, inadequate to-morrow. But what we are trying to do will remain the same. We must continue to ask how to protect those among us whose need of protection is the greatest, how to supplement the immigrant's previous training and experience so that he can most successfully meet American conditions, how to make the best that is in him available for community use.

An attempt has been made in the preceding chapters to recommend some of the measures that would, at the present time, serve to make the immigrants of the present day better and more useful citizens. The adoption of such measures as have been recommended is justified in the light of the information and experience we now have. They must be undertaken if we are to give to every group as well as every individual in the community the largest possible opportunity for self-development and for participation in American life. Because we have failed to enact such measures in the past, and have isolated the immigrant by our narrow prejudices and suspicions, we have regarded our complex population a source of national confusion.

The Immigrant and the Community

If the immigrant is given intelligent consideration in the making of a social program, this complex population may become a source of new national strength, a means of translating into reality our American ideals.

INDEX

Abbott, Edith, *Women in Industry*, quoted, 209
Abbott and Breckinridge, *Truancy and Non-Attendance, in the Chicago Schools*, 229, 234
Accidents, industrial, 193, 204
Addams, Miss, 242, 256
Adjustment, 292, 296
Age distribution of immigrants, 55-56, 192, 221
Agriculture. *See* Farm Land; Farm Work
Albanians, 44-45
Altgeld, Governor, 247
American Federation of Labor, 215
Americanism, 223, 235, 271-274, 281, 295
Americanization, 67, 68, 235-236, 285, 287
Assimilation, 277-278, 285, 289, 296
Assisted immigration, 166, 171
Austria, 53, 59, 60, 191, 270

Banks and bankers, immigrant, 82-94, 129, 135, 196
Bilingual schools, 230-233
"Black Hand," 118-119
Boarders, 69
Boas, Franz, *The Mind of Primitive Man*, quoted, 273-274, 289
Bohemians, 50, 66, 67, 230, 231, 270
Bondsmen, professional, 135, 137
Borden, Hannah, 209
"Boss," political, 256, 264

Breckinridge and Abbott, *The Delinquent Child and the Home*, quoted, 225
Brown, C. M., quoted, 203
Bulgarians, 33

Cabmen, 19-20
California Commission on Immigration and Housing, 101, 102, 103
Canada, 167, 186-187
Casement, Sir Roger, 279
Castiglione, G. E. di Palma, quoted, 96
Castle Garden, 7
Casual labor problem, 47, 256
Causes of immigration, 57, 59
Central Howard Association, 118
Chicago Council Committee on Crime, 111-113, 117, 136
Chicago Immigrant Station, 22
Chicago School of Civics and Philanthropy, 237
Citizenship, 248-252
Class feeling, 59
Cleveland Foundation Survey, 227, 242
Cleveland Immigration Office, 101, 102, 103
Commons, Professor, quoted, 210-211
Compulsory education laws, 229, 232
Construction camps, 31-35, 196-198, 245-246
Contract labor laws, 48, 216-219
County Jail, 130-131

Index

Courts, the immigrant in the, 105–137
Crime and the immigrant, 105–137, 166; statistics of, 108, 110–114, 137
Croatia, 57, 270
Cross, Professor, quoted, 284

Dance halls, 72
Davenport, C. B., *Heredity in Relation to Eugenics*, quoted, 109
Debarred *See* Exclusion and excluded classes
Delinquency, juvenile, 74, 225–226
Deportation, 76–77, 107, 178–188, 193–194
Devine, E. T., *Principles of Relief*, 176
Disease, 138–141
Distribution, Federal Bureau of, 53
Distribution of labor, 42, 53
Domestic Relations, Court of, 127
Domestic service, 27, 28, 50, 51, 73
"Dumping," 183, 185, 186

Education of the immigrant, 221–246
Ellis Island, 8, 9, 10, 12, 22, 65, 78, 183, 228
Emigration statistics, 288
Employment agencies, 5, 7, 26–54
England, 4, 53, 162–163, 167, 174–175
English language: ignorance of, 31, 43, 49, 71, 119–121, 124, 137, 193, 237; teaching of, 222, 224, 237, 241–245
English race, 33, 166, 167

Evening schools, 237–245
Exclusion and excluded classes, 6, 76, 107, 139–143, 171–173, 179, 183, 193, 282
Exploitation, 3, 5, 6, 7, 12, 14, 20, 26, 39, 53, 81–104, 135, 199, 202, 222, 282

Fairchild, H P., *Immigration*, quoted, 166, 204
Fall River boats, 10
Family immigration, 82
Farm lands, sale of, 95–100
Farm work, 51–52, 274–275
Feeble-minded, 173, 188–189
Fraud *See* Exploitation

Galicia, 12, 55, 57, 58, 60, 181
Germans, 6, 50, 143, 144, 145, 166, 169, 170, 252, 253, 270, 275, 287
Girl, immigrant, special problem of, 7–18, 55–80, employment agencies, 27–31, 50–51; moral exploitation, 7, 24, 29–30, 71–78; statistics of nationality, 55–56
Greeks, 33, 73, 112, 113, 227, 231, 232, 254, 293

Hale, Edward Everett, *Letters on Irish Immigration*, quoted, 168–171
Hammond, *The Village Labourer*, quoted, 175
Head tax, 6, 21, 24
Health, public. *See* Public health
Hindu, 186
Hotel work, 28, 29, 32
Hourwich, I. A, *Immigration and Labor*, 206
House work *See* Domestic service
Housing conditions, 69–71, 143, 203
Howe, Frederic C., 10

300

Index

Hull-House, 121, 242, 293
Hungary, 55, 57, 60, 81, 270
Husband, W. W., quoted, 97

Illiteracy, 62, 228, 238
Immigrant banks and bankers. *See* Banks
Immigrant Homes, 30, 79
Immigrant stations, 21
Immigrant trains, 9, 10, 14, 20, 23
Immigrants' Protective League investigations of: compulsory education, 228-229; employment agencies, 26-54; evening schools, 237-239; immigrant banks, 84-94; midwives, 148-164; supervision of arrivals, 19-21; unaccompanied girls, 17-18, 61-71
Immorality, 71, 115. *See also* Prostitutes and prostitution
Industrial democracy and the immigrant, 196-220
Industry, immigrant in, 26-54, 196-220
Infant mortality, 145, 150, 158, 262
Insane, 188-189, 191
"Intelligence offices," 28, 50
Internationalism and the immigrant, 267-281
Interpreters, 31, 34, 48, 54, 91, 117, 124-129, 137
Irish, 3, 6, 33, 35, 83, 143, 144, 145, 166, 167, 168, 169, 191, 252, 253, 269, 287
Italians, 28, 33, 52, 68, 96, 112, 119, 127, 129

Jenks and Lauck, *Immigration Problem*, quoted, 214
Jews, 28, 62, 67, 158, 210-211, 231, 270

"Job," first, problem of finding, 26-54
Job selling, 38
Johnson, S. C., *History of Emigration*, quoted, 166, 167
Journey of the immigrant, 3-25
Justices of the peace, 124
Juvenile Court, 127, 225
Juvenile delinquency, 74, 225-226
Juvenile Protective Association, 128

Kapp, Friedrich, 3
Know Nothing Party, 247, 253, 287

Labor. *See* Industry
Labor agencies. *See* Employment agencies
Labor unions. *See* Trade unions
Land frauds, 95-101
Laws of Settlement, 173-177
Lawyers, 128, 129-135, 137
Legal Aid Society, 132, 133
Legislation, federal, 4, 5, 6, 10, 21-23, 24, 47-48, 75-78, 106, 107, 139, 142, 170, 173, 176, 177, 179, 216-219, 249
Legislation, state, 5, 6, 14, 44, 46, 92-93, 150, 170-171, 204, 231, 233
Lemberg, 57, 66
Lincoln, President, 217, 253
Literacy test, 219
Lithuanians, 52, 66, 69, 230, 270
Lodgers, 69
Lumber camps, 41, 42

McMaster, John B., quoted, 166, 169
Maguire, John F., *The Irish in America*, quoted, 83
Martineau, Harriet, 208

Index

Massachusetts Immigration Commission, 10, 11, 38, 42, 46, 95, 100, 102, 110, 115, 125, 161, 223, 233, 241, 246
Matrons in Immigration Service, 78
Medical inspection, 140, 142, 183
Mental defects, exclusion for, 141-142
Merriam, Professor, 260
Midwifery, schools of, 152, 153, 159, 164
Midwives, 146-164
Migratory workers, 29, 32
Military service, 272
Miller, H A, *The School and the Immigrant*, quoted, 242
Miners, 46, 202-205
Munsterberg, Professor, quoted, 290
Municipal building, 71
Municipal courts, 124, 127, 135
Municipal Voters' League, 258, 260

National labor exchange, 48
Native American Party, 168, 253, 287
Naturalization, 248-252
New York Citizens' Association, Report of Council of Hygiene and Public Health, 143
New York Bureau of Industries and Immigration, 94, 101
New York Commission on Immigration, 110
New York Department of Health, 159, 160
New York State laws, 5, 6, 23
Newer immigration, 248, 275, 284, 285, 288, 290
Night schools *See* Evening schools
Non-family groups, 70, 71, 115
Notaries public, 94, 178

Occupations of: immigrant women, 27-30, 62, 64, 65, 66, 67, 68, immigrant men, 26-54, 200-202
Olander, Victor A., quoted, 203
Older immigration, 83, 248, 285, 288, 290
Olmsted, Frederick Law, 275

Page, T. W, quoted, 14, 200, 274
Parochial schools, 230-234
Pauperism, 166, 189-193
Peace, 279-280
Poles, 33, 52, 55, 61, 63, 64, 69, 72, 230, 231, 270
Police, 117, 118, 120, 121, 125, 128, 130, 135, 255, 260
Police judges, 124
Police stations, 13, 16, 117, 120, 260
Politics, immigrants in, 247-266
Poor laws, 167
Ports of arrival, protective machinery at, 7
Postal Savings Bank, 92
Poverty problem and the immigrant, 136, 137, 166-195, 284
Private schools. *See* Parochial schools
Prostitutes and prostitution, 24, 29, 30, 75
Public defender, 135
Public health and the immigrant, 138-165
Public health nurses, 145

Race prejudice, 79, 122, 193, 211, 253, 271, 278, 284, 290, 296, 297
Railroad construction work, 32, 33, 35, 196, 197
Railroad journey *See* Journey
Restaurant work, 28, 29, 32, 72, 73
Rhodes, J F, quoted, 252

302

Index

Ripley, Professor, quoted, 285
Ross, Professor, quoted, 220, 283
"Runners," 5, 7, 46, 128, 137
Russians, 33, 52, 60, 66, 67, 69, 97, 191
Ruthenians, 55, 56, 57, 66

Sailing vessels, steerage conditions, 3
Scandinavians, 50, 56, 97, 252, 253, 274
Schools. *See* Bilingual; Evening; Parochial
Servians, 267, 269
Settlement, Laws of. *See* Laws of Settlement
Slovaks, 50, 66, 67, 69, 81, 230
Smith, Adam, quoted, 175
Social program, place of immigrant in, 282-298
Socialist Party, 265
State regulation. *See* Legislation, state
Statistics of: arrivals, 55-56, 172; crime, 110-114, 137; criminals debarred, 108; evening schools, 239, excluded classes, 171-173; feeble-minded, 173, 188; foreign born, 221, 237, 285-286; industry, 200-202, insane, 188-189, 191; naturalization, 248; paupers, 189-192
Steamship ticket agents, 89
Steerage conditions, 3, 4, 5, 10
Steerage legislation, 4, 5
Strikes and strikebreakers, 46, 47, 48, 120, 202, 203, 205, 207, 208, 212-213
Sumner, W. G., *Folkways*, quoted, 271, 273
Swiss, 166

Trachoma, 140, 185
Trade unions, 31, 49, 167, 204, 205, 206, 210, 211, 212, 215, 220, 265
Traditions, immigrant, 68, 79, 145, 226-227, 228, 296

Ukrainians. *See* Ruthenians; Russians
Unemployment, 29, 32, 48, 52, 87, 219
United Charities of Chicago, 132
United States Immigration Service, 6, 21, 22, 48, 53, 55, 78, 101, 107-108, 171, 173, 177, 178, 187, 228
United States Immigration Commission, 30, 75, 109, 110, 114, 214, 228, 248
Unmarried mothers, 71

Van Blarcom, Carolyn C., quoted, 159, 163
Visiting teacher, 245
Von Holst, H., quoted, 253
Voyage. *See* Journey

Wages, 28, 34, 48, 197, 202, 205, 206, 207
War and immigration, 60-61, 62, 83, 179, 236, 267-269, 279
Warne, Frank J., *Immigrant Invasion*, 205, 209
White Slavery. *See* Prostitutes and Prostitution
Williams, Dr J. W, quoted, 156
Women: and trade unionism, 213-214; education of, 244; in Immigrant Service, 78. *See also* Girls; Occupations

Ziegler, Dr. C. E, quoted, 157

Lightning Source UK Ltd.
Milton Keynes UK
UKHW022057110521
383564UK00003B/193